Contesting the
Body of Christ

Contesting the *Body of Christ*

Ecclesiology's Revolutionary Century

MYLES WERNTZ

FOREWORD BY EPHRAIM RADNER

Baker Academic
a division of Baker Publishing Group
Grand Rapids, Michigan

© 2025 by Myles Werntz

Published by Baker Academic
a division of Baker Publishing Group
Grand Rapids, Michigan
BakerAcademic.com

Printed in the United States of America

All rights reserved. No part of this publication may be reproduced, stored in a retrieval system, or transmitted in any form or by any means—for example, electronic, photocopy, recording—without the prior written permission of the publisher. The only exception is brief quotations in printed reviews.

Library of Congress Cataloging-in-Publication Data
Names: Werntz, Myles, author.
Title: Contesting the body of Christ : ecclesiology's revolutionary century / Myles Werntz.
Description: Grand Rapids, Michigan : Baker Academic, a division of Baker Publishing Group, [2025] | Includes bibliographical references and index.
Identifiers: LCCN 2024051870 | ISBN 9781540960085 (paperback) | ISBN 9781540969149 (casebound) | ISBN 9781493449941 (ebook) | ISBN 9781493449958 (pdf)
Subjects: LCSH: Church—Marks—History of doctrines—20th century. | Church—History of doctrines—20th century. | Church—Forecasting.
Classification: LCC BV601 .W47 2025 | DDC 262.009/04—dc23/eng/20250216
LC record available at https://lccn.loc.gov/2024051870

Unless otherwise indicated, Scripture quotations are from the New Revised Standard Version Bible, copyright © 1989 National Council of the Churches of Christ in the United States of America. Used by permission. All rights reserved worldwide.

Scripture quotations labeled NIV are taken from the Holy Bible, New International Version®, NIV®. Copyright © 1973, 1978, 1984, 2011 by Biblica, Inc.® Used by permission of Zondervan. All rights reserved worldwide. www.zondervan.com. The "NIV" and "New International Version" are trademarks registered in the United States Patent and Trademark Office by Biblica, Inc.®

Cover art: Fresco of Jesus on the Cross with Saint John and Mary, Modena, Italy / Jozef Sedmak / Alamy Stock Photo

Baker Publishing Group publications use paper produced from sustainable forestry practices and postconsumer waste whenever possible.

25 26 27 28 29 30 31   7 6 5 4 3 2 1

To those who made the space possible for this book to exist:
Randy, Bob, Carson, Ken, Craig, Teresa

Contents

Foreword by Ephraim Radner   ix

Acknowledgments   xv

Introduction   1

1. The Rending of the Cloth:
   The Church as One   13

2. To Be Like God:
   The Church as Holy   55

3. In All Times and All Places:
   The Church as Catholic   91

4. In the Past, the Present, and the Future:
   The Church as Apostolic   125

    Conclusion: *On Earth as It Is in Heaven; A Modest Proposal for the Twenty-First-Century Church*   157

Index   181

Foreword

Ephraim Radner

Not long ago, I was sitting in the basement of a local Catholic church. It was the beginning of the Week of Prayer for Christian Unity, and the parish priest was giving a short introduction to the ecumenical movement. There were about twenty-five of us there. Half were Latino immigrants of one kind or another, and the talk was being translated into Spanish by a young woman. The priest gave an excellent presentation. He laid out the way the Catholic Church had changed her views about and attitudes toward non-Catholic Christians over the past seventy-five years. "We may be in imperfect communion with one another," he said, "but we're all Christians. God gives his saving gifts and works his grace in lots of churches." Then he asked, "Do you have a child who is going to a Pentecostal church? Don't worry. Maybe you can learn something about God from them." There were lots of smiles; heads nodded. Half the folk in the basement, in fact, went to Pentecostal or evangelical churches themselves from time to time, maybe frequently. The priest had said something they understood, welcomed, and knew already deep down. "How did this happen?" the priest continued. "When I was growing up, the Protestants around me were all 'heretics.' They were going to hell. Now we can see Christ alive in them." The answer he gave was simple: the Holy Spirit. "The past century has been the century of the Holy Spirit," he asserted. "For the church, anyway. The church's life is the Holy Spirit's. And the church is living again in a new way." There were more smiles, even broader now; more nodding. The Anglos and Latinos looked at one another with wide and happy eyes.

I have spent most of my adult career worrying about the church: her divisions, her crimes and sins, her weakness. That is in part because I began my own professional ministry in a place—Burundi—where the connection between the churches' failures and human misery, in the form of war and murder as well as moral paralysis, was a throbbing sorrow. I ended up following this thread backward, sideward, and forward; into the past and around the world; and even in my neighborhood. In all of this, I also searched for the Holy Spirit's life and presence, hidden in the corners of these difficult and obscured histories. The whole task proved wearying, and surely too narrow, too focused, even obsessive. I have needed wide grins and nods across aisles, streets, and altars. What I, and many others like me, have needed is the lived assertion, caught up in credible testimony, that the Spirit has awakened us and lives in the church and churches of today. The testimony is there for the taking.

Myles Werntz's study is thus a tonic for the weary. If the past century was a kind of ecclesial "century of the Holy Spirit" (surely an exaggeration, but never mind that), Werntz provides the theological analysis such a truth demands. Weary though I may be, I am not unrealistic. The past century was not a good one on many fronts: horrendous wars, massive displacements of people, unraveling cultures, tottering governments, climatic upheaval. Furthermore, many of these problems have continued into the twenty-first century, often in exacerbated forms. The churches have not gleamed in the midst of this turmoil in a way that has dispersed the shadows. In many cases, just the opposite. But "the darkness did not overcome [the light]" (John 1:5). The church and her churches have survived. More than that, in fact: in some cases, they have thrived. As a whole, in any case, martyrs, ministers, and baptized Christians—the people of God—have somehow moved closer to one another, crossed the road to enter one another's buildings, sat in prayer together. They have been moved by the Holy Spirit, surely; and they have recognized this movement at work among others. Like me, Werntz is not unrealistic. He knows well how Christians have dealt death to one another, literally and figuratively. But knowing this, he is, nonetheless, simply attentive to the Spirit. He is also openly grateful. This book is the fruit of such gratitude.

Werntz's working presupposition derives from a thought experiment. Let us say that the Spirit really is at work in the church and her churches. (After all, the promise that the Spirit will be is a fundamental Christian claim.) If we take that reality as a starting point, what will we see, and how will we describe it? His experiment, however, is more than an imaginative exercise: he traces the ways that things of the Spirit are in fact being seen in the churches and how, as a result, we are morally pressed to describe them. There are the feats of ecumenical rapprochement, noted above. There are remarkable movements of renewal, life-giving reorderings of social relations within churches, and acts of astonishing courage and compassion. They are all around us. The presupposition of pneumatic life in the church turns out to be an axiom that the sceptic is compelled to accept as a relatively concrete descriptive conclusion. Deductive theological reasoning, in Werntz's analysis, coincides with inductive discovery.

The century of the Holy Sprit, however, is more than the collection of pneumatic effects, the laying out of gifts that we can identify here and there, among Catholics, Orthodox, Protestants, Pentecostals, and so on. The gifts didn't just show up, as if, within this specific period, new things happened that had not happened before. Werntz also wants to describe *the shape of recognition*, focusing not so much on why we didn't see this before but on how we can see it truthfully now and in the future. The answer to this latter question is also a matter of the Spirit's life, but in the form of an ascesis, a discipline.

Among Werntz's most illuminating proposals is the suggestion that the church's traditional "marks" of identity or character—unity, holiness, catholicity, and apostolicity (as the creed puts it)—are bound up, not to essences, but to a two-sided reality. First, the marks of the church are themselves given and ordered by the Spirit. Hence, we should expect to find them somehow within the diversity of Christ's churches. If the Spirit is indeed the giver of gifts to Christians in their common life, then among these gifts are, eminently, the features that make up the marks of the church. But there is a second aspect to the reality of these Spirit-sourced marks: to be *marks* at all, they must be recognizable, we must *see* them. And this requires training, as it were, given in the habits of Christan life and formation. When laying out a call to the church of the twenty-first century, Werntz suggests that virtues like temperance, prudence, fortitude, and justice ground the habits of Christians as they turn toward one another in the midst of what have too often been deemed simple separations and divisions. To see and receive the Spirit's gifts is to be shaped as a certain kind of people, made up of certain kinds of persons. Temperate (moderate) Christians or churches are, paradoxically, more open to the other than intemperate ones, because the former are able to discern more truly what counts as too much or too little of some relational practice. This is bound to habits of unity. Prudence, not to be confused with timidity, understands the need to grow, to move forward, in a carefully measured way. The practice of this virtue, it turns out, reinforces the temperance that fosters unity. And so on. In forming and being formed as these *kinds* of people, the church enacts her own pneumatic character.

Here is where Werntz's realism is properly tethered, and in a way that can both challenge the weary and explain their weariness. Werntz's discussion is rarely abstract. This book, in fact, can be viewed as a focused training of its own sort, aimed at refocusing our habits of vision (and hence the virtues of our relational perceptions). This kind of training is, like most formation, utterly concrete, bound to exercising our capacities with regard to real things, real people, real histories, and their questions. This book excels at taking apart our assumptions about our churches' pasts and reframing people and events in ways that take seriously the promise of the Spirit's work in their midst. We hear about Christian churches in the East, in Africa, in this or that situation and challenge; we are presented with witnesses of faith in the midst of contexts we are forced to think through more carefully. In Werntz's presentation, the twentieth century doesn't really emerge as a "new age of the Spirit." Rather, Werntz helps unveil before our eyes how the century has been characterized by more brilliant pneumatic colors than we were trained to recognize or wont to imagine. That is partly also because Werntz wants us to learn to see the Spirit working more consistently across *all* eras in which the churches' lives must, in fact, be engaged by the Spirit's life, according to the Spirit's promise. The church *looks* better, not because it is, but because we are becoming better witnesses of the Spirit in her midst. In its own way, Werntz's volume is an enchiridion of the church for the present, like Augustine's and Erasmus's were for previous eras, a guide "ready-at-hand" for the active life of the faithful.

Whether or not one agrees with all the historical and social-psychological interpretations that Werntz provides in this rereading of the church's larger life, much of it is plausible enough to render the weary less self-confident in their accepted fatigue. This is so especially as his challenges are founded on compelling theological bases. In whatever arenas of questioning this might occur, Werntz, through his analysis of the actual pneumatic life of the church and its participants, is actually issuing a call to repentance. This is something that those who "despair" of the church (Werntz's own characterization of our moment's slippage in faith) are apt to run from. Whether weary or blithely self-confident, we should not—for the sake of our lives themselves!—run from this call. Like Barnabas, Werntz would put all of us through a program of profound reinvigoration, itself one of the Spirit's greatest gifts (Rom. 12:8).

Acknowledgments

This book has been written in many different places and has benefited from innumerable conversation partners. My first and enduring gratitude goes to my parents, David and Kathy Werntz, who raised me in Methodist, charismatic, and Baptist churches, giving me my first view of the breadth of the Christian life and of what it means that the Spirit makes alive these bodies of Christ. The writing of this book was made possible by the generous support of my deans at Logsdon Seminary and at the Graduate School of Theology at Abilene Christian University: Bob Ellis and Carson Reed. The explorations in this book have been nourished over the last decade by conversations with my students at Baylor University, Palm Beach Atlantic University, Hardin-Simmons University, and Abilene Christian University. To these students: I hope that you can see yourselves in these arguments and digressions from our courses on ecclesiology. Finally, my deepest gratitude goes to my friends and colleagues—too many to name here—who have helped sharpen my thinking, who have challenged my parochialism, and who have (hesitantly) asked if this book would ever be completed. The manifold arguments made in these pages are a result of the time with friends and colleagues. Through conference conversations, book recommendations, happenstance insights over coffee, and strong convictions argued over, my thinking on this topic has changed for the better, I hope. All errors in judgment remain my own. The book is done, but the arguments over the church go on.

Introduction

An Origin Story

This is a book that asks what we learn about the nature of the church from looking at how ecclesiology in the twentieth century discussed, embodied, and contested the four marks of the church: one, holy, catholic, and apostolic. It is a book that, among other things, introduces what the church is by looking at how churches have enacted their vocation to be the church over the long course of the twentieth century. For the twentieth century was a time of both great upheaval and great renewal in Christianity and in the doctrine of the church. During the twentieth century, ecumenism came into full swing, the Pentecostal movement emerged, indigenous churches sprang up as colonialism ended, and long-standing arrangements globally between churches were forged and dissolved. Watching how churches navigate these waters gives us insight into how we might understand the nature of the church under these headings of one, holy, catholic, and apostolic.

Explaining how this book came to be will help clarify what kind of book this is. In 2015, I was teaching at Palm Beach Atlantic University, and my dean assigned me a course on global Christianity. As anyone who has been on a faculty knows, you frequently learn as you go, but global Christianity was not somewhere I had ever been, intellectually speaking. I had traveled widely and seen churches living and ministering across the world, but that had never materially affected how I thought about what the church is. In being tasked with this course, I had come into a crisis: I had come up short intellectually in a way that opened up major questions regarding my own scholarship.[1] For if I was ignorant of what global Christianity was, how had this limited how I understood one of my primary interests: the doctrine of the church?

When my dean asked me to teach this course on global Christianity, I had already wanted to continue learning about the doctrine of the church. I had written my dissertation on the intersection of ecclesiology and Christian ethics of nonviolence, which led me into ecclesiologies of three American theologians and deepened my understanding of how a doctrine of the church frames Christian responses to social questions. The question of what the church is had framed how I taught the history of twentieth-century theology elsewhere. But this course on global Christianity exposed for me the ways in which my understanding of ecclesiology was parochial: My narration of the Christian church was nearly exclusively focused on events in the United States and Europe. This was a problem.

In that course, the students and I read Japanese, Ghanian, Argentinian, and Thai theologians. We began asking questions about Caribbean, Central American, and Chinese writers. Many of these questions were fresh and live for me. It occurred to me that I knew nothing about large swaths of churches. At that point, I had not yet been to Greece and heard the Orthodox liturgies, nor seen Armenian evangelicals preaching, nor asked what it meant that Lebanese Baptists seemed to care little about the kinds of questions American Baptists were asking.

And so, I set out to learn what I did not yet know.[2] After returning from Florida to teach at the now-disbanded Logsdon Seminary at Hardin-Simmons University, I sketched out what such a book might look like. Perhaps it was in God's providence that my ambition outstripped my wisdom for such a project. For if I had known that the next years would include job expansion, followed

---

1. Dustin Benac's description of crisis as "coming up short" is instructive here. A crisis invites us to consider the interplay between divine and human realities and exposes complexities about human realities that otherwise go unnoticed. In Benac's rendering, crisis offers opportunity for recognition, expansion of horizons, and an invitation to give account for a different description of the world. See Dustin Benac, "Theology for Crisis: Practical Theology and the Practice of Giving an Account," *Practical Theology* 16 (2023): 747–60.

2. As Augustine put it, "I endeavor to be one of those who write because they have made some progress, and who, by-means of writing, make further progress." *Letter 143*, trans. J. G. Cunningham, in vol. 1 of *The Nicene and Post-Nicene Fathers*, Series 1, ed. Philip Schaff (Buffalo, NY: Christian Literature Publishing, 1887), rev. Kevin Knight for New Advent, https://www.newadvent.org/fathers/1102143.htm.

by the dissolution of the seminary, a global pandemic, and beginning a new position at Abilene Christian University from the ground up, I doubt I would have taken up this work to begin with.

A projected three-year project was started and stopped multiple times,[3] and it would be nearly eight years after writing the first words of this book that I wrote the last ones. Along the way, many things have shifted for me intellectually and personally, not least of all the fact that my own Baptist tradition continues to change and my two children are now part of the story described here. This, then, is a book born out of a desire not to teach but to learn—and it is my hope, first, that I have learned.

The Present Work: Limits and Liabilities

Having committed to write about a topic as big as ecclesiology in the twentieth century, I immediately encountered problems. One was the problem of scope. Any book on the doctrine of the church and the twentieth century will either be two hundred pages or fifteen volumes, risking treatment that is either overly simplistic or exhaustive to the point of being exhausting. This meant, then, that in order to tell this story in a way that both honors the variegations of church in the twentieth century and does some justice to ecclesiology as an ongoing work of the Spirit in creation, I made three decisions.

First, while landmark events such as the founding of the World Council of Churches and the Second Vatican Council are discussed, many others were left out. This was not because events such as Orthodox-Anglican dialogues were not significant, but because there were quite simply other stories to tell—from South Africa, Korea, and Bulgaria, and other localities. Omissions in the story here are legion: readers will find discussions of Latin American responses to the Second Vatican Council, but not Indonesian responses.[4] Various Orthodox communions are omitted, as are fulsome discussions of the intimacies of various Protestant bodies. The present work aims to characterize the doctrines

---

3. It was in the middle of writing this that COVID occurred, leaving me at home without a library and yet still thinking about the puzzle of ecclesiology. It was then that I wrote *From Isolation to Community* (Grand Rapids: Baker Academic, 2022). Readers who have read that work will detect similar themes, particularly around what it means that churches endure, change, and sometimes end, and what this might mean theologically.

4. Emanuel Pranawa Dhatu Martasudjita, "The Indonesian Catholic Church 50 Years after Vatican II: Seven Models of Church Life," *International Journal for the Study of the Christian Church* 15 (2015): 123–38.

of the church in the twentieth century as they were lived, which means that I have tried to anchor discussions of the marks of the church in key documents, discussions, and movements that elucidate what the four marks of the church look like from the vantage point of the last century. But this also means there were more stories to tell than were feasible for this project.

Second, as a theologian writing about the church, I tried to avoid, as much as possible, the "Great Man" version of storytelling,[5] wherein the ideas of theologians are front and center, and to emphasize the stories of what churches are. For ecclesiology is different than a history of ideas; it is, instead, a history of how churches take root in particular times and places and, in God's providence, bear out the work of the Spirit in those particular contexts.[6] Ecclesiology begins with God's giving of the Spirit so that the Spirit may shape a body in the world that is God's people. Such work of the Spirit takes ordinary form, working with the praise and actions of the people and, sometimes, theologians. Many familiar names from twentieth-century theology, therefore, do not appear in this book, apart from a few whose writings illustrate what is happening within these ecclesiological circles.

Third, I decided to lean into selectivity. Telling a story requires a storyteller, and that teller has limits. As indicated above, intentionally focusing on smaller, illustrative stories meant omitting other stories and angles that would be fruitful. But in doing so, I have tried to be *representatively* selective. The stories of many particular Protestant groups, such as Lutherans and Presbyterians and Mennonites, are minimally addressed or altogether absent. The same is true for the stories of various Orthodox gatherings. This is not because they are unimportant, but because many of the dynamics that, for example, created the Lutheran Church of America or that split the Presbyterians into the Presbyterian Church in America (PCA) and the Presbyterian

---

5. This perspective on history is summed up by Thomas Carlyle in "Lecture I: The Hero as Divinity. Odin. Paganism: Scandinavian Mythology," in *On Heroes, Hero-Worship, & the Heroic in History: Six Lectures* (London: James Fraser, 1841), 1–2:
> Universal History, the history of what man has accomplished in this world, is at bottom the History of the Great Men who have worked here. They were the leaders of men, these great ones; the modellers, patterns, and in a wide sense creators, of whatsoever the general mass of men contrived to do or to attain; all things that we see standing accomplished in the world are properly the outer material result, the practical realisation and embodiment, of Thoughts that dwelt in the Great Men sent into the world: the soul of the whole world's history, it may justly be considered, were the history of these men.

6. Because I am a theologian and ethicist, my interest in doctrine is not that of the historian: it is important to be accurate with respect to events, places, and persons, but I want to be accurate because I take it that we are dealing with God's actions in the world.

Church (U.S.A.) (commonly referred to as the PCUSA) are covered, though not by telling those particular events. While I take it that the overall shape of the story I tell concerning these four marks of the church is true, it is not exhaustive. I leave it to members of those communions to add their own voices to the chorus. There is nothing magical about the limits established here, for stories do not somehow begin in 1900 and end in 2000. While I have intentionally left the concerns of the twenty-first century to the side in this book, focusing instead on what the twentieth century offers us, the stories here continue today.

Beginning with the Spirit: The Marks of the Church

When organizing a story about twentieth-century ecclesiology, any number of options are available. One could write it as a story of a period of great reunion and convergence, emphasizing the ecumenical impulses that came alongside new divisions. One could characterize the twentieth century as a time of institutional decline and rebirth, with global forms of Christianity, and especially charismatic ones, expanding rapidly. One could, alternatively, chart a story of contextual challenges and local solutions. But the risk one runs in telling a story about ecclesiology—about the work of God to create a body in the world—is that in the process one's story can become *only* sociological. This is not to diminish the careful work of historians, but to offer a caution that to tell a story about church is to account for what we see as the work of God and, specifically, of the Holy Spirit.

The organizing motif of this book, then, is the marks of the church, considered as organizing characteristics that help us see, first and foremost, what the twentieth century might teach us about the nature of the church. Readers may be skeptical of some of the inclusions made here, but I have made them out of a broad principle of "innocent until proven guilty": that until a church proves itself to be an inheritor of "another gospel"—to borrow Saint Paul's phrase—it falls to Christians to name that church as an assembly of fellow members of Christ's body. By "the marks of the church," I mean those articulated in the Constantinopolitan Creed in 381: one, holy, catholic, and apostolic. These marks, used in liturgies across the Christian world—Presbyterian, Orthodox, Catholic, Methodist, Anglican, Lutheran, and so on—provide a composite sketch of what is confessed about this body and what the church then aspires to be in its faith and life.

But observers of these discussions know that there are not one but *two* sets of marks associated with ecclesiology: the four marks (used here) and the seven marks articulated by Martin Luther.[7] These seven marks—Scripture, baptism, the Lord's Supper, church discipline, biblical offices, worship, and suffering—offer a compelling account of the conditions that sustain the church over time and identify its worship as that which helps "the poor believer" (an important criterion for distinguishing between true and false gatherings in the name of Jesus Christ). When teasing out a doctrine of the church, it is instructive to ask whether a church self-consciously lacks some of these marks, and then to ask why they would choose to neglect them.

I have chosen not to focus our inquiry into the church on the second set of marks for two reasons. First, to focus on the conditions of a church's validity is to discuss what is lacking, not whether what is present is in fact of God. It is, I think, to begin from a place of suspicion rather than of inquiry and (arguably) of charity, to assume that a body claiming to be a church is guilty until proven innocent. But second—and more to our own age—discussions in ecclesiology have become tired affairs, creating statements that compare social practices instead of inquiring into what makes these practices possible to begin with. Discussions of this nature have tended to become less theological than sociological. For these reasons, I focus on the four marks, which exist not as freestanding statements but as statements under the subheading of the third article of the Constantinopolitan Creed: that having to do with the Holy Spirit. For in the creed, confessing the Holy Spirit—the one who makes Christ known to us—is the prerequisite to believing that there is such a thing as the church at all.

As Scripture teaches, it is possible to proclaim that Christ is Lord, to confess that the Holy One of Israel has come in the flesh, only because of the work of the Holy Spirit. This is a very minimal place to begin, but perhaps the most important place. This does not mean that bodies confessing in earnest that Christ is Lord cannot be in error about what that entails—the history of Christian doctrine is rife with debates that illustrate they can. And this does not mean that a body cannot be in error about what it lacks, for there are churches that are imbued with the Spirit that self-consciously downplay one or more of the four marks. Rather, this means that if a church has been called into being by the Spirit, these four marks are, in a very real sense, parts

---

7. Luther's account can be found in Martin Luther, *Luther's Works*, ed. Jaroslav Pelikan and Helmut T. Lehman, 55 vols. (Philadelphia: Muhlenberg and Fortress), 41:148–66.

of its being. It falls to us, then, to ask not *whether* these marks are present but *in what way* they are present.

By beginning with this basic assumption—that the Holy Spirit is present among those who confess that Christ has come in the flesh—we can then approach these churches with a sense of charity and curiosity, asking what we might learn from how they have existed over time with respect to these four marks. In his comments on true and false reform, Yves Congar puts it this way, which signals the kind of realism I am proposing here:

> These principles are essentially the faith (the revealed doctrine) and the sacraments of the faith, then the apostolic powers derived from the sovereign energies of Christ as king, priest, and prophet (related to the faith and sacraments). . . . We are dealing here, then, with gifts and promises from God that flowing from God, participate in divine infallibility. . . .
>
> But here I am not considering the personal reception or personal use that persons make of these gifts. Rather, I am looking at the gifts in themselves, such as they are in coming forth from the hand of God and as they exist by his goodness. In this respect, even if gifts are given or communicated through the mediation of a human being, the infallibility of God remains in place with respect to his gifts, because the human intermediary has a purely instrumental role here. . . . This is what happens to creatures if God extends his goodness to the point of using them to produce his own divine work.[8]

Congar's emphasis on the divine gift of God to the churches is instructive here. For Congar, these infallible gifts of God, present in and through the sacraments as their precondition, open up broader questions regarding the role of sacraments in churches. But these questions belong more to the framing represented by Luther than to the one I have proposed.[9] For insofar as the church is the gift of the Spirit, Congar would have to concede that the question is not whether churches lacking sacraments are churches but what work needs to be done amid the plurality and divisions of churches.[10]

---

8. Yves Congar, *True and False Reform in the Church*, trans. Paul Philibert (Collegeville, MN: Liturgical Press, 2011), 92–93.

9. This is not to say that Luther is original in articulating these concerns, or that Congar is parroting Luther, but to indicate that the framework that Congar and Luther share begins in a different place than the one this present work adopts.

10. This is indeed the posture taken by the Second Vatican Council, stating how the Catholic Church views members of churches that lack the pope (and thus, by its view, the sacraments as well). In Paul VI, *Unitatis Redintegratio* (Vatican City: Holy See, 1964), 3, https://www.vatican.va/archive/hist_councils/ii_vatican_council/documents/vat-ii_decree_19641121_unitatis-redintegratio_en.html,

By beginning with this double assumption—that (1) the Spirit makes possible our confession of Christ and the constitution of a church and (2) the Spirit's presence brings with it these marks of what a body of Christ is—we can begin to ask new kinds of questions born out of curiosity, asking *how* this is so rather than presuming that it is not so. Approaching ecclesiology in this way opens up the possibility of discovering a fuller range of what these marks can, and in fact do, look like. In examining twentieth-century ecclesiology as taken up by church bodies, we see an expanded vision of what these four marks are and how they might inform our understanding of what it means to be participants in Christ's church.

In his *Sanctorum Communio*, Dietrich Bonhoeffer offers an important account of this dynamic, of how the Holy Spirit constitutes the church and yet churches retain characters rooted in the particularities of history, culture, and time. The Holy Spirit, Bonhoeffer writes, works not only in the particularities of a person but through the particularities of relational bonds of churches, church relations to creation, and the bonds between churches. The Spirit's work here is that of bringing holiness and the knowledge of Christ into the contours of the world, but in a way that does not extract them from creation but brings the work of Christ into ten thousand fields.[11]

As Bonhoeffer puts it, "The Holy Spirit *uses* the objective spirit [of the church] as a vehicle for its gathering and sustaining social activity."[12] This means, in turn, that the Spirit does not overcome time, but works within it

---

we see both the recognition of the Spirit's work in such churches and a critique of how they lack the seven marks:

> The children who are born into these Communities and who grow up believing in Christ cannot be accused of the sin involved in the separation, and the Catholic Church embraces upon them as brothers, with respect and affection. For men who believe in Christ and have been truly baptized are in communion with the Catholic Church even though this communion is imperfect. The differences that exist in varying degrees between them and the Catholic Church—whether in doctrine and sometimes in discipline, or concerning the structure of the Church—do indeed create many obstacles, sometimes serious ones, to full ecclesiastical communion.

11. Here I have in mind something less akin to "letting a thousand flowers bloom" than to assuming that some of the things that occur in and among the churches are weeds within the wheat (Matt. 13:24–43). Plurality as a feature of time is, in Scripture, frequently more a matter of divine patience than of an idealized state; therefore, it belongs to Christians to examine what is present and perhaps to see it as a strange form of wheat.

12. Dietrich Bonhoeffer, *Sanctorum Communio*, ed. Clifford Green, trans. Reinhard Krauss and Nancy Lukens (Minneapolis: Fortress, 1998), 215. For a full exposition of this theme, see Michael Mawson, "The Spirit and the Community: Pneumatology and Ecclesiology in Jenson, Hutter, and Bonhoeffer," *International Journal of Systematic Theology* 15 (2013): 453–68.

to bring the body of Christ to maturity in and through the workings of time, culture, and particularity. For us to tell a story of ecclesiology in the twentieth century that does justice, then, not only to the one work of the Holy Spirit, but also to the various ways in which that one Spirit works means neither telling a story of liberal tolerance masquerading as the Holy Spirit's diverse work nor dismissing the role that time and culture play in theological discourse in favor of reaching conceptual agreement. Telling the story well means presuming that the Spirit *is* working toward unity and that disagreements over what it means to be the body of Christ in the world are part of how that unity is achieved.

The chapters before us will proceed in the following way. We will follow the traditional ordering of the marks—one, holy, catholic, and apostolic—describing not only the ways in which these marks were explicitly contested in denominational and confessional conversations but also how they were implicitly discussed. In each chapter, I have attempted to let the mark be discussed on its own terms, rather than annexing it to another mark, for treating each one singularly allows us to see what is foreclosed when concerns for unity (to take the most frequent example) dominate discussion of the other marks. The aim of each chapter, then, is to offer a composite sketch of the dimensions of each mark, showing that there is surprising overlap in concerns, but also that by asking what lies behind us, we might regain more fully what it means to be the church today. As I state above, the marks are what we find confessed as signs of the Spirit's presence. This approach does not mean that churches cannot be in error about important things, only that God works in, through, and in spite of error to offer gifts nonetheless. We are poorer when we turn these gifts away.

A Final Note: The Twentieth Century in View of the Present

In our own age, anxieties abound concerning the future of church, and particularly about whether an emergency situation is at hand. Questions concerning the future of theological education, decline in church attendance, degraded knowledge by churchgoers—these are not new questions, and they present a temptation toward despair. But despair is partly fueled by the stories we tell about the past: about its glory or richness.

It will be one of the unspoken assumptions of this book that such despair is misplaced for two reasons. First, the past was no less tumultuous than the present. We will be looking at a century that saw not only the rise of the World Council of Churches but also the decline of many established churches in the wake of colonialism's decline. We will be looking at how charismatic influences reconfigured denominations, how gender and race troubled the waters, and how Orthodoxy weathered Communist reversals of fortune. That the twenty-first century has seen numerical declines is, in this view, part of a larger history, and hardly the full picture.

Second, the past does not provide, I argue, a picture only of fragmentation and division. It also provides a vision of hope—hope that church denominations, working out their witness through the guidance of the Holy Spirit, can do so in ways that produce surprising overlap. In the coming chapters, for example, we will see how struggles over nationalism are the common property of both liberal Protestants and the Orthodox. We will also see that common strengths emerge between unlikely partners, such as Orthodox and charismatic churches, Baptist and Methodist churches, Catholic and African Independent churches. Being able to see these convergences offers us a way to name how those unlikely pairings might help us today. If this book was written first of all as an exercise in learning, it has also become, through this, an exercise in hope—hope that God's promise to have a people and to be present to those people does not depend on them either being maximally faithful or availing themselves of all possible riches offered to them by the Spirit through the people of God across time.

None of this obviates the difficulties that have been a part of ecclesiology since time immemorial. There is no golden age to reach back to that gets behind the dynamics of contestation. Churches have experienced rising and falling tides with respect to cooperation, communion, and overlap, but distinctions and differences—particularly over how the body of Christ lives faithfully in creation—are perennially part of what the one body of Christ is. As noted earlier in connection with Bonhoeffer, the Spirit's presence does not override the material shape of churches; rather, the Spirit works within the creaturely realities of churches in ways that invite our curiosity and, indeed, our charity.

That Paul describes the vocation of Christians as being "living sacrifices" is not, then, exclusive of such difficulties, but includes the need to navigate these difficulties well. These differences between churches are not, on this reading, only the result of sin and breaking faith; they are part of what it is to be living sacrifices, to have what we are as creatures caught up in the work of the Holy Spirit, through time, to the praise of the Father and in the unity of the Son. In being living sacrifices, churches offer what God, by the Spirit, has given churches to be in their time and place as they work toward mutual understanding in and through divisions, knowing that ecclesial life is intrinsic to our healing as creatures. But all of this invites us to ask questions of *how*, rather than *if*, the Spirit is at work.

Let us begin the asking.

1

The Rending of the Cloth

The Church as One

The Persistent Pursuit of Unity

The question of unity has long surrounded questions of ecclesiology. Echoing Jesus's prayer in John 17, Cyprian writes in the third century, "He cannot possess the garment of Christ who parts and divides the Church of Christ."[1] But even then, less than two hundred years removed from the world of Scripture, Christian unity was not simple or without its problems. For while the important controversies of the early church—particularly, those with the Donatists and the Marcionites—represent divisions created by denying God's action in baptism or by dividing the Scriptures, respectively, not all divisions among Christians are so easily accounted for or so directly overcome.

It is important to mention these events to remind us that there was no golden age of Christian unity, but that the church's actual unity has always been a work in progress, at times less complicated and less divided, but never simple. In this way, the twentieth century posed no less of a challenge for the church's claim to unity than any previous era, and in some ways it posed more challenges. As

---

1. Cyprian, "On the Unity of the Church," 7, in *The Ante-Nicene Fathers: Translations of the Writings of the Fathers down to A.D. 325*, ed. Alexander Roberts and James Donaldson (Peabody, MA: Hendrickson, 1995), 5:423.

the global state of the Christian faith became a recognized reality, old doctrinal questions emerged, now accompanied by new social questions. Common tenets of the faith did not always guarantee theological agreement, nor did common practices mean universal agreement on what it means for the church to be one.

In this chapter, we will address two primary questions: (1) In what ways were Christian divisions overcome, and (2) in what ways did Christians remain divided? We will look at the major ecumenical ventures of the century, including the emergence of the World Council of Churches, the National Council of Churches, and the mid-century rapprochement between Protestants and Catholics. But approaching these questions will also mean exploring the ways in which various ethical challenges, such as apartheid, the civil rights movement, the World Wars, and decolonialization, divided the churches institutionally and ethically.

In naming the distinctions concerning unity, I aim to help us to begin asking questions about what constitutes unity, and particularly, the limits of the approaches envisioned here. Insofar as no conversation begins from scratch, it is appropriate for us to see these approaches as works in progress, differing both in light of their conversation partners and because of the conditions on the ground. Unity is, in other words, a gift present to the churches in various ways and under the conditions in which they emerge. This acknowledgment is not to negate the unity that appears here, but to have a way to name it well, as the gift that is needed at the time.

Assessing Unity: The Roman Catholic Contribution

The first decades of the twentieth century saw Roman Catholicism describing unity in a way that frequently emphasized the juridical structures of the Church, characterizing reunion among Christians as a return to Rome. Since the mid-nineteenth century, the popes had emphasized that Christian unity remained the unfinished task of the modern era; as *Christi Nomen* (1894) indicates, the work of Christian unity entailed "return to the One Church."[2] The scope of these early conversations was often limited to Anglicans, seen in the Oxford Movement and the Malines Conversations.[3] Throughout the

---

2. George H. Tavard, *Two Centuries of Ecumenism: The Search for Unity* (Notre Dame, IN: Fides, 1960), 70. Other encyclicals emphasizing this theme include *Grande Munus* (1880), *Praeclara Gratulationis* (1894), and *Provida Matris* (1895).

3. Tavard, *Two Centuries of Ecumenism*, 32–55.

early decades of the twentieth century, movements to initiate dialogue between Catholic and Protestant teaching faculties, and even to open conversation with Lutherans, were not unheard of.[4] Indeed, even the "Faith and Order" movement that emerged after the 1910 Edinburgh Conference was commended by Pope Benedict XVI (though Catholic participation was absent at the conference).[5]

This is not to say, however, that these early conversations were unproblematic from a Catholic vantage point. Pius XI's *Mortalium Animos* (1928), which forbade Catholic participation in the nascent work of the ecumenical movement, displays the deep difference between Protestants and Catholics in conceiving church unity. The logic of *Mortalium*—that the unity of doctrine could not be divided into discrete pieces around which Christians could unite, inasmuch as Christ's person cannot be divided—stood in stark contrast to reunion as occurring through discursive reasoning, which is an approach one sees in the World Council of Churches.[6] And yet, on the ground, there remained deep interest in reunion: an institute for the study of Eastern Orthodox theology came into existence in 1922, and the Amay monastery (dedicated to ecumenical reunion) was founded in 1925.[7]

Given the early engagements between Catholics and various Protestant groups, what then posed the problem? Theologically, the nub of the issue can be summed up by Yves Congar's 1939 assessment:

> The oneness of the Church is a communication and extension of the oneness of God Himself. The Life which is in the bosom of the Father is not only

---

4. In the universities of Tübingen and Heidelberg, for example, there were separate Catholic and Protestant theological faculties. On the roots of their relationship see Bradford E. Hinze, "Roman Catholic Theology: Tübingen," in *The Blackwell Companion to Nineteenth-Century Theology*, ed. David Fergusson (Malden, MA: Blackwell, 2010).

5. Hinze, "Roman Catholic Theology," 78.

6. *Mortalium Animos*, 8: "This being so, it is clear that the Apostolic See cannot on any terms take part in their assemblies, nor is it anyway lawful for Catholics either to support or to work for such enterprises; for if they do so they will be giving countenance to a false Christianity, quite alien to the one Church of Christ." See Pius XI, *Mortalium Animos* (Vatican City: Holy See, 1928), http://w2.vatican.va/content/pius-xi/en/encyclicals/documents/hf_p-xi_enc_19280106_mortalium-animos.html. As William Henn describes, the WCC's approach in the early 1920s was one of comparative doctrine rather than seeking points of doctrinal convergence. "The Achievements of Faith and Order," in *Celebrating a Century of Ecumenism: Exploring the Achievements of International Dialogue* (Grand Rapids: Eerdmans, 2012), 41.

7. See also Pius XI's encyclical *Rerum Orientalium*, which orders the introduction of courses studying Orthodox theology in Catholic seminaries. *Rerum Orientalium* (Vatican City: Holy See, 1928), available at Papal Encyclicals Online, https://www.papalencyclicals.net/pius11/p11reror.htm#:~:text.

communicated within the Godhead itself, thus constituting the Divine *Societas* of the Three Persons of the Blessed Trinity. . . . The church is precisely this extension of the divine life to a multitude of creatures, not as a result of their own exertions to develop their religious sense or to lead a life similar to God's, but by the imparting to them of the very life of God itself, so that they actually share the life and participate in the purposes of God.[8]

In Congar's words, we can observe that for Roman Catholicism, the church's unity could not be broken into separate discussions of doctrine and polity, as, from Congar's perspective, these are interwoven realities: confession of the One God could be mirrored only by a unified liturgical life. As Congar notes, the oneness of the church was not about "develop[ing] the religious sense" (Faith and Order) or "lead[ing] a life similar to God's" (Life and Work) in a first-order sense, but about receiving the life of God in a sacramental way, participating in the gift of God in a way that *then* gave rise to the "religious sense" and "life similar to God's."

Early conversations and ecumenical overtures stalled during two world wars, reignited by the 1964 landmark decree *Unitatis Redintegratio*, at the Second Vatican Council. In that decree, the council addressed the burgeoning question of Christian division, stating that God "has been rousing divided Christians to remorse over their divisions and to a longing for unity."[9] *Unitatis*'s concerns, however, should not be read overoptimistically, as the concerns of *Unitatis* must be held together with the statement in *Lumen Gentium* that "the one Church of Christ . . . subsists in the Catholic Church, which is governed by the successor of Peter and by the Bishops in communion with him."[10]

Even so, the admission that church unity "subsists" in Rome signaled a different way forward than previous statements on church unity. Previous councils, such as the First Vatican Council, contained little language about intrafraternal unity, while the Second Vatican Council documents explicitly address the implications of Christian division for liturgy, mission, and social

---

8. Yves Congar, OP, *Divided Christendom: A Catholic Study of the Problem of Reunion* (London: Centenary Press, 1939), 48.
9. Paul VI, *Unitatis Redintegratio* (Vatican City: Holy See, 1964), 1, https://www.vatican.va/archive/hist_councils/ii_vatican_council/documents/vat-ii_decree_19641121_unitatis-redintegratio_en.html.
10. Paul VI, *Lumen Gentium* (Vatican City: Holy See, 1964), 8, https://www.vatican.va/archive/hist_councils/ii_vatican_council/documents/vat-ii_const_19641121_lumen-gentium_en.html.

action. *Unitatis*, for example, declares that "men who believe in Christ and have been truly baptized are in communion with the Catholic Church," though their baptism outside of the Catholic Church is accompanied by structural and doctrinal differences.[11] This fraternal unity, however, remained a kind of unity-in-separation, insofar as naming Protestants and Orthodox as "separated brethren" involved naming them as family, yet *estranged* family. Worship in common was not prescribed indiscriminately, baptisms still lacked fullness of unity, and moral teachings remained disjointed between Protestants and Catholics.[12]

What should become clear in this discussion is that the Second Vatican Council does not reject alternate approaches to the oneness of the church; rather, it operates out of a vision of the church's oneness not as an *achievement* but as a *gift* in which liturgy and life coinhere. As Congar indicates, because the church emerges as the corresponding image of God's own unity, the oneness of the church is not a matter of bricolage. Various touchpoints between aspects of Catholicism and other Christians can be seen in liturgy, doctrine, and common witness, but each of these aspects bears witness to a more complex whole. Additional declarations on the role of the laity, on the nature of the church in the modern world, and on the liturgy broadened out conciliar definitions of the church, creating more touchpoints between Catholics and other Christians, but without walking back this fundamental point. Material disagreements persisted over any number of topics, but the role of the pontiff at Rome continued to loom over these ecumenical discussions.[13]

In sum, Vatican II offered recognition of non-Catholic churches because of their possession of those things common to all churches (Scripture, prayer, doctrine), but since unity names a coinherence of teaching and worship, full unity would remain elusive: analogies may exist, but unity was not just a matter of finding analogous positions. Even so, the remainder of the twentieth

---

11. Paul VI, *Unitatis Redintegratio*, 3.
12. Paul VI, *Unitatis Redintegratio*, 8, 22, 23. This understanding stems from the church not simply as a juridical institution but as an entrance into the mystery of Christ. For a cogent articulation of this, see Pius XII, *Mystici Corporis Christi* (Vatican City: Holy See, 1943), http://w2.vatican.va/content/pius-xii/en/encyclicals/documents/hf_p-xii_enc_29061943_mystici-corporis-christi.html.
13. As put by Pope Paul VI, "The pope, we well know, is without doubt the most serious obstacle on the road to ecumenism" (*Acta Apostolicae Sedis* [Vatican City: Holy See, 1967], 497–98). For one proposal on resolving this, see Jean-Louis Leuba, "Papacy, Protestantism and Ecumenism," *Ecumenical Review* 46 (1994): 467–74.

century saw the emergence of evangelical-Catholic alliances,[14] Catholic-Lutheran dialogues,[15] Catholic-Orthodox dialogues,[16] and Pentecostal-Catholic dialogues[17]—to name but a few of these ventures, committed to the unity of Christians despite material differences of doctrine and polity.

Assessing Unity: The World Council of Churches

The contribution of Roman Catholicism opens up an important question: What is the role of *discovery* in the search for unity? In knitting together liturgical realities with moral action, Catholicism appears as an integral whole that is self-interpreting: unity is that which is received as a whole, though there may be echoes elsewhere of that particular form. Therefore, ecumenical ventures that do not propose this starting point, even serious ones, have an uncertain purpose. Alongside the "receptive ecumenical" proposals of Walter Kasper, the president of the Pontifical Council for Promoting Christian Unity—which emphasizes seeing divided Christians as offering gifts to be received to and from one another[18]—were alternative proposals emphasizing a need to "return to Rome," that unity required leaving particular communions for the Roman Catholic Church. In the World Council of Churches, however, we find a different approach—that through contestation, unity might be *discovered*, for in the midst of a fractured Christianity, such an approach offers reparation in the pursuit of unity.

The World Council of Churches—which would become the largest ecumenical body among Protestants—grew out of a distinctly different set of

14. Dennis R. Hoover, "Ecumenism of the Trenches? The Politics of Evangelical-Catholic Alliances," *Journal of Ecumenical Studies* 41 (2004): 247–71.

15. For a cataloging of these efforts, see Jeffrey Gros, "Hope for Eternal Life: The Lutheran-Catholic Dialogue," *Journal of Ecumenical Studies* 46 (2011): 259–69. Most preeminent among the work in this area was the *Joint Declaration on the Doctrine of Justification*, produced by the Lutheran World Federation and the Catholic Church. See *Joint Declaration on the Doctrine of Justification* (Vatican City: Dicastery for Promoting Christian Unity, 2018–22), http://www.christianunity.va/content/unitacristiani/en/dialoghi/sezione-occidentale/luterani/dialogo/documenti-di-dialogo/1999-dichiarazione-congiunta-sulla-dottrina-della-giustificazion.html.

16. John Borelli and John H. Erickson, *The Quest for Unity: Orthodox and Catholics in Dialogue* (Crestwood, NY: St. Vladimir's Seminary Press, 1996).

17. See the dialogue documents from the Dicastery for Promoting Christian Unity, Catholic Pentecostal International Dialogue, https://www.christianunity.va/content/unitacristiani/en/dialoghi/sezione-occidentale/pentecostali/dialogo/documenti-di-dialogo.html.

18. For an overview of the approach, including Kasper's work, see Paul D. Murray, *Receptive Ecumenism and the Call to Catholic Learning: Exploring a Way for Contemporary Ecumenism* (Oxford: Oxford University Press, 2008).

concerns, directed no less toward the divisions that plagued Christians at the dawn of the twentieth century, but conceiving a different road forward than pre–Vatican II Catholicism. Since the late sixteenth century, non-Catholic Christianity had proliferated into a variety of movements, some of which traced their roots back into Catholicism and some of which proffered a new way to be Christian entirely. Groups as disparate as Anglicans, Baptists, Pentecostals, Lutherans, and Mennonites spread out globally, bringing a new challenge to the Christian claim of unity: In what sense, in the face of multiplying denominations, was it even possible to speak of Christian unity?

By the early part of the century, the issue of Christian division was affecting one of the central concerns of many Protestant bodies: missionary work. And so, in 1910, twelve hundred delegates from across a variety of Christian denominations gathered together at the World Missionary Conference, in Edinburgh, to explore the variety of issues facing Protestant missionaries in the field. The conference, the result of nearly three years of planning, was largely pragmatic in nature, assessing what had been done in the previous decades and determining what work remained.[19] In the wake of the Edinburgh conference, it became apparent that, rather than a one-time meeting, an ongoing labor was needed if the divisions over mission were to be healed both theologically and practically. In 1927, the first World Conference on Faith and Order convened in Lausanne, paired later with the Universal Christian Council on Life and Work in 1934, emerging as the World Council of Churches (WCC) in 1948.

Other aspects of the WCC will be addressed in later chapters, but one assumption operated here that would offer a significant divergence from the Catholic approach: the plurality—and parity—of the ecclesial bodies who composed this group. Rather than assume a common structure among the attendees, who ranged ecclesiastically from Presbyterians and Anglicans to free church missionaries and the Christian Missionary Alliance, the gathering focused on the sending capacity of the "home base" of each group, and how each home base could facilitate mission.[20] Protestant groups differed widely with respect to both theological views and polity; while these theological differences could be productively discussed, the ecclesiological nature of these

---

19. For a full account of the conference, see Brian Stanley, *The World Missionary Conference, Edinburgh 1910* (Grand Rapids: Eerdmans, 2009).

20. See David G. Dawson, "The Church and the Edinburgh Missionary Conference," *Missiology* 39 (2011): 157–73.

missions could not be questioned without undermining the very foundation of the gathering itself.

This affected, and continues to affect, the World Council's vision of church unity in two ways. First, the WCC constituted itself by working with local denominational forms as opposed to national councils of churches.[21] This decision, which the council made in order to be able to incorporate the broadest possible base of Christian groups, meant in turn that the starting point of unity it was able to envision was more practical than liturgical; by choosing to maintain ecclesiastical parity among its members, the WCC has no authority over its members doctrinally.[22] Put more positively, this decision has also meant that the WCC has been able to incorporate as many voices as possible into its meetings, respond to geopolitical concerns to unity more quickly, and thus to undertake the needs of its global constituency in a timely fashion.

Second, the WCC, from the beginning, saw both issues of polity and issues of social witness as issues of significance for Christian unity. By adopting these two foci, the WCC enabled its members to key in on specific modes of Christian division, some of which stem from specifically liturgical issues and some from the material and social issues surrounding the church's worship. This separation from doctrinal questions and from social questions allows for the WCC to have a dual approach to how unity might be found, while still seeking a comprehensive unity of both liturgy and social witness. This is to recognize that the unity that the Spirit brings might begin prior to a mutual recognition liturgically.

The difference between Vatican II and the WCC with regard to the unity of the church should not be cast in terms of one (the WCC) being concerned with mission and the other (Roman Catholicism) being concerned with unity as a matter of institution. Instead, the fault line between the two approaches lies with the relationship *between* liturgical unity and social action. Whereas Vatican II is quite clear that church unity requires more than social action, the WCC has been less clear on this point. Because the two tracks of the WCC (Faith and Order / Life and Work) constitute two distinct sets of concerns (liturgy / social witness), questions have been raised as to whether the WCC

21. S. Wesley Ariarajah, "Achievements and Limits of the World Council of Churches," in *Celebrating a Century of Ecumenism: Exploring the Achievements of International Dialogue*, ed. John A. Radano (Grand Rapids: Eerdmans, 2012), 5–7.

22. As articulated in the 1948 Amsterdam assembly: "The Council disavows any thought of becoming a single unified church structure independent of the churches that have joined in constituting the Council." Ariarajah, "Achievements and Limits," 6.

sees a connection between these two dimensions of unity, or whether these constitute two unrelated barriers to church unity, such that the unity of the church can be facilitated at *either* a liturgical or a social level.

The WCC's response to this criticism is best articulated in the 1951 statement "The Calling of the Church to Mission and to Unity," which frames the question of Christian unity very much in terms of its mission: "The division in our thought and practice between 'Church' and 'Mission' can be overcome only as we return to Christ Himself in whom the Church has its being and its task, and to a fresh understanding of what He has done, is doing, and will do. . . . The obligation to take the Gospel to the whole world, and the obligation to draw all Christ's people together both rest upon Christ's whole work, and are indissolubly connected. Every attempt to separate these two tasks violates the wholeness of Christ's ministry to the world."[23]

It is here, I suggest, that we see how these dual elements of the WCC cohere. While issues of social witness and liturgy are significant areas of unity, missions (the founding concern of the WCC) constitutes the true hope for Christian unity in this arrangement. Absent a commitment to the fullness of the Spirit's presence in and through newer churches, unity would continue to be foreshortened to those liturgical and moral issues and to the ecclesial partners already present. As the WCC's partners became more global in scope, without abandoning its theme of unity-in-mission, the acknowledgment began to grow that many of the WCC's prior meetings had neglected many of its global partners.

Beginning in New Delhi (1961), the interrelationship between unity and local ecclesial forms became a more significant part of WCC discussions. This meant emphasizing the familiar themes of "one committed fellowship, holding the one apostolic faith, preaching the one Gospel, breaking the one bread," but also addressing the ways in which this apostolic faith was appropriated in an increasingly global church.[24] Actualizing this in various global settings, for example, meant allowing for latitude among the members with regard to doctrine and ethics, while still coming together for common missions.[25] At this juncture, the response of the Second Vatican Council seems apparent: common

---

23. World Council of Churches, "The Calling of the Church to Mission and to Unity," in *A Documentary History of the Faith and Order Movement 1927–1963*, ed. Lukas Vischer (St. Louis: Bethany Press, 1963), 173–74.
24. World Council of Churches, "The Calling of the Church to Mission and to Unity," 144–45.
25. World Council of Churches, "The Calling of the Church to Mission and to Unity," 151.

witness, while important, cannot sidestep questions of whether or not a church is marked by the fullness of God's presence; such issues, as we have already seen, create limits to what kind of ecclesial unity the Spirit might materially bring.

Assessing Unity: The Eastern Orthodox Churches

This picture of the twentieth-century drive toward Christian unity would not be complete without bringing in the Eastern Orthodox churches. This is difficult, however, for two reasons. First, there is no directly corresponding event in the twentieth century among the Orthodox that is quite like the founding of the World Council of Churches or the Second Vatican Council.[26] The Orthodox churches, unlike the Protestant members of the WCC, have never seen their independence from other Christian communions as conditioned by the need to preserve "autonomy" in quite the same way, and unlike Catholics, they do not have a hierarchy within which there is a titular head of all Orthodox churches. Operating as a unified series of patriarchs, metropolitans, and archbishops, Orthodox churches have generally not seen the need for "reunion" movements like the WCC or for the reforming events of Vatican II. As John Meyendorff observes, the Orthodox churches have broadly prioritized unity of faith and confession in such a way that each of the autocephalous churches has its own contextual history, liturgical variances, and moral questions that do not always materially affect its unity with the other Orthodox communions.[27]

The second major difficulty with drawing Eastern Orthodoxy into this discussion, from a twentieth-century vantage point, was suspicion of "the West" present among many Orthodox churches during the early twentieth century. Having developed historically in the shadow of both Islamic and Catholic persecution, the Orthodox churches were proportionally less concerned with reuniting the fragments of Western Christendom than they were with nurturing their local communions. Through the late Middle Ages and Reformation years, Orthodox churches and their Western counterparts would dialogue on occasion, but these occasions usually resulted in mutual frustration and

---

26. The Fourth General Assembly of *Syndemesmos* (a federation of Orthodox youth) created an office for Orthodox unity and missions in 1958, but this, as Meyendorff notes, was more concerned with intra-Orthodox unity and missions, not primarily with relations between the Orthodox and other Christians. See John Meyendorff, *Catholicity and the Church* (New York: St. Vladimir's Seminary Press, 1983), 106–8.

27. John Meyendorff, *The Orthodox Church: Its Past and Its Role in the World Today* (Crestwood, NY: St. Vladimir's Press, 1981), 64–67.

further mistrust.[28] As the twentieth century unfolded, these historical wounds were not entirely mitigated, as various Orthodox communions found themselves having to carefully navigate new nationalist regimes rising out of the remnants of the old Byzantine and Ottoman empires. Whereas, in western Europe, strong nation-states had often aided the emergence of Protestant denominations, the emergence of nationalism proved to be a cause of great suffering for many Orthodox churches, particularly the Armenian communion.[29]

This complicated relationship to the West can be best seen in Russian Orthodoxy. In the late nineteenth century, the Russian Orthodox revival turned on an explicit rejection of "the West" and a turn toward a fully Slavophilic Orthodox church.[30] In practice, Russian Orthodoxy followed the lead of various other Orthodox communions and was fully indigenized in language, organization, and leadership. But among some of its luminary theologians, a new openness began to be expressed for engaging with Western philosophy and theology. The writings of Sergius Bulgakov, though recapitulating patristic themes, began to critically engage with German idealism and Western theology, as did the work of other Orthodox thinkers such as Georges Florovsky and John Zizioulas.[31] Though historical wounds and suspicion about Western corruption of the ancient faith remained, and motivated detractors,

---

28. Meyendorff, *Orthodox Church*, 91, describes reunion attempts made in 1454 and 1484 on behalf of the Eastern Orthodox churches toward Roman Catholicism, rooted not in mutual recognition so much as the desire for Catholics to abandon the papacy and return to Orthodoxy. Overtures made by a group of Lutheran theologians in 1574 toward ecumenical patriarch Jeremias II met with similar ends. On the Reformation-era relations between Orthodox churches and the Reformation churches, see Ernst Benz, *Wittenberg und Byzanz: Zur Begegnung und Auseinandersetzung der Reformation und der Östlich-orthodoxen Kirche* (Marburg: Elwert-Gräfe und Unzer Verlag, 1949).

29. For an overview of the Armenian Orthodox communion in the modern era, see S. Peter Cowe, "Church and Diaspora: The Case of the Armenians," in *The Cambridge History of Christianity*, vol. 5, *Eastern Christianity*, ed. Michael Angold (Cambridge: Cambridge University Press, 2006): 430–57.

30. For overviews of the Russian Orthodox church and its ambivalent relationship with Western nationalism, see Nathaniel Davis, *A Long Walk to Church: A Contemporary History of Russian Orthodoxy* (Boulder, CO: Westview, 2003); and Edward E. Roslof, *Red Priests: Renovationism, Russian Orthodoxy, and Revolution, 1905–1946* (Bloomington: Indiana University Press, 2002). On the depiction of "the West" in Russian Orthodoxy in the late nineteenth and early twentieth centuries, see Vera Shevzov, "The Burdens of Tradition: Orthodox Constructions of the West in Russia (late 19th–early 20th cc.)," in *Orthodox Constructions of the West*, ed. George E. Demacopoulos and Aristotle Papanikolaou (New York: Fordham University Press, 2013), 83–101.

31. See Aristotle Papanikolaou, "Eastern Orthodox Theology," in *The Routledge Companion to Modern Christian Thought*, ed. Chad Meister and James Beilby (London: Routledge, 2013), 538–49. For Bulgakov's idealist engagements, see Sergius Bulgakov, *The Comforter*, trans. Boris

others in Eastern Orthodox communions continued to evince openness to the West during the twentieth century.[32]

Despite some movement, Eastern Orthodox and Roman Catholic dialogue remained stalled over one of the central ecclesiological tenets that we saw in Vatican II: the role of the papacy. To assert the see of Peter as preeminent over other centers of Christianity flew in the face of Eastern Orthodox ecclesiology, which envisioned each autocephalous church as equal to the others. The communion theology that emerged during Vatican II, however, promised a new way forward. Briefly, communion theology emphasized the centrality of the local church, that the fullness of Christ was present in each legitimate communion of the church.[33] Such was the promise of this new emphasis that Ecumenical Patriarch Athenagoras joined with Paul VI during the final session of Vatican II in lifting the mutual anathemas of 1054 that had divided the Eastern Orthodox churches from the Roman Catholic ones.

If these authorities jointly recognized each other at the landmark event of twentieth-century ecumenism, what could keep these two Christian traditions apart? Broadly, it is an issue looked at in two ways. From the Orthodox vantage point, papal primacy remains a stumbling block for conversations: to place the pope in an elevated position is a non-starter. But from the Catholic vantage point, as Joseph Ratzinger wrote, the papacy is part of God's work that the East must come to terms with: it is part of the historical experience of the church in the West, part of God's own work, and not a corruption of the original faith.[34] In the same way that Eastern Orthodoxy had developed in

---

Jakim (Grand Rapids: Eerdmans, 2004); Bulgakov, *The Lamb of God*, trans. Boris Jakim (Grand Rapids: Eerdmans, 2008).

32. Consider two opposing volumes, both published in the wake of the Second Vatican Council, both from within the Greek Orthodox Church: Athenagoras, *Introduction to the Theological Dialogue of Anglicans and Orthodox*, report of a commission of the Fourth Pan-Orthodox Conference, Belgrade, 1966 (Athens: n.p., 1967); and Alexander Kalomiras, *Against False Union: Humble Thoughts of an Orthodox Christian concerning the Attempts for Union of the One, Holy, Catholic, and Apostolic Church with the So-Called Churches of the West*, with a prologue by Photios Kontoglou, trans. George Gabriel (Boston: Holy Transfiguration Monastery, 1967).

33. Christ is "truly present in all legitimately organized local groups of the faithful, which insofar as they are united to their pastors, are also quite appropriately called Churches." Paul VI, *Lumen Gentium* (Vatican City: Holy See, 1964), 26, https://www.vatican.va/archive/hist_councils/ii_vatican_council/documents/vat-ii_const_19641121_lumen-gentium_en.html.

34. Joseph Ratzinger, *Church, Ecumenism, and Politics* (New York: Crossroads, 1988), 81–82:
 It is no use expecting the concept of the papacy to change quickly or easily to an image of the Pope comparable with our image of an Eastern Patriarch as primus inter pares in our sense. We must understand and accept the fact that papal primacy has over the

multiple cultures, producing deep wellsprings of theological wisdom that the whole could now benefit from, so Western Christianity (including, arguably, non-Catholic Christianity) had its own history of God's living and active work that the East could not readily disavow without negating God's past work.

Beyond Catholicism, the WCC, and Eastern Orthodoxy

That Ratzinger—later Pope Benedict XVI—would make the argument about the need for openness toward Catholicism as a matter of contextual faithfulness creates an intriguing opening not only for this conversation between Catholics and Orthodox but for a response to the divide posited between Catholicism and the World Council of Churches, as well as for openness toward other configurations of unity.

For if context is allowed to play into how unity develops, then a new vista for the oneness of the church appears. This is a thread that will continue into other marks of the church, particularly catholicity, but must be noted here. For even within conversations about how the church is one, a new and haunted kind of discussion emerges: what happens in the spaces beyond the older conversations between Catholics, Orthodox, and mainline Protestants may be of significance not because it is "contextual" but because it is through contexts that the one Spirit draws out unforeseen dimensions of this mark of the church.

If we look beyond the most prominent approaches of the twentieth century, we find a variety of alternate approaches, such as spiritual unity, a unity of missions, or hermeneutical unity. In the approaches above, issues of doctrinal and practical unity were identified but largely kept as separate discussions; other movements and groups identified these dynamics of disunity as well, but yielded different results. When one turns to other forms of Christianity not typically associated with the WCC, the picture of the church's unity in the twentieth century becomes increasingly complex, if not altogether overwhelming. In the following section, I will draw out these three approaches to the church's unity, placing them into conversation with

---

course of the Western Church's history, become a constitutive element in Roman Catholicism. What we must decide is whether we cannot still move towards communion, while accepting that that primacy is an internal affair of the Roman Church. As long as Rome does not force it upon the other churches, it can remain merely a problem for her own people, to the extent that they themselves decide to accept or reject it.

the approaches we have already seen. The examples here are by no means exhaustive, but they indicate some of the manifold ecclesiological developments of the era.

Unity of the Spirit

The birth of Pentecostal Christianity,[35] for example, introduces a new variety of Christianity that describes the unity of the church as a matter of the Holy Spirit's working, and not a matter of transdenominational mechanisms such as the WCC or Vatican bilateral dialogues. Though appearing in various forms and theological shades, Pentecostal churches hold to the priority of the Spirit's work for establishing the church and its unity. Calling themselves simply "the Apostolic Faith" early on, Azusa Street Pentecostals emphasized the spiritual and invisible unity of the faith.[36]

The American Pentecostal movement developed apart from formal ecumenical bodies until they, along with the Assemblies of God and the Church of God (charismatic denominations), joined the National Association of Evangelicals in 1943.[37] This American development finds parallels on a grassroots level throughout Europe and, in recent years, has become more prominent as more Latin American and African Pentecostal groups join with the WCC's efforts.[38] But for many years, the Pentecostal appeal to the spiritual and invisible unity of Christianity, apart from the need for further clarification, along with widespread prejudices against Pentecostalism among American

---

35. In this section, I will use the designations "Pentecostal" and "charismatic" loosely and as rough equivalents, though I recognize there is disagreement among scholars about whether a distinction between the two should be made, and if so, what kind. As Allan Anderson notes, the distinction between the two typically refers to whether a church identifies with the institutional bodies of Pentecostalism or subscribes to its tenets outside the denominations that identify as Pentecostal (*An Introduction to Pentecostalism* [Oxford: Oxford University Press, 2004], 144). There are innumerable churches—as we will see in chap. 2—where the effects of the charismatic movement are seen, but as features *among* Baptists, *among* Episcopalians, and so forth, not as fundamental to ecclesial life. In this section, I will reference the former groups, which do not identify with a second ecclesiological framework.

36. Anderson, *Introduction to Pentecostalism*, 249.

37. Anderson, *Introduction to Pentecostalism*, 250.

38. See Walter J. Hollenweger, *Pentecostalism: Origins and Developments Worldwide* (Peabody, MA: Hendrickson, 2007), 334–69. On the globalization of Pentecostalism, see Donald E. Miller, Kimon H. Sargeant, and Richard Flory, eds., *Spirit and Power: The Growth and Global Impact of Pentecostalism* (Oxford: Oxford University Press, 2013); and Karl Poewe, ed., *Charismatic Christianity as a Global Culture* (Columbia: University of South Carolina Press, 1994).

denominations, hindered whatever contributions Pentecostals might have made early on to the church's unity.[39]

Pentecostals and other charismatic groups, though participating in larger doctrinal discussions (such as with the WCC), more frequently envisioned Pentecostal and charismatic experience as a spiritual gift to all the churches, in two senses. First, Pentecostals offered to churches a vision of the actuality of many biblical things that European churches frequently took to have been mythological, such as miracles and glossolalia. David J. Du Plessis, a leader in the South African Pentecostal churches and general secretary of the World Pentecostal Conferences between 1949 and 1958, illustrates this point.[40] For Du Plessis, and many other Pentecostals, the supernatural occurrences described in Scripture are, rather, "part and parcel of a Christian's life," and thus not strictly for those of Pentecostal denominations. By demonstrating the actuality of healings, miracles, tongues, prophecy, and other aspects of Scripture that moderns typically take as "mythological," Du Plessis contended that Pentecostals provide a vision that could be captured by other Christians as well. In other words, unity is not so much achieved through a common doctrinal position (though these aspects matter), but through a common participation in the one Spirit.

The Pentecostal movement, though distinct in theology and teaching, finds its position regarding church unity echoed by a variety of charismatic groups across the twentieth century. American groups such as the Vineyard Fellowship and Calvary Chapel formed networks of congregations across the country; while their churches formed associations with one another on the basis of doctrine, their unity was often articulated in terms of its invisible basis. But as one of the members of William Seymour's congregation noted,[41] this unity is difficult to achieve, for every name given to a movement—even one as

---

39. Late twentieth-century developments in Pentecostal dialogues attempted to rectify many of the century-long prejudices. As the report from the dialogue between the Pontifical Council for Promoting Christian Unity and some classical Pentecostal Churches (1985–1989) affirmed, "Pentecostals tend to view denominations as more or less legitimate manifestations of the one, universal Church. Their legitimacy depends on the degree of their faithfulness to the fundamental doctrines of the Scripture. We both agree that the Holy Spirit is the Spirit of unity in diversity (cf. *1 Cor* 12:13ff.) and not the Spirit of division." *Perspectives on Koinonia* (Vatican City: Dicastery for Promoting Christian Unity, 1989), 34, http://www.christianunity.va/content/unitacristiani/en/dialoghi/sezione-occidentale/pentecostali/dialogo/documenti-di-dialogo/testo-in-inglese1.html#:~:text=Pentecostals%20tend%20to%20view%20denominations,1%20Cor%2012:13ff.

40. Hollenweger, *Pentecostalism*, 351ff.

41. Seymour is one of the key figures in the origination of Pentecostalism.

innocent as "the Apostolic Faith"—re-creates divisions that are then overcome not through institutional structures but by appeals to spiritual unity.[42] This caveat aside, what is notable about the Pentecostal mode of the church's oneness is how this emphasis on spiritual (and not confessional) unity has been allowed to take root in various places and cultures and to exercise influence on various other traditions.[43]

The Pentecostal/charismatic ethos of the church's unity provides an important counterpoint to the traditioned approach of twentieth-century Catholicism and the dialogical approach of the WCC. By emphasizing the common spirituality of the Christian life, a Pentecostal approach speaks to the common root of Christian unity in the encounter of God, prior to the articulation of this unity in doctrine or common witness. To be sure, Pentecostal theology is governed by the Scriptures, but doctrinal explication of the Scriptures passes through the fulcrum of the experience of "Spirit-baptism," the reception of the Holy Spirit that connotes the beginning of the Christian life. By Pentecostal lights, while doctrine is essential in naming and giving reasons for Pentecostal beliefs, the various groups associated with the Pentecostal movement began to divide precisely when doctrinal self-definition took precedence over the unity of experience of the Spirit.[44]

Though Pentecostals would divide institutionally over any number of doctrinal issues, producing alternative charismatic movements, the Pentecostal ethos of unity—the affirmation of a common recognition of the Spirit across denominations—took root globally. Following the Nigerian civil war, for example, Anglicans and neo-Pentecostals found themselves deeply at odds over issues of clerical authority, the role of tradition in church life, and emergent strains of "prosperity gospel" in some Nigerian charismatic

---

42. Anderson, *Introduction to Pentecostalism*, 249.

43. Hollenweger, *Pentecostalism*, 41–129; Miller, Sargeant, and Flory, *Spirit and Power*, 185–224. Movements inspired by Pentecostalism, ranging from the Catholic charismatic movement to the Reformed Church–based Pentecostalism in France, show the way in which Pentecostalism has influenced other traditions, while the resources above attest to the global and cultural reach of Pentecostalism.

44. Terrence Robert Crowe, *Pentecostal Unity: Recurring Frustration and Enduring Hopes* (Chicago: Loyola University Press, 1993), 180ff. See also Anderson, *Introduction to Pentecostalism*, 45ff. This is not to say that these doctrinal differences were not worth the struggle. Groups such as the "Oneness" Pentecostal movement, founded less than a decade after Azusa Street, emphasize a nontriune God—that "Father," "Son," and "Spirit" are three names of God rather than three persons of the One God. Similarly, divisions between Pentecostals and the Assemblies of God emerged over issues of how to define the work of Christ as final or open to further revelation by the Spirit.

churches.[45] By the late 1990s, however, many Nigerian Anglican churches had begun adopting charismatic practices, such as prophecy, speaking in tongues, and ecstatic worship styles. This could be read as shrewd adaptation by the Anglicans, but more charitably, this seems to be an instance of the core spirituality of the neo-Pentecostals—characterized by vibrant, ecstatic religious experience—being shared across denominational lines where other questions of liturgy proved more durable obstacles to unity.[46]

Criticisms of this form of unity, most notably by Anglican ecumenist Lesslie Newbigin, were not uncommon. Newbigin noted that Pentecostals could be prone to a "non-historical mysticism in which the work of the Holy Spirit in the heart is regarded as practically independent of Christ's work in the flesh, the Scriptures, and the sacraments."[47] The emphasis on a common work of the Spirit—the basis of many Pentecostal visions of church unity—required, Newbigin held, corresponding attention to order, lest attention to the gifts of the Spirit be pitted against the unitive work of the Spirit.[48]

As Newbigin indicates, this is not to negate the Pentecostal emphasis, but to warn against visions of church unity that cohere only at an invisible, mystical level. From the view of Catholicism, "spiritual ecumenism" took a slightly different approach, emphasizing the doxological dimensions of ecumenism; in the words of Walter Kasper, "It is significant that Jesus did not primarily express his desire for unity in a teaching or in a commandment but in a prayer to his Father."[49] Agreeing with the Pentecostal principle that unity is a "gift from above," Kapser differs by stating that the prayer for unity leads once again to looking for a visible shape to that unity, so that unity might move forward.

The explicitly pneumatological basis for this form of invisible unity was not the only way in which this pursuit of unity took place. The African independent church movement, in its various forms, has also been characterized in this manner. The multiplicity of African cultures yielded—both before and

---

45. As Jesse Zink describes, this conflict between Nigerians was due in no small part to the influence of American prosperity gospel preachers who had invested significant resources in Nigeria during the late 1980s and beyond. Jesse Zink, "'Anglocostalism' in Nigeria: Neo-Pentecostalism and Obstacles to Anglican Unity," *Journal of Anglican Studies* 10 (2012): 237–38.

46. Zink, "'Anglocostalism' in Nigeria," 246.

47. Lesslie Newbigin, *The Household of God: Lectures on the Nature of the Church* (London: SCM, 1953), 98–99.

48. On this point, see Geoffrey Wainright, "The One Hope of Your Calling? The Ecumenical and Pentecostal Movements after a Century," *PNEUMA* 25 (2003): 14.

49. Walter Kasper, *A Handbook of Spiritual Ecumenism* (New York: New City Press, 2007), 10.

after decolonialization—a plurality of local churches that reflected their locality, but without many of the institutional or formal mechanisms of unity characteristic of European churches. Far from declining, Christianity in Africa multiplied over the course of the twentieth century, though not solely through traditional churches, which were frequently associated with colonial pasts.[50]

Throughout the century, alongside traditional denominations, new congregations of Zionist, Pentecostal, and independent evangelical varieties began to appear, as new forms of Christianity began to develop.[51] The sociocultural reasons for the development of these churches differed from country to country, but the African Independent Church (AIC) movement, as it came to be known, is broadly brought together in the assumption that the Holy Spirit raised up individual leaders who then would lead the congregations and that the Holy Spirit worked within congregations to contextualize the faith to their cultural moment.[52]

As M. L. Daneel observes, a common feature of many within the AIC is that of call-dreams, visions, and divinely inspired church leaders.[53] This focus on church leaders as divinely inspired is not a shrewd cover for building up personality-focused ecclesiastical bodies but is, Daneel argues, for the sake of renewing that particular culture in and through the church body. For example, by appealing to the Spirit's vision, churches are able to chart new directions in their contexts that do not need to first receive sanction from existing church bodies.

This could be read as spawning division, but according to Daneel, it is more appropriate to see this as diverse churches being birthed by the same Spirit. It is in this sense that the unity among AI churches is not found in

---

50. For overviews on the expansion and plurality of Christianity in the African continent following decolonization, see David Maxwell and Ingrid Lawrie, *Christianity and the African Imagination: Essays in Honour of Adrian Hastings* (Leiden: Brill, 2002); and Elizabeth Isichei, *A History of Christianity in Africa: From Antiquity to the Present* (Grand Rapids: Eerdmans, 1995), 323–53.

51. For a history of African Zionist and Pentecostal churches, see Joel E. Tishken and Andreas Heuser, "'Africa Always Brings Us Something New': A Historiography of African Zionist and Pentecostal Christianities," *Religion* 45 (2015): 153–73.

52. This is a sweeping assertion and subject to challenge at any number of points by the historiographic literature of various regions in the continent. On this point of the charismatic prophet in AI (African Independent) Christianity, see M. L. Daneel, *Question for Belonging: Introduction to a Study of African Independent Churches* (Gweru, Zimbabwe: Mambo Press, 1987); and N. I. Ndiokwere, *Prophecy and Revolution: The Role of Prophets in the African Independent Churches and in Biblical Tradition* (London: SPCK, 1985).

53. M. L. Daneel, "African Independent Church Pneumatology and the Salvation of All Creation," *International Review of Mission* 82 (1993): 146.

having overarching structures, as their Anglican counterparts in the same region might have. Rather, the unity among AI churches—like that of Pentecostals—is one that is assumed; because the same Spirit is at work in diverse cultural settings, unity does not need to be facilitated by additional structures.

Unity of Mission

In distinguishing the visible nature of the church's unity from its pneumatological dimension, put forward most clearly by Pentecostalism, we saw an argument for unity emerging that can be summarized accordingly: divided churches, with distinct cultural origins, are filled by the same Holy Spirit. This is a good floor for church unity, but not a very desirable ceiling. The criticism is that this leaves much to be desired in terms of concrete articulation. Earlier, I briefly discussed how the World Missionary Conference of 1910 provided a vision of Christian unity grounded in actual, concrete forms not of doxology but of mission. Here, I will build on that meeting as describing a different kind of model that appears: one grounded in common mission.

It is easier, however, to *say* that the unity of the church consists of mission than it is to live in accordance with that principle.[54] The twentieth century offers a number of promising visions in this respect, albeit not without various challenges. The first problem emerges when mission remains separate from ecclesiological concerns for unity. As exemplified by the 1910 World Missionary Conference, mission then becomes the occasion not for unity but for further division among churches. The second problem, which will be discussed momentarily, is that discussing mission apart from ecclesiology can lead to the marginalization of ecclesiology (as exemplified by the American Social Gospel).

The World Missionary Conference of 1910 (WMC) is largely viewed as the forerunner of the WCC. But as Brian Stanley has shown, this is largely a mythological remembrance of the WMC. Initially, the WMC was conceived as an opportunity for Christian denominations and mission-sending organizations to address practical and theological issues associated with evangelism. The meeting was amply attended by representatives from numerous European and American denominations and missionary agencies, though lacking ample representation from the Anglicans and drawing none from Catholic

---

54. For a recent, more comprehensive survey of this theme, see Norman E. Thomas, *Missions and Unity: Lessons from History, 1792–2010* (Eugene, OR: Cascade Books, 2010).

or Orthodox circles. Ecclesiological concerns dividing the participants were noted, but set to the side. Out of the eight commissions established prior to the meeting, only one dealt with issues of unity.[55] Indeed, the original name of the conference, "Third Ecumenical Missionary Conference," shows that the conference leadership saw their ecumenism as referencing a *geographic* comprehensiveness rather than a theological one. Working out noncompetition with other Christian groups was an important aspect of the WMC, but establishing a theological or ecclesiological basis of unity among the groups was not the primary intent of the meeting.[56]

As the meeting unfolded, two complications of the meeting's simple thesis—to focus on global evangelization—appeared. First, missionaries who had offered input to the meeting planners emphasized that mission and church had to go hand in hand; the days of individualist missions had to give way to missions in which the church was not "a mere by-product of mission work, but rather . . . 'the most efficient element in the Christian propaganda.'"[57] As the preconference surveys distributed among missions personnel indicate, ecclesiology radically changed on the mission field (where mission was the priority), and often in largely ecumenical directions. Baptist missionaries reported adopting a more Presbyterian structure; Anglicans reported developing an ecclesial structure that gave more space for lay voices and influence.[58] Put differently, the discussions of the WMC initially envisioned the unity of the church as a side concern for missions, while missions personnel saw the church's unity unfolding within their acts of mission. Discussions of ecclesiology could not be sidelined indefinitely.

The second difficulty that became apparent at the WMC came in the form of the implicit colonialism that haunted the meeting. Reports indicate that national churches from traditional mission fields—that is, non-European countries—were often not viewed as full partners in the missions venture; though invited to the WMC, Christians from India, Japan, China, Korea, and elsewhere were included in the conference program but not in the conference planning.[59] These delegates from "younger churches," as exemplified by a ser-

55. Stanley, *World Missionary Conference*, 32–33.
56. Stanley, *World Missionary Conference*, 71–72.
57. Stanley, *World Missionary Conference*, 133.
58. Stanley, *World Missionary Conference*, 136. See also Stanley, "The Re-Shaping of Christian Tradition: Western Denominational Identity in a Non-Western Context," in *Unity and Diversity in the Church*, ed. R. N. Swanson (Oxford: Blackwell, 1996), 399–426.
59. Stanley, *World Missionary Conference*, 91–94.

mon given by Indian representative V. S. Azariah, were looking not to receive sacrifices from the West but to be received as friends.[60] If these delegates came from national churches, sponsored by Western missions agencies, how was it that their plea would be effectively ignored?[61]

Initially, it seems, the focus on unity in mission was an effort to draw in the "younger churches." For if mission is conceived of as an extension of ecclesiology, the "younger churches," who may or may not have the experience necessary to broach theological discussions of mission and church identity, find themselves as *unequal* partners. But if mission is viewed as an extension or outgrowth of the life of a congregation, all churches—whether coming from the "sending" world or not, whether "younger" or more established—have a more *equal* part to play in mission.

Enacting this vision of unity-in-mission was easier said than done. For elevating mission as the unifying force over ecclesiological concerns arguably blunted the revolutionary, unitive power that might be realized through common mission. For mission is always for the sake of bringing new believers into *some particular body*: endlessly lifting mission simply defers the difficult questions of ecclesial division, particular theologies in particular ecclesial cultures, disparity of resources, and historical prominence, all of which are lying in wait. The result of this elevation of mission was that non-Western Christians would continue to develop indigenous forms of Christianity that represent competitive, rather than complementary, visions of Christianity to their Western counterparts. The initial WMC concluded by emphasizing that Christians on mission *should* be unified, without specifying any particulars of how, having worked toward unity while sidestepping many of the material questions that would help unity be manifest on the ground.[62]

This is not to say that missions would have no role to play in fostering church unity. As the WMC gave way to the WCC, mission found itself in a supporting role. In the subsequent meetings following the WMC, the newly formed commissions of Faith and Order and Life and Work met alongside the International Missionary Council (IMC). In 1961—nearly fifty years after the original WMC—the IMC would become folded into the ongoing ecumenical work of the WCC, initially leaving missions as a neglected topic within the

---

60. Stanley, *World Missionary Conference*, 124–25.
61. Stanley, *World Missionary Conference*, 126. Stanley notes the various ways in which the recording presses of the conference saw the speech as "unfortunate, most unfair."
62. Stanley, *World Missionary Conference*, 280.

first two WCC assemblies. But in the third assembly, the IMC folded into the work of the WCC, and missions emerged again as one of the key foci in the 1968 Assembly at Uppsala.

Mission, Unity, and Politics

The WMC represents a way in which, when ecclesiology and mission are maintained as *separate* concerns, common mission can actually work *against* the unity of the churches, deferring particular (and difficult) conversations that need to happen. In the Social Gospel movement in the United States in the early twentieth century, we find a different approach (with a different set of problems): common mission *in particular societies*, with social concerns as a central focus. The Social Gospel movement, arising among largely Protestant churches in the late nineteenth and early twentieth centuries, emphasized the social implications of the gospel, that Christ's work was not only to atone for souls but to be a model for sociopolitical relationships.[63] Walter Rauschenbusch, a Baptist minister and the best-known figure of the movement, was instrumental not only in highlighting the relationship between the New Testament and socialist philosophy but in envisioning how what he termed "the work of the Kingdom of God"—that is, social reform and witness—was an ecumenical force transcending denominational concerns.[64]

The Social Gospel movement was not solely Rauschenbusch's invention; it was the collaborative work of a number of like-minded ministers in the late nineteenth and early twentieth centuries from a variety of denominational backgrounds. Their concern, put simply, was this: church life was disconnected from its social context. The combination of church life with social ministry is as old as churches themselves, and indeed more socially minded movements, such as the Salvation Army (which opened its doors in 1865), long preceded the American Social Gospel movement. But what the Social Gospel movement

---

63. For the historical roots of the Social Gospel, see Ronald C. White and C. Howard Hopkins, *The Social Gospel: Religion and Reform in Changing America* (Philadelphia: Temple University Press, 1976). Not discussed in this section are the parallel moves made by their African American counterparts. For this, see Gary Dorrien, *The New Abolition: W. E. B. Dubois and the Black Social Gospel* (New Haven: Yale University Press, 2018).

64. For the ways in which the modern ecumenical movement inherited themes and theology of the movement, see Melanie A. May, "The Kingdom of God, the Church, and the World: The Social Gospel and the Making of Theology in the Twentieth-Century Ecumenical Movement," in *The Social Gospel Today*, ed. Christopher H. Evans (Louisville: Westminster John Knox, 2001), 38–52.

brought to the table was that this might also be a way of uniting churches across denominational and doctrinal lines.

Churches had the opportunity to contribute, more than any other institution, to the betterment of society, Rauschenbusch wrote, but their "ecclesiastical" commitments often get in their way.[65] These ecclesiastical commitments to bureaucratic maintenance divided the church not only from social concerns but also from other churches who might well be allies for bringing forth the kingdom of God into society. The Federal Council of Churches (the forerunner of the National Council of Churches), founded in 1908, was "a child of destiny," Rauschenbusch wrote, that could facilitate churches from divergent denominations coming into a singular movement that could benefit the nation.[66]

In contrast to the efforts of the WMC, we must note that the backdrop of the unity that could come through the Social Gospel movement was not one ordered toward transnational unity but one ordered toward the *national good*.[67] In contrast to the WMC, for whom the concept of national benefits of church unity was an afterthought, Rauschenbusch's version of Social Gospel held this front and center. Churches, after all, existed to move human society toward God and not to perpetuate itself; therefore, in his proposals for social action, Rauschenbusch sought to demonstrate again and again how churches working together to produce persons who were attended to physically and assisted economically might benefit society and how this benefit was also in the best interest of churches. A society that is more economically equitable, for example, reduces economic competition between churches, so that ministers will go not to the most financially lucrative church.[68]

The approach of the Social Gospel movement moved beyond the WMC in two respects, then. First, in uniting mission to ethics, instead of separating them as in the WMC model, the Social Gospel movement achieved a comprehensive and pragmatic ecumenism, albeit a short-lived one. Second, the Social Gospel movement, by contrast to the WMC, was relatively uninterested

---

65. Walter Rauschenbusch, *Christianity and the Social Crisis* (orig. 1907; New York: Harper and Row, 1964), 348: "The social movement could have no more powerful ally than religious enthusiasm; it could have no more dangerous ally than ecclesiasticism."

66. See Christopher H. Evans, *The Kingdom Is Always but Coming* (Grand Rapids: Eerdmans, 2004), 244.

67. I will return to the Social Gospel again in my discussion of the mark of holiness.

68. In *Christianity and the Social Crisis*, 299–302, Rauschenbusch argues that leveling society's income inequality gap makes possible more church cooperation, for churches will no longer be economically competing with one another.

in a *theory* of ecumenical cooperation and was more interested in a praxis of ecumenism. These gains, however, came at the cost of joining the fate of society with the church's reason for being. For if material benefit is ultimately the church's reason for being, there is no reason to consider liturgy, theology, or any particular ecclesial framework as necessary. Church becomes, in the end, only a different kind of social benevolence organization.[69]

Throughout the century, other interdenominational cooperative ventures emerged, such as the National Council of Churches[70] and the birth of the parachurch movement—both of which emerged in the American scene as nondenominational, practice-centered Christian movements in the wake of fundamentalist divisions over doctrine.[71] Interdenominational missions organizations, international relief organizations (such as Christian Aid), and ecumenical social agencies all provided examples of this form of unity-in-mission. These groups, in identifying a common work that Christians can all partner in across doctrinal divisions, continue to grow well into the twenty-first century.

Unity of Hermeneutics

The Social Gospel approach, which fostered church unity through "kingdom building," was not without its detractors. The pastor of the First Baptist Church New York City, just blocks from Rauschenbusch's home in Hell's Kitchen, published a pamphlet criticizing the Social Gospel as denying scriptural authority in favor of historical action.[72] This criticism—that the Social Gospel had bought engagement in the world at the expense of faithfulness to Scripture—would soon find a larger cultural standard-bearer, and with it, a different variety of unity: hermeneutics.

At the same time that Rauschenbusch authored his best-selling *Christianity and the Social Crisis*, a group of theologians associated with the Bible Institute

---

69. Alongside this, in having such an explicitly social orientation, the movement arguably became uncritically nationalist in its orientation, focusing exclusively on American concerns, as opposed to international ones. See Miguel A. De La Torre, *Latina/o Social Ethics: Moving beyond Eurocentric Moral Thinking* (Waco: Baylor University Press, 2010), 7–10.

70. See Jill K. Gill, *Embattled Ecumenism: The National Council of Churches, the Vietnam War, and the Trials of the Protestant Left* (DeKalb: Northern Illinois University Press, 2011).

71. See Wesley K. Willmer, J. David Schmidt, and Martyn Smith, *The Prospering Parachurch: Enlarging the Boundaries of God's Kingdom* (San Fransisco: Jossey-Bass, 1998); and Robert Wuthnow, *The Restructuring of American Religion: Society and Faith since World War II* (Princeton: Princeton University Press, 1988).

72. Evans, *Kingdom Is Always but Coming*, 225.

of Los Angeles began publishing a series of essays simply entitled *The Fundamentals*, defending Scripture over against a bevy of modernist corruptions of doctrine. As George Marsden observes, the overwhelming focus of *The Fundamentals* was the authority of God in Scripture, as opposed to modern science and German historicism (to which Rauschenbusch's work was deeply indebted), which they saw as undermining traditional scriptural doctrines.[73] *The Fundamentals* left a deep and permanent mark on twentieth-century Christianity, emphasizing premillennial and dispensationalist hermeneutics, but also offering a counter-vision of how Christian unity happened: Scripture, and particularly, a rightly rendered reading of Scripture.

The authors of *The Fundamentals* came from a variety of Protestant backgrounds, including Baptists, Presbyterians, Bible Churches, and Churches of Christ. Despite manifold tensions among the various authors of *The Fundamentals* on issues such as whether Christianity should have any stake in preserving American society, the authors were united in a common vision of Scripture's authority and a common rejection of modernist approaches that would posit an external authority for Christians beyond Scripture.[74]

The unity of the early fundamentalists did not, as with the Social Gospel, relativize the roles of denominations because of their common commitments; rather, over the course of the first quarter of the twentieth century, fundamentalists began to seek to influence the direction of various denominational institutions, for it was through denominational structures that Christianity in a broader sense could be rescued from the modernist influences of biblical criticism.

But by 1925, the irony of this approach was apparent: in multiple denominations, fundamentalist approaches—while creating a transdenominational movement—were helping to *divide* denominations. Over the course of the twentieth century, new denominations would be created by this movement, amplifying the problem of Christian disunity.[75] In other words, the

---

73. George Marsden, *Fundamentalism and American Culture: The Shaping of Twentieth-Century Evangelicalism, 1870–1925* (Oxford: Oxford University Press, 1981), 120. Other introductions to American fundamentalism include Matthew Avery Sutton, *American Apocalypse: A History of Modern Evangelicalism* (Cambridge, MA: Harvard University Press, 2015); Paul Maltby, *Christian Fundamentalism and the Culture of Disenchantment* (Charlottesville: University of Virginia Press, 2013); Barry Hankins, *Evangelicalism and Fundamentalism: A Documentary Reader* (New York: NYU Press, 2008).

74. On these internal tensions among the authors of *The Fundamentals*, see Marsden, *Fundamentalism and American Culture*, 124–38.

75. Marsden, *Fundamentalism and American Culture*, 178ff. Among the traditions affected were the Disciples of Christ, the Lutherans, the Protestant Episcopalians, the Methodists, the

ecumenically authored *Fundamentals* posited a unity of Scripture, as opposed to the modernist-inflected unity represented within American denominations, but created new divisions in the process.[76]

The global legacy of fundamentalism, creating both unity and disunity, was borne out in the mission field, both in the ways that it affected unity among missions groups and in the ways that fundamentalism affected congregations in other parts of the world. Some events were more flamboyant, such as when J. Gresham Machen, author of the fundamentalist broadside *Christianity and Liberalism*, famously broke away from the Presbyterian Board of Foreign Missions and founded his own missions society and denomination. But as Joel Carpenter writes, most fundamentalist missions work happened through newly established interdenominational agencies, outside of traditional denominational structures.[77] The old waters were troubled, and new waters coalesced.

Sending agencies, publications, training schools, and churches formed a new nexus for sending out fundamentalist missionaries in a way that complicated the mission field. For as we have seen already, with events such as the Edinburgh Missionary Conference and movements such as the World Council of Churches, unity on the mission field was paramount in a time of Christian division. Fundamentalism, by sidestepping the denominational approach to church unity and opting for a self-defined orthodoxy, operated outside of this broad concern for unity on the mission field.[78]

Alongside this movement of fundamentalism arose another hermeneutically united movement: evangelicalism. In the twenty-first century, who counts as an "evangelical" may very well be a heated dispute,[79] but in the early years

---

Presbyterians, and the Canadian Baptists. While not creating new denominations in every instance, various theological educational institutions were created during this period that would sustain the fundamentalist ethos, including Dallas Theological Seminary, Bob Jones University, and Westminster Theological Seminary (193–94).

76. Fundamentalism, though suffering institutional setbacks in the early decades of the twentieth century, would prove resurgent in the decades after the Second World War. On this history, see Joel A. Carpenter, *Revive Us Again: The Reawakening of American Fundamentalism* (New York: Oxford University Press, 1997).

77. Joel Carpenter, "Propagating the Faith Once Delivered: The Fundamentalist Missionary Enterprise," in *Earthen Vessels: American Evangelicals and Foreign Missions, 1880–1980*, ed. Joel A. Carpenter and Wilbert R. Shenk (Grand Rapids: Eerdmans, 1990), 92–132.

78. For an overview of the global forms of Christian fundamentalism sent out from the United States, see Steve Brouwer, Paul Gifford, and Susan D. Rose, *Exporting the American Gospel: Global Christian Fundamentalism* (New York: Routledge, 1996).

79. Thomas S. Kidd, *Who Is an Evangelical? The History of a Movement in Crisis* (New Haven: Yale University Press, 2019).

of the twentieth century, "evangelicalism" designated a broad coalition of Christians committed to the authority of Scripture, social engagement (both cultural and evangelistic), the ongoing conversion of the self, and the centrality of Christ's work for salvation.[80] The relationship between evangelicalism (as a broad canopy) and fundamentalism as movements is debated and need not preoccupy us here.[81] To be sure, there was overlap between these groups: the National Association of Evangelicals and Youth For Christ—two of the largest American "evangelical" groups of the 1930s and 1940s—were both largely populated by dispensationalist fundamentalists, and it would not be until the late 1950s that fundamentalism and a broader evangelicalism would become more distinct.[82]

The unity among a broader evangelical coalition was largely under a scriptural vision of conversion, but not necessarily under doctrine, as seen in the specifically dispensationalist vision of the fundamentalists.[83] This would be important to the survival of evangelicalism, but also a source of difficulty for its unity going forward in two ways. First, because evangelicalism drew from nearly every Protestant denomination (and later, from Catholicism), evangelicalism had no central ecclesial body to unite its members, but rather relied on

80. This has been classically defined by David Bebbington in *Evangelicalism in Modern Britain: A History from the 1730s to the 1980s* (London: Routledge, 1989). George Marsden, in *Understanding Fundamentalism and Evangelicalism* (Grand Rapids: Eerdmans, 1991), 4, offers a slightly different grouping, separating biblical authority and the historical nature of Scripture into two different markers. It is this second marker that, Marsden argues, allows for fundamentalists to be a subset of evangelicals.

81. Key works attempting to sort out this relationship include Marsden, *Understanding Fundamentalism and Evangelicalism*; David Bebbington and David Cerci Jones, *Evangelicalism and Fundamentalism in the United Kingdom during the Twentieth Century* (Oxford: Oxford University Press, 2013); and Harriet Harris, *Fundamentalism and Evangelicals* (Oxford: Oxford University Press, 2008).

82. Marsden, *Understanding Fundamentalism and Evangelicalism*, 71–73.

83. One of the issues that helped to distinguish these groups—and that would affect the question of how to conceive of Christian unity—was the basic nature of history: Was history getting more corrupt? Traditional dispensationalist theology—characteristic of early fundamentalism—held that the world was in cultural decline and that any attempt to "Christianize" or convert the culture was misguided scripturally. By the late 1940s, many prominent names in the evangelical movement, such as Carl Henry, Charles E. Fuller, and Billy Graham, were no longer comfortable with this theological persuasion. The "neo-evangelicals" of the 1950s embraced cultural change as a scriptural mandate, using political and cultural connections to this end. The most notable example here is the ongoing relationship between Billy Graham and the US presidents. See Richard V. Pierard, "Billy Graham and the U.S. Presidency," *Journal of Church and State* 22 (1980): 107–27. For a broader (and critical) account of the relationship between evangelical Protestants and American economic culture, see Kevin Kruse, *One Nation under God: How Corporate America Invented Christian America* (New York: Basic Books, 2015).

parachurch institutional bodies that would help them sustain their vision over time, including the publication *Christianity Today*, educational institutions such as Fuller Theological Seminary and Wheaton College, and international bodies such as the World Evangelical Alliance. But none of these were envisioned as governing bodies as much as intellectual resources for evangelical Christians and rallying points for the diverse interests of evangelicalism.

Second, because evangelicalism represented a broad set of scriptural commitments, but not an ecclesial denomination, its appropriation internationally left the question open: How far do the limits of hermeneutical unity stretch? The emergence of Latin American evangelicalism will help demonstrate this point. Distinct from both Catholics and Pentecostals, South American evangelicals existed as a minority within South and Central American nations.[84] Distinguished by their voluntarist ecclesiology, indigenous leadership, and Anabaptist-inflected belief in the equality of all members in leadership, evangelical churches in Latin America operated theologically in ways similar to their North American counterparts. However, unlike American evangelicals—who have long enjoyed influence within political life—South American evangelicals were seen as largely fringe actors compared to the established Catholic Church.[85]

This state bias against evangelicals pushed evangelical churches more decidedly toward their own indigenous resources, ones not immediately shared with their American counterparts. The contextuality of evangelical churches globally—which range from charismatic megachurches to small communions—is broadly brokered by commitments to Scripture similar to those of American evangelicals. But it is hard to name what ongoing union there is between American and Argentine evangelicals in that case, apart from the claim to a common mode of reading Scripture. But even within common national and cultural parameters, the unity of a common reading of Scripture is no guarantee of unity. During the 1970s, the broad hermeneutical unity of evangelicalism was threatened again by the introduction of a specification to that unity: the question of whether Scripture's truthfulness was best described as "inerrant."[86]

---

84. C. Rene Padilla, "Latin America," in *Global Evangelicalism: Theology, History and Culture in Regional Perspective*, ed. Donald M. Lewis and Richard V. Pierard (Downers Grove, IL: IVP Academic, 2014), 177ff.

85. Padilla, "Latin America," 187.

86. For a summary of the issues, see Harold Lindsell, *The Battle for the Bible* (Grand Rapids: Zondervan, 1976).

The lingering ecclesiological question concerning both the evangelical and fundamentalist movements is that they have primarily existed transdenominationally, having no ecclesial homes to call their own. Because evangelicalism became a kind of church-from-churches, made up of various individuals, churches, and persons *within* churches, the socially unifying bodies became not ecclesial organs but parachurch institutions and events: schools, publications, and conferences. Whereas other modes of church unity drew on common confessions or common practices, a common scriptural hermeneutic enabled transdenominational unity, but a unity that could be disrupted by hermeneutical nuance. As seen in cases such as dispensationalism or inerrancy, however, unity among evangelicals became fractured even within a common basic commitment to the authority of Scripture.[87]

This being said, evangelicalism proved to be one of the most potent and theologically unifying forces in the twentieth century. As the WCC continued to grow in prominence after the Second World War, evangelicals were largely dismayed that missions—which had been one of the primary impetuses for the WCC—was given less attention in the structuring of the WCC; the International Missionary Council was finally folded into the WCC at the 1961 meeting in New Delhi, but in the eyes of many evangelicals, the IMC remained a secondary focus of the WCC.[88] The Lausanne Movement, created by evangelical stalwart John Stott, established widely read covenants and committees for evangelism, becoming an evangelical alternative to the largely mainline-Protestant WCC.

By comparison to other varieties thus far, unity of hermeneutics appears to be the most contentious version, a gift in motion and one in which there is always a contest on the horizon. But a contest can be either a threat or an entrée to a different ecumenical future. Consider one example of the latter. The Lausanne Conference indicates that such a practical focus, rooted in a common hermeneutic, does not need to be equated with dissension even if it is characterized by contention. If this relatively new movement of evangelical unity can both be new and appear in and through existing church bodies, then evangelicalism might be

---

87. On the lingering question of space and visibility and how it affects evangelical ecclesiology, see John Webster, "The Visible Attests the Invisible," in *The Community of the Word: Toward an Evangelical Ecclesiology*, ed. Mark Husbands and Daniel J. Treier (Downers Grove, IL: InterVarsity, 2005), 96–113; and William Dyrness, "Spaces for an Evangelical Ecclesiology," in Husbands and Treier, *Community of the Word*, 251–72.
88. R. David Nelson and Charles Raith II, *Ecumenism: A Guide for the Perplexed* (Edinburgh: Bloomsbury T&T Clark, 2017), 80–81.

seen as a church-based movement that creates a home for the plurality of themes of unity we have already rehearsed. For in this brief history of evangelicalism, we find that the other unifying motifs—missions, social witness, a common reading of Scripture—are all drawn together. What a hermeneutical form of unity lacks in terms of a singular liturgical frame it makes up for by occupying multiple ecclesial homes that infuse its hermeneutic with new possibilities.

The Practical and Ethical Challenges to Christian Unity

If churches are bodies of Christ in motion through the world, then material questions of culture and ethics are not side concerns to how ecclesiology functions, but very real factors in a church's identity. Particularly, questions of culture and ethics shape the possibilities a church has for confessing the marks. This much should be clear in our first chapter already, whether seen under the auspices of Orthodox engagements with Western thought, Catholic histories of division from Protestants, or Protestant engagements with context via evangelicalism or the Social Gospel movement.

Put differently, moral challenges become occasions for illuminating ways in which we have foreshortened our understanding of the Spirit's work in drawing out Christ's body in the world: if divisions of wealth, cultural mores, and sexuality shaped the Corinthian church, we must also allow ourselves to ask how these questions shape the present church. Accordingly, an assessment of twentieth-century ecclesiology cannot be complete without asking about the ways in which material questions of culture and ethics affect our vision of *how* the church is one.

This chapter began with a discussion of the three dominant movements of the twentieth century: Vatican II, the rise of the World Council of Churches, and Eastern Orthodoxy. While these three strands may have divergent visions of Christian unity and, particularly, of what would occasion reunion, they stand together in seeing the question of Christian unity as one involving both doctrine and practice. As Union Seminary theologian and Protestant ecumenist John C. Bennett noted just after Vatican II, social teaching had been both a point of unity and a bone of contention between Protestants and Catholics in the first part of the century.[89]

---

89. John C. Bennett, "Ecumenical Cooperation on Public Issues," in *The Future of Ecumenism*, ed. Hans Küng (New York: Paulist Press, 1969), 64.

But he also found that they were proving to be vehicles of convergence. While not glossing over the difficult doctrinal issues that remained, Bennett found that the post–Vatican II convergence between Protestants and Catholics over issues of war, development aid, and nuclear proliferation were promising points of unity. Similarly, Catholic and Protestant cooperation in Bible societies linked a renewed emphasis on Catholic lay piety with long-standing Protestant concerns for Bible translation in missions.[90] But other ethical issues that separated Protestants and Catholics—such as the use of birth control—pointed to doctrinal divisions that persisted behind otherwise convenient points of convergence.[91]

It is these separations on social issues that show both the promise and the limit of social ethics for bringing about ecclesial unity. As we have seen, Vatican II and member churches of the WCC had done much work to bridge the ecumenical divides—including their common acknowledgment of the dual role of doctrine and ethics in articulating Christian unity. But other ecclesiological concerns (which persist into the twenty-first century) show that doctrinal parity and ethical union alone remain insufficient for true ecclesiological unity.

In proposing common ventures that multiple Christian traditions could join in together (without naming these ventures as full ecumenical recognition), Vatican II had the effect of naming a variety of ethical challenges that posed, in their own ways, important material concerns that do affect Christian unity. Insofar as human unity exists only through the person of Christ, the challenges addressed at Vatican II, such as nuclear war, industrialization, and economic globalization, pose alternate forms of human unity that seek to replicate that which is available only through Christ.

Consider the following example. When *Gaudium et Spes*, in 1965, declared that recent developments in mass media were usurping the slowly forged

---

90. Walter Abbot, SJ, "Common Ecumenical Work for the Bible," in *The Future of Ecumenism*, ed. Hans Küng (New York: Paulist Press, 1969), 29–36.

91. The touchstone for this argument is the 1968 encyclical *Humanae Vitae*, which condemned the use of artificial birth control as separating the procreative act from the possibility of children (Paul VI, *Humanae Vitae* [Vatican City: Holy See, 1968], https://www.vatican.va/content/paul-vi/en/encyclicals/documents/hf_p-vi_enc_25071968_humanae-vitae.html). Most Protestant groups had no official statement on the use of birth control prior to the Anglicans, who made a pro-contraception statement in 1930 at the Lambeth Conference. See Kathryn Blanchard, "The Gift of Contraception: Calvin, Barth, and a Lost Protestant Conversation," *Journal of the Society of Christian Ethics* 27 (2007): 225–49. The question behind contraception, as Blanchard points out, is not simply practical but evinces deeper theological divisions over how Christians understand the nature of personhood and whether sex is fundamentally ordered toward welcoming children.

bonds of family and community, quickly manufacturing bonds "without, however, a corresponding personal development, and truly personal relationships (personalization),"[92] it was articulating this very insight: doctrine was one vanguard of the church's unity, but ethics was the frequently neglected flank. New forms of unity, such as nationalism and cultural unity, posed challenges for the unity that the church had spoken of as found centrally in the person and work of Jesus Christ. Emphasizing the "communitarian vision" of human life, *Gaudium et Spes* notes the ways in which Christ calls for care for the common good and human dignity but also insists that this vision would not be possible if God were excluded from public life in the ways that atheist humanitarian movements proposed.[93]

The central failure for alternative proposals for human unity is their presupposing of unity as a purely creaturely act, absent a sense of God drawing persons together into a mystical bond. As Dorothy Day put it in reflecting on the difference between her Communist past and her Catholic present: "But our unity, if it is not unity of thought, in regard to temporal matters, is a unity at the altar rail. We are all members of the Mystical Body of Christ, and so we are closer, to each other, by the tie of grace, than any blood brothers are. . . . But of course the tie that binds Catholics is closer, the tie of grace. We partake of the same food, Christ."[94]

In closing this chapter, we will look at examples of two twentieth-century challenges to church unity that emerged as unattended wounds of the past:

---

92. Paul VI, *Gaudium et Spes* (Vatican City: Holy See, 1965), 6, https://www.vatican.va/archive/hist_councils/ii_vatican_council/documents/vat-ii_const_19651207_gaudium-et-spes_en.html.

93. Paul VI, *Gaudium et Spes*, 20–21:
One form of modern atheism which should not be ignored is that which looks to people's economic and social emancipation for their liberation. It holds that religion, of its very nature, frustrates such emancipation by investing people's hopes in a future life, thus both deceiving them and discouraging them from working for a better form of life on earth. That is why those who hold such views, wherever they gain control of the state, violently attack religion, and in order to spread atheism, especially in the education of young people, make use of all the means by which the civil authority can bring pressure to bear on its subjects. . . . The church holds that to acknowledge God is in no way to diminish human dignity, since such dignity is grounded and brought to perfection in God. Women and men have in fact been placed in the world by God, who created them as intelligent and free beings; but over and above this they are called as daughters and sons to intimacy with God and to share in his happiness. It further teaches that hope in a life to come does not take away from the importance of the duties of this life on earth but rather adds to it by giving new motives for fulfilling those duties.

94. Dorothy Day, *Catholic Worker*, May 1948, 1.

racial division and war. In naming these two particular challenges, it is important to see these not as *external* factors affecting the unity of the church, but as *internal* ones. There are any number of other avenues we might explore—the relationship of Communism to Christianity, Solidarity (the political movement that unified Poland in the 1980s), and environmental degradation—social issues that both divided Christians and united them in sometimes helpful ways. But race and war remain perennial issues of Christian division then and now and thus warrant closer attention here.

Race and Christian Unity

The racial inequality that challenged the consciousness of White American churches with the American civil rights movement was only one of many challenges of its kind for Christian unity in the twentieth century.[95] For the twentieth century was the century of decolonialization and the emergence of new independent countries across the globe, and with them, new forms of Christianity attuned to how race and racism had been key factors in their emerging histories. And so, the unity of the church in a postcolonial age proved to be a lingering question, both in terms of the divisions of race that appeared in former colonial settings and in terms of how the colonial question exposed and sharpened the wound of previously unresolved racial divisions.

In the wake of the Second World War, new waves of international cooperation emerged, affecting international relations of the churches as well. The World Council of Churches (WCC), officially coming into being just years after the United Nations, would quickly have to turn its attentions from global missions to the emergence of world Christianity, from simply propagating the faith to attending to how to keep diverse forms of global faith from fracturing into multiple faiths.[96] As is seen in the WCC Life and Work discussions from

---

95. On the role of churches in the civil rights movement, see in particular Charles Marsh, *God's Long Summer: Stories of Faith and Civil Rights* (Princeton: Princeton University Press, 2008); Marsh, *The Beloved Community: How Faith Shapes Social Justice, from the Civil Rights Movement to Today* (New York: Basic Books, 2004); and Carolyn Renée Dupont, *Mississippi Praying: Southern White Evangelicals and the Civil Rights Movement, 1945–1975* (New York: NYU Press, 2013).

96. In designating the plurality of Christianity across the globe as "world Christianity," I am following the distinction made by Lamin Sanneh between "world Christianity" (the emergence of various, and often unconnected, forms of Christianity) and "global Christianity" (the emergence of Christianity through the world as projected outward by Europe and America into colonial spaces). Sanneh, *Whose Religion Is Christianity?* (Grand Rapids: Eerdmans, 2002), 22–23.

the 1960s forward, ethical tangles over issues of race and economics came to illustrate the cultural and theological divides emerging between European churches and churches of the so-called Global South.

Robert McAfee Brown, an observer at these meetings, writes of the issue of apartheid coming to the forefront during the 1968 Uppsala meeting of the World Council of Churches (WCC). American delegates, in the wake of the civil rights movement, wrote of the need for South Africa to likewise be "self-determined" in its government, meaning that South African Black people should be able to negotiate their own destiny. From the Black South African perspective, however, calling for "self-determination" was inadvertently appealing to Whites in South Africa, as it relieved the nation from international pressure and left the South African Black population in an even worse place.[97]

The work of the WCC's Programme to Combat Racism (PCR) serves as a poignant example of the difficulties that racism posed for Christian unity, and particularly of how institutional efforts to address one injustice could pit church bodies against one another.[98] Though the WCC was founded in 1948, it was not until 1968 that the PCR emerged as an official arm of the WCC, at the Uppsala gathering, only weeks after the assassination of Martin Luther King Jr. As one of its first actions, the fledgling PCR began to press international financiers to withdraw funds from segregated South Africa as a means to force political change.[99] In time, the PCR shifted its work toward mobilizing local churches to address racist policies in their own countries, with successes most notably in South Africa.

Critics note that, by focusing their work on Black-White racism, the PCR neglected other dimensions, such as the declining land rights of Indians in Latin America or of the Maori in New Zealand.[100] The problem of limited resources forced the PCR to prioritize some efforts over others, leaving issues

---

97. Robert McAfee Brown, "Uppsala: An Informal Report," *Journal of Ecumenical Studies* 5 (1968): 647.

98. As Claude Welch astutely observes, the internationalism promoted by the founding of the United Nations lent itself to the founding of the WCC, as a Christian offshoot of this sentiment for international cooperation. See Welch, "Mobilizing Morality: The World Council of Churches and Its Program to Combat Racism, 1969–1994," *Human Rights Quarterly* 23 (2001): 868.

99. Welch, "Mobilizing Morality," 898–99. In one of the more intriguing episodes of the PRC's timeline, Andrew Young, PCR member and former lieutenant of Dr. King, had changed his mind about this approach and undertook a trip to South Africa in a time when the PCR was engaging in an extensive isolationist strategy in order to force the hand of the Afrikaners, setting off a furious debate over whether isolationist strategies were the appropriate course.

100. Welch, "Mobilizing Morality," 907.

such as Australian discrimination against the Aborigines and continued racism in the United States to the side in its work. But even while a unified Christian body emerged to engage racism, it was not apparent that a unified approach could be agreed on. Even in the PCR's central point of concern—South Africa—the question of how to deal with institutionalized racist policies continued to divide Afrikaner and Black South African churches.

This particular South African struggle over how to address the divisions of racism was multiplied out repeatedly in the years following UN Resolution 1514 (1960), which granted independence to colonies. As former colonies gained political independence, what to make of their Christian heritage, where racism was intertwined with churches, remained a live issue. In places, for example, where Christianity had a lengthy and indigenized history, chances were greater that indigenous churches would retain ties to the churches of the home country, as was the case in Kenya and the Democratic Republic of the Congo.

South Africa once again proves an instructive case of these difficulties. The Zion Christian Church (ZCC), one of the largest of the "Zionist" churches in Africa (churches originating from the missions work of the Christian Catholic Apostolic Church in Zion, Illinois), became by virtue of its size a key player in the 1992 ending of apartheid.[101] With nearly forty thousand registered members, the ZCC was sought out by F. W. de Klerk and other Afrikaner leaders as negotiations over the ending of apartheid were going forward. The church, however, though one of the largest, found itself at odds with other independent churches who backed the work of the African National Congress (ANC). Because of their long-standing relationship to North American White churches, ZCC members tended to favor a more quietist approach toward political involvement, giving them the appearance of siding with the White establishment, despite leadership statements to the contrary.[102] Churches who supported the ANC, by contrast, saw the ZCC as operating in bad faith. Racism, far from dividing only White churches from Black South Africans, played a role in dividing Black South African Christians from one another.

Racial and cultural divisions were not the province only of Protestants. The Catholic Church in mainland China had enjoyed communion with Rome since the seventeenth century. But in 1958, internal pressures on the Catholic

---

101. See Allan H. Anderson, *African Reformation: African Initiated Christianity in the 20th Century* (Trenton, NJ: Africa World Press, 2001), 103–8.
102. Anderson, *African Reformation*, 106.

Church of China led to the separation of the Chinese Catholic Church from Rome, with the dioceses self-electing bishops.[103] With postwar suspicions of foreign influences within China growing, the Chinese Catholic Church, like other Christian movements, positioned itself as an indigenous movement; such a movement was designed by Chinese Catholic leaders to preserve Catholicism, but ultimately led to a no more favorable outcome during the Cultural Revolution.[104] Orthodox Christianity initially fared somewhat better in China across racial lines due to congenial relations between Russia and China, though the Orthodox churches, too, suffered loss and division from other communions due to concerns of outside influence from the West.[105]

In the United States, divisions of racism illuminated by the American civil rights movement were reflected in national divisions between churches. For example, although the movement drew support from some White churches, it remained largely a movement centered in Black church denominations and traditions.[106] The lament over this division is best embodied in Dr. Martin Luther King Jr.'s statement that he was "gravely disappointed with the white moderate . . . who lives by a mythical concept of time and who constantly advises the Negro to wait for a 'more convenient season.'"[107] In ways analogous to the WCC's emphasis on how social divisions affect ecclesial unity, King keenly identified the way in which—while united in confession—White churches remained divided from Black churches in social witness.

Attempts to repair this breach between Black and White churches in the United States took multiple forms. The work of James Cone, best known as one of the pioneering voices of Black theology, contended that union between White and Black churches was indeed possible in spite of the racist legacies of some White churches, provided that White churches joined in the Black church struggles for racial equality and justice.[108] Joseph H. Jackson, president of the National Baptist Convention USA, saw Cone's work as polarizing and

---

103. We will return to this story in chapter 4, as an example of claims to apostolicity becoming complicated.

104. See Ying Fuk-tsang, "Mainland China," in *Christianities in Asia*, ed. Peter C. Phan (Malden, MA: Wiley-Blackwell), 149–70.

105. Ying, "Mainland China," 159–61.

106. For some of the ecclesio-logics in play here, see Dupont, *Mississippi Praying*; and Stephen Haynes, *The Last Segregated Hour: The Memphis Kneel-Ins and the Campaign for Southern Church Desegregation* (Oxford: Oxford University Press, 2012).

107. Martin Luther King Jr., "Letter from Birmingham Jail," in *The Radical King*, ed. Cornel West (Boston: Beacon Press, 2015), 135.

108. James Cone, *God of the Oppressed* (Maryknoll, NY: Orbis Books, 1997), 221–23.

as distracting from the basis of true unity found in common confession of a Christ who is beyond race.[109] But for Cone, setting aside the dividing issue of race was not possible: true unity could not be found between White and Black churches absent a unity of ethics. Any true confession of Christ must be made from within social action, not prior to it.[110]

These representative examples help us to see the ways in which racism operated not simply as external but as *internal* fissures among Christian churches. For it was not only the ways in which White racism created the need for there to be Black and Indigenous churches; remedying racism likewise created new division even among those directly affected by racism to begin with. As a material concern for how church unity was enacted, racism appears not as a side issue but as a question that caused new churches to come into being and to be divided.

Conflict and Christian Unity

One of the great incongruencies of the twentieth century is that, while great strides were made on various fronts of unity—both ecclesially and politically—this was also a time of surging nationalism. Alongside the more notorious examples of the World Wars, conflicts among Middle Eastern nations and regime changes in South America posed grave challenges for daily life, not to mention the question of Christian unity. Others have adequately detailed the devastation of the "bloodiest century," and so here we will look only at the ways in which twentieth-century conflicts created difficulties for thinking of the church as one. While not a twentieth-century phenomenon alone, the link between national unity and war between Christians posed an international threat to Christian unity in a way that was unique to the twentieth century.

The rise of the conditions of the Second World War and the near cessation of activities by the World Council of Churches during this period is not a coincidence; the quieting of ecumenical activities in the face of brewing war among the nations central to the WCC shows how fragile that unity could

---

109. Raphael Warnock, *The Divided Mind of the Black Church: Theology, Piety and Public Witness* (New York: NYU Press, 2014), 126–28.

110. James Cone, *Speaking the Truth: Ecumenism, Liberation, and Black Theology* (Maryknoll, NY: Orbis Books, 1996). One need only read King's "Letter from Birmingham Jail" to see the degree to which Jackson's argument about the unity of the church is mirrored in the approach taken by the White ministers addressed by King, in Martin Luther King Jr., *Why We Can't Wait* (New York: Signet Books, 1963), 76–95.

prove to be. The war was devastating for Christian unity in at least two interrelated ways. First, as with the First World War, nations with Christian heritages and with robust participation in international ecumenical activities found themselves bitter enemies before, during, and after the conflict. As seen in the case of Dietrich Bonhoeffer, ecumenical relationships between Germany and England, once celebrated, were viewed suspiciously and negatively.[111]

The destruction wrought on churches and ecumenical relationships during this period was due in part to viewing the nation as more able to foster unity than other institutions, including the church. In contrast to the claim of Christians that Christ is the one in whom "all things hold together" (Col. 1:17), insurgent nationalism on both sides of the Atlantic operated in such a way as to claim the allegiance of Christians and call on them to view their fellow Christians elsewhere as enemies. But perhaps nowhere was this as tragic as in the events of Nagasaki in 1945. For centuries, Christian missionaries had struggled to make inroads into Japan, and with great difficulty, a thriving Catholic community had developed in Japan. Its administrative and geographical center? Nagasaki.[112] Within seconds, what Christians had labored for centuries to bring to fruition was obliterated with the atomic bomb.[113]

But consider a different example as well, occasioned by the Nazis: that war rended not only Christian unity across traditions but Christian unity within particular confessions as well. The German National Church movement arose as a way to lend the support of the Lutheran church to the national struggle for reconstruction in the wake of the First World War. Documents from within the German National Church movement show the manner in which the German National Church saw the rise of Germany as a providential act of God as well as an act that divided Christians from Judaism.[114] Terming the presence of Jews in Germany as "the Jewish problem," the German National Church movement—in pamphlets, articles, and public pronouncements—described

---

111. See Keith Clements, *Dietrich Bonhoeffer's Ecumenical Quest* (Amsterdam: World Council of Churches, 2015).

112. Eduardo Berdejo, "Atomic Bomb Dropped on Nagasaki Killed Two-Thirds of the City's Catholics 78 Years Ago," *Catholic News Agency*, August 9, 2023, https://www.catholicnewsagency.com/news/255054/atomic-bomb-dropped-on-nagasaki-killed-two-thirds-of-the-city-s-catholics-78-years-ago.

113. On the development of Japanese Christianity, its decimation in the Second World War, and its resurgence in the years afterward, see Mark R. Mullins, *Handbook of Christianity in Japan* (Leiden: Brill, 2003).

114. See Mary M. Solberg, *A Church Undone: Documents from the German Christian Faith Movement, 1932–1940* (Minneapolis: Fortress, 2016).

the Jews as effectively incompatible with Christianity and, by extension, incompatible with Germany. In the notorious "Aryan paragraph," which spelled out the incompatibility of Judaism and Christianity, German Christians divorced the New and Old Testaments, effectively creating a new canon for themselves.[115]

Wars between Christians for nationalist reasons were not limited to the most egregious examples of the World Wars. Internal conflicts, such as the Rwandan genocide of 1994 and the Yugoslavian civil war of the 1980s, pitted Christian groups against one another under the auspices of ethnicity.[116] During the 1970s and 1980s, the state of El Salvador sponsored the murders, by "death squads," of Catholic dissidents—Salvadorans who opposed the junta; the killings were often done by other Catholics in the name of the state.[117]

The aftermath of war often proved to be as divisive for churches as the wars themselves, as churches then had to narrate what had happened during the war. As Anna Peterson observes with respect to El Salvador, Catholics struggled to name what had happened there: Were Catholics killed by the state martyrs or not?[118] When Archbishop Óscar Romero was murdered while celebrating Mass, it seemed clear-cut, but what about the deaths of ordinary Catholics who were involved in opposing an unjust government? Divisions in politics created divisions over how, in the aftermath of violence, to value the sacrifices Christians had made.

The twentieth century provided many chances to observe the church-splitting effects of war, whether in the two World Wars, in the Cold War, or in many of the intranational conflicts. In each of these cases, the unity of Christians was subsumed beneath another kind of unity, whether sociopolitical or ethnic, resulting in the killing of Christians by Christians. But in an intriguing and ironic development, the production of Christian unity was itself the unintended result of violence, at least in one case. Japanese imperialism during the early twentieth century precipitated large portions of East Asia coming under Japanese rule in the first half of the century. In 1940, the

115. Solberg, *Church Undone*, 53–81.
116. See Carol Rittner, John K. Roth, and Wendy Whitworth, eds., *Genocide in Rwanda: Complicity of the Churches* (St. Paul: Paragon House, 2004). On the role that Christian identity played in the Yugoslavian Civil War, see Jure Kristo, "Relations between the State and the Roman Catholic Church in Croatia, Yugoslavia in the 1970's and 1980's," *Occasional Papers on Religion in Eastern Europe* 2, no. 3 (1982).
117. See Anna L. Peterson, *Martyrdom and the Politics of Religion: Progressive Catholicism in El Salvador's Civil War* (Albany: SUNY Press, 1997).
118. Peterson, *Martyrdom and the Politics of Religion*, 93–96.

Church of Christ in Japan was created by the law, folding thirty-two different churches into the union by government mandate.[119] Regional unions of churches after 1940 in Indonesia likewise began, for better or worse, as the result of Japanese conquest.[120]

What we are to make of this relation between war and the church's unity, particularly in cases of enforced ecumenism, is complicated. On the one hand, the wars of the twentieth century furthered Christian division, built on existing divisions, and hampered movements toward unity. But war also unexpectedly proved to be the impetus for renewed energy toward Christian unity. Aside from the aforementioned churches formed in Indonesia and Japan, one of the most celebrated movements after the Second World War, the founding of the Church of South India, came in the wake of national celebrations and religious violence after India's independence.[121] The structural uniting of the Church of South India, in which former Presbyterians and Congregationalist ministers entered into a new ecclesial world together, was one of the century's greatest ecumenical moments.

Taking Stock: Christian Unity in the Twentieth Century

As we look back on the attempts to articulate not only why Christians should be unified but *how*, it should be apparent that movements for international unity during the twentieth century were attuned not only to issues of worship but to those of culture as well. The difficulty with this acknowledgment, however, is that though doctrinal issues may have remained relatively stable, doctrine is only ever practiced, preached, and taught in embodied form. And so, as seen in the discussions of the World Council of Churches in particular, as more and more partners came to the table from across the globe, it became more and more difficult to ignore the material issues surrounding church doctrine.

Whether in the form of war, race, or the assumed priority of the concerns of Western nations over those of their former colonies, the struggle of the twentieth century with respect to unity began as one of doctrine and, over time, began to encompass the more material aspects of doctrine. For example,

---

119. Scott W. Sunquist, *Explorations in Asian Christianity: History, Theology, and Mission* (Downers Grove, IL: IVP Academic, 2017), 44.
   120. Sunquist, *Explorations in Asian Christianity*, 44.
   121. Sunquist, *Explorations in Asian Christianity*, 45.

both Vatican II and discussions in the WCC treat issues of ethics distinctly from issues of ecclesiology. In *Gaudium et Spes*, issues of war are treated as issues of church witness, subsequent to more properly ecclesiological issues, which are sorted out in other documents. Likewise, the WCC developed commissions to deal with issues of life and work as issues separate from faith and order. This is not to condemn the work of previous generations but to offer an observation for future discussions: church unity cannot be so easily sorted out from the material conditions in which the church seeks to be one, and therefore material conditions should be considered as internal conversation partners for these conversations.

Other visions of church unity, which locate unity in mission, Scripture, or Spirit, by contrast, tended to fall into self-selectivity with respect to pursuits of unity. As seen in both fundamentalism and evangelicalism, unity in the Scriptures became unity *in a certain reading* of the Scriptures; those whose hermeneutics differed were not necessarily written off as non-Christians, but they were often treated as secondary partners in terms of church unity. The same could be said with respect to missions: both the nascent foreign missions movement and the Social Gospel—as disparate as they are—operated in a kind of self-selectivity that bound together churches from across denominational lines even as they separated themselves from others. The unity of the Spirit, as present in Pentecostalism and in the AIC movement, while perhaps the most theologically basic one, likewise tended to operate within certain understandings of what counts most directly as the Spirit's work, whether with respect to glossolalia or with respect to cultural appropriateness; those whose understandings of the Spirit's operation differed were not dismissed, but they were not included in that vision of unity.

In sum, what occurred throughout the twentieth century, in various ways, was a struggle for how to articulate Christian unity amid myriad material conditions that divided Christians; the degree to which unity between Christian bodies succeeded, it appears, depended on their facility in addressing these material issues. This is not to say that Christian unity is simply a material matter—of aligning doctrines or of joint social action. But it is to acknowledge that Christian unity rose and fell as these issues were addressed, or not, among Christians as contributing factors to their divisions. We may be tempted to retrospectively valorize other ages as being more united, but what must be kept in front of us is not the statement or judgment of another age upon our own unity, but the promise that, in all things, the Christ who calls his church to be one is the Christ who operates within his church to make that so. It is in this sense that we might learn from our recent past and recognize the new challenges of our present for what they are: opportunities to manifest unity in ways that are doctrinal and cultural, missional and hermeneutical, partial and full.

At this point, we must move away from questions of unity and ask, What kind of people are called into this unity? This takes us now from questions of the practice of unity into the question of holiness. For it does little good for us to entertain notions of unity if the content of our unity is something other than that which God gives: holiness. And so, to the second mark we go.

2

To Be Like God

The Church as Holy

In Your Light, We See Light: The Holiness of God and the Holiness of the Church

In at least two ways, our discussion of holiness is already too late. First, as Paul O'Callaghan points out, holiness is the mark of the church that, according to the oldest creeds, encapsulates all the other marks.[1] The fact that holiness was present in ancient descriptions of the church even when apostolicity was not mentioned emphasizes holiness's priority among the marks, at least for some early Christians. In naming the difference between the church and its neighbors, holiness encapsulated what the life of the church offered in contrast to the Roman Empire.

Second, holiness, as much as unity, describes the nature of God, and thus that which is, by analogy, most central for the church's existence. Frequently, ecclesiological arguments will point to the prayer that Jesus prays for his

---

1. Paul O'Callaghan, "The Holiness of the Church in Early Christian Creeds," *Irish Theological Quarterly* 54 (1988): 59–65. As we have noted already, the marks were most likely viewed as inseparable realities of the church, but holiness as a quality and an inalienable property of the church was descriptively the mark most often present in the creeds, even if other marks were omitted descriptively.

followers: that they would be one as he and the Father are one. But this unity of Father and Son is not one of *practiced* unity but one of essence, with holiness being one of the descriptors of the nature of God.[2] Without holiness standing alongside unity as descriptive of the singular essence of God, much is lost both in our doctrine of God and in our doctrine of the church.

I bring these two points up to indicate that, in God, holiness and unity of persons are revealed together. The one God is the one holy God: Father, Son, and Spirit. Holiness is not somehow derivative of unity within God. And yet, the marks of the church, ordered as they are, come to us in *sequential* form, with holiness following after oneness. But this is not without its costs: to turn to holiness as a characteristic of the church after discussions of unity threatens to treat the holiness of the church as a derivative feature, annexed to unity, suggesting that the church can be holy *only insofar* as it is one.

But all is not lost, even if we are now conditioned to see holiness as dependent on unity. Holiness is inseparable from the other marks and may exert pressure on other marks of the church. If a church is known by these four inseparable features, this means that we can ask not only, Can an ununified church be holy? but also, Can an unholy church be unified? Holiness, as I will describe it, is different than moral purity alone. Morality is certainly *part* of what is meant by holiness; in both Old and New Testaments, the vision of the people of God as holy entails not being like other peoples with respect to behavior. But to speak of the *church* as holy is to attribute to it a quality that pertains to the whole of the church body together, independent of the actions of one of its members—a quality not funded by the behaviors of believers.

Consider two examples from Scripture here: Jesus's eating with sinners in Luke 10 and the presence of God in the temple in Ezekiel. In both cases, the presence of God is described hand in hand with the lackluster moral condition of those in the presence of God. The holiness of God is first about the redeeming and life-giving presence of the power of God on display in creation, and second, about the kind of moral behaviors consistent with that presence. Far from notions of "holiness" as a kind of moralism, holiness names what the church is by virtue of God having sanctified the church in Jesus Christ: before it is a task, it is an indelible gift of God's own presence.[3]

---

2. Put differently, if the Father and the Son were not one in essence (sharing in the one divine essence), then whatever unity they had would be the unity of two different gods. This argument is pervasive in early trinitarian arguments.

3. David Willis, *Notes on the Holiness of God* (Grand Rapids: Eerdmans, 2002), 25.

Though we are only now directly considering the question of the church as holy, the question of the church's holiness has been on the table all along. For as we looked at the question of Christian division, we were also asking the question of holiness—of how the church's unity reflects not just a pragmatic task but the church's character as *God's* church. Likewise, when we explore questions of catholicity, of the church's connection to the breadth of created life, we will ask questions about what it means that the church is both connected to creation and yet distinct from it, as the firstfruits of what creation is meant to be. Holiness, though second in order in these explorations, is never far from the surface.

Two sets of questions will help us explore holiness as it appears in twentieth-century ecclesiology. First, what does it mean that holiness is a property of the *whole* church? The twentieth century is a century rife with populism, concerns for lay involvement, and mass mobilization of Christians for missions, relief work, and lay ministry. Viewing these under the mark of holiness causes us to ask, In what ways does this revival of interest in the church being the work of *all* of the people shape the church? But alongside this, in the twentieth century the church reckoned with its past in a way that it had not in previous centuries. There have always been those, both inside and outside the church, who have criticized Christian practice, but in the twentieth century, a second set of questions began to be asked more directly and more urgently: Can a church that has contributed to social sin claim to be the bearer of the triune God's holiness in the world? Can the church's holiness be compromised, and if so, how? And what is the appropriate posture of a church when it fails? It is these clusters of questions that we will take up in this chapter.

Holiness and Unity: How Do They Relate?

The holiness of the church is, like its unity, a borrowed attribute; the church—as a member of creation—does not intrinsically possess anything that distinguishes it from the rest of creation on this count. This is simultaneously a daunting claim (in that this frail body of people is the bearer of the power of God) and a claim that relieves us (in that our own moral failures do not reflect the nature of God). As Brian Flanagan puts it, we "become what we receive"; we become the bearers of God's holiness as we receive the gift of holiness from God.[4]

---

4. Brian P. Flanagan, *Stumbling in Holiness: Sin and Sanctity in the Church* (Collegeville, MN: Liturgical Press, 2018), 101. This concept goes back at least to Augustine, who writes,

But is the holiness of the church conditioned upon its unity? Do we become holy to the degree that we are unified? The stakes of this question are high, in that those who are properly unified (see chap. 1) are those who are unified in God's presence, bearers of God's holiness. In *Lumen Gentium* (a "dogmatic constitution on the church"), from Vatican II, for example, the mystery of the church as "a kind of sacrament or sign of intimate union with God, and of the unity of all mankind," establishes the nature of the church as an organization in which laity and hierarchy are united and yet distinguished.[5]

It is not until after this point that *holiness* emerges as a theme of the document. The gifts of the Holy Spirit, variegated in the hierarchy and laity, manifest the holiness as a predicate of unity; to be the holy people of God is to mirror the unity of God. At this point, the manifestations of holiness beyond the substance of the church as holy-as-such proliferate: "In their walk of life, [individuals] strive for the perfection of charity, and thereby help others to grow.... This holiness shines out in the practice of the counsels customarily called 'evangelical.' Under the influence of the Holy Spirit, the practice of the counsels is undertaken by many Christians, either privately or in some Church-approved situation or state, and produces in the world ... a shining witness and model of holiness."[6]

The forms of lay holiness envisioned here in *Lumen Gentium* are universal in scope: holiness is that which is envisioned for all manners of work, and the virtues therein are to be mirrored in the hierarchy, with all encouraged to pursue analogous holiness in their own lives, "the perfect fulfillment of their proper state."[7] Much ink has been spilled on what to make of the hierarchical nature of holiness, with some states (which "derive more abundant fruit" from the grace bestowed in baptism[8]) designated as more perfect because of their singular devotion to the church. The unity that enables a differentiated life within the church (hierarchy and laity) is replicated in terms of the holiness available to its members: differentiated according to station.

---

speaking on the Eucharist, "Be what you see; receive what you are." Augustine, *Sermon 272*, Early Church Texts, https://www.earlychurchtexts.com/public/augustine_sermon_272_eucharist.htm.

5. Walter M. Abbott, SJ, ed., *The Documents of Vatican II* (New York: Guild Press, 1966), 15. The document deals, in logical order, with the mystery of the church's union with God (chap. 1), then the people of God (chap. 2), who are variously divided into hierarchy (chap. 3) and laity (chap. 4).

6. Abbott, *Documents of Vatican II*, 66.
7. Abbott, *Documents of Vatican II*, 72.
8. Abbott, *Documents of Vatican II*, 74.

Is the description of the church's holiness here overly conditioned by the mark of unity? The work pastorally accommodates to persons' "states," with certain kinds of holiness appropriate to various life stations: not all are monks or celibates. And by being attentive to the different stages of life, and yet naming each stage as "fullness of the Christian life," *Lumen Gentium* assumes that a person's own holiness, proper to their own bodily life, is a shared holiness. But if a person's holiness is tied into the unified holiness of the church, the shape that their holiness can take is prescribed by their status as laity or clergy. In this case, unity takes the form of unity between hierarchy and laity, with the holiness of particular members conditioned by this kind of unity in such a way that any disruption of the structure of *unity* calls the character of *holiness* into question.

Unity and Holiness: An Alternate Approach

But this is not the only possible relationship between holiness and unity. While other churches are attuned to the need for unity, this is not to say that holiness is an extension of prior liturgical and structural unity. It is possible that holiness reconfigures how unity occurs.

As described in the previous chapter, many charismatic churches give the name "unity" first to a unity of charismatic giftings and relations, not to a structural unity—if indeed they consider unity to be structural at all. In this arrangement, unity follows from holiness and the presence of the Spirit, which create unity along the way; in the words of Albert Schenkel, in this way, the charismatic movement was possibly "the most important ecumenical development of this century."[9]

Charismatic emphases and influence, though most closely associated with the Pentecostal churches, could be seen in nearly every denomination, including Roman Catholicism, with the Catholic charismatic renewals of the 1960s.[10] But among non-Catholic groups, two predominant approaches appeared with

---

9. Albert Frederick Schenkel, "New Wine and Baptist Wineskins," in *Pentecostal Currents in American Protestantism*, ed. Edith L. Blumhofer, Russell P. Spittler, and Grant A. Wacker (Urbana: University of Illinois Press, 1999), 154.

10. The Spiritan movement—which, most notably, founded Duquesne University in Pittsburgh—predates the charismatic renewal in Catholicism by nearly 250 years, but the origin of the modern Catholic Charismatic Renewal is typically traced to the experiences of two professors at Duquesne and a student group at the University of Notre Dame. See René Laurentin, *Catholic Pentecostalism* (New York: Doubleday, 1977).

respect to the relation of holiness and unity. Some (such as the Methodist and Holiness denominations, including the Church of the Nazarene and the Church of God) incorporated charismatic teachings as legitimate expressions of the Christian life, while others (such as Baptist and Christian Missionary Alliance churches) treated charismatic expressions as that which could be counted, but only within a rightly ordered faith.[11] Following Grant Wacker's approach, we can say that these two approaches—while both valuing holiness and unity—produced two different understandings of what holiness does with respect to church unity.

The first approach—which incorporated charismatic renewals and expressions as a way of *vivifying* unity—can be seen in the example of the Korean Holiness Church (KHC). Founded in the first decade of the twentieth century as an indigenous Korean expression of the holiness traditions, the KHC emphasized Wesleyan themes of justification and sanctification, with the central emphasis on the Christian seeking total sanctification. The denomination's founding coincided with the Korean Revival of 1907, but while it was undoubtedly strengthened by the revival, the KHC ordered the charismatic experience to preexisting Wesleyan doctrine such that the charismatic experience infused the preexisting liturgical patterns with new insights and gifts.[12]

The KHC emphasized the "full gospel," which incorporated healings and baptism into the Holy Spirit into the core teachings of the movement, subsequent to the regenerative work of baptism.[13] In doing so, the KHC indicated that the work of holiness was conditioned by the work of baptism and did not emphasize holiness as an experience unrelated to the

---

11. Grant Wacker, "Travail of a Broken Family: Radical Evangelical Responses to the Emergence of Pentecostalism, 1906–16," in Blumhofer, Spittler, and Wacker, *Pentecostal Currents in American Protestantism*, 25.

12. The KHC was founded in no small part due to the work of missionaries from the thriving Tokyo Bible Institute, which emphasized the "fourfold gospel," taught by the Oriental Missionary Society and their American counterparts in the Christian Missionary Alliance (CMA). For the history of the Korean Holiness Church, see Meesaeng Lee Choi, *The Rise of the Korean Holiness Church in Relation to the American Holiness Movement* (Lanham, MD: Scarecrow, 2008). The denomination would eventually birth two smaller denominations (Korea Evangelical Holiness Church and Jesus Holiness Church of Korea) in 1962. For the history of the early twentieth-century revivals in Korea, see Wiliam N. Blair and Bruce F. Hunt, *The Korean Pentecost and the Suffering Which Followed* (Edinburgh: Banner of Truth Trust, 1977).

13. The KHC is different from American Holiness churches most particularly on the question of speaking in tongues. Compare with the Articles of Faith of Pentecostal Holiness Church, which emphasizes speaking in tongues as initial evidence of the Spirit's renewal, in *Discipline of the Pentecostal Holiness Church* (Franklin Springs, GA: Board of Publication, Pentecostal Holiness Church, 1945), 13.

core doctrines of Wesleyan holiness; the Christian life is one of increased holiness, as a participation in the work of God between regeneration and Christ's return.[14] In this way, as the variegated charismatic experiences of the believers found orientation within the norming work of baptism, unity became expansive, incorporating expressions of the Spirit's work that were not universally experienced. As opposed to Vatican II, which describes the holiness of the church as a structurally narrated feature of the church's unity, the Korean Holiness Church simply assumed that the holiness of believers will bear the fruit of unity across churches. Put differently, the structural form of unity for the KHC is a product of holiness, not its presumption.

The charismatic emphasis offers a second dimension to this understanding of the relationship of holiness to unity: as the movement grew and deepened its ties to Korea, it simultaneously moved further from the purview of the missionaries, at least for a time.[15] In forming itself as a thoroughly Korean church, the KHC simultaneously established theological continuity with the apostolic movement of the New Testament and discontinuity with any missionary governance. This is not to say that the KHC was unconcerned about unity with the missionaries, but that its relation to them was established by a primary concern for holiness that cut against the grain of the existing institutional relationships. The KHC's emphasis on divine healings, millennialist eschatology, and baptism of the Holy Spirit, as enshrined in its constitution and bylaws, breaks with some of the Reformed tendencies present in the early influential figures of the KHC.[16] What emerges is a unity of holiness as opposed to a unity of order *first*.

As Grant Wacker indicates, holiness and unity might relate in a second, albeit more initially disruptive, way as well: holiness producing new forms. The charismatic movement, where it appeared in various forms, was often labeled as heretical, troublemaking, or disquieting for denominational unity. Among American Baptists and Southern Baptists in a North American context, the pervasiveness of charismatic gifts such as speaking in tongues was viewed with suspicion as unbiblical or perhaps demonic in origin. While the Southern Baptists rejected a motion at their national convention in 1975 to

14. *Discipline of the Pentecostal Holiness Church*, 106.
15. One dimension to the birth of the KHC yet undiscussed is the "self-born" nature of the denomination, which refers both to the charismatic roots and to the Minjung theology intrinsic to the movement. See Choi, *Rise of the Korean Holiness Church*, 103.
16. Choi, *Rise of the Korean Holiness Church*, 106.

denounce charismatics, they likewise reaffirmed their 1963 doctrinal statement that affirms "God cultivates Christian character, comforts believers, and bestows the spiritual gifts by which they serve God through His church."[17] Put differently, so long as expressions of holiness, such as charismatic ones, did not become the framing question for how church order proceeded, the expressions could be carried out in local settings.

Among North American Black Baptists, the charismatic emphases eventuated, in one case, in a reformulating of unity, similar to that seen in the KHC: the founding of the Full Gospel Baptist Fellowship (FGBF) in 1993. The founding church, Greater St. Stephen Missionary Baptist (renamed Greater St. Stephen Full Gospel Baptist Church), was at the time the largest Baptist Church in New Orleans, with over ten thousand attendees. Joining hands with a dozen like-minded pastors, a new denomination emerged that, according to historian C. Douglas Weaver, was a hybrid of Baptist local church autonomy and Pentecostal emphases on spiritual gifts and Holy Spirit Baptism.[18] The group's initial convention gathered over thirty thousand people in 1994 and would grow to almost two thousand churches in the decades to come.

While the FGBF is better known for its prosperity-gospel teaching, the FGBF represents an intriguing example of the way in which holiness—particularly when calibrated toward experience—reconfigures ecclesiological forms of unity. Many FGBF churches, for example, dually aligned with either Southern Baptist churches or American Baptist churches; given the struggles within the Southern Baptist Convention over that which is celebrated in the FGBF, the holiness emphasis here created a broader network for churches, after *initially* creating a breakaway group. Church holiness, then, when manifested in spiritual gifts that become the core identifying mark of church holiness, has the capacity to create a pneumatologically *expansive* vision of the church rather than a *divisive* one.

The Problem of Holiness

In these examples, we see some of the difficulties that emerge when unity follows from the charismatic expression of holiness. The Baptist emphasis on

---

17. *The Baptist Faith and Message* (Nashville: Sunday School Board of the Southern Baptist Convention, 1963).
18. C. Douglas Weaver, *Baptists and the Holy Spirit: The Contested History with Holiness-Pentecostal-Charismatic Movements* (Waco: Baylor University Press, 2019), 385–89.

local autonomy of churches allowed for the proliferation of the charismatic movement, creating a form of unity within that was rooted in the Spirit's gifting rather than in eucharistic liturgy. But unlike in the Korean Holiness Church, because of the presumption of church autonomy, the diffuse charismatic experiences among Baptist churches bore no common theological or liturgical pattern that could account for these divergences. With the absence of a common liturgical or denominationally binding framework, the charismatic infusion in Baptist life was sometimes seen as renewing institutional unity and sometimes seen as producing new forms of unity, with the charismatic renewal troubling simplistic unity and pushing churches toward a more receptive form of unity structured by the emerging gifts of the Spirit.

A more minimalist approach to navigating this question of holiness and unity can be seen in the WCC. In 1947, following the first World Pentecostal Conference in Zurich, Pentecostal representatives began to approach the WCC with a desire to be included in the work of the council.[19] Such sentiments of cooperation were not universal among Pentecostals, some of whom saw the unity of the WCC as purely formal and not organized by the Spirit's work.[20] In the next three decades, only a handful of Pentecostal churches became formal members of the WCC, many of whom encountered strong pushback from within the particular churches of the WCC themselves. But what emerged as a fruit of this longer dialogue was, in 1991, a new consultation to incorporate the particular emphases of the Pentecostal churches into the WCC's concerns.[21]

How did this larger incorporation of Pentecostals occur? There were, prior to 1991, Pentecostal churches involved in the WCC, and so the WCC's approach could be seen as keeping the peace that had been breached elsewhere, for the sake of unity. A more interesting framing, though, is that the WCC was welcoming charismatic renewal, but only insofar as charismatic renewal cohered first not to church order but to *triune confession*: God gives holiness to a church in forms appropriate to what that church is in the midst of time. By viewing charismatic renewal as a triune gift first (a gift that we must receive, even if we do not know what to do with it), the WCC navigated a

---

19. For an overview of this history, see Martin Robra, "The World Council of Churches and Pentecostals," *Ecumenical Review* 71 (2019): 161–74.
20. Robra, "World Council of Churches and Pentecostals," 164.
21. Robra, "World Council of Churches and Pentecostals," 168. The report can be read in Michael Kinnamon, ed., *Signs of the Spirit: Official Report, Seventh Assembly, Canberra, Australia, 7–20 February 1991* (Geneva: WCC Publications; Grand Rapids: Eerdmans, 1991), 107–8.

different road than what we saw either with the Korean Holiness or the Black Baptist examples.

The incorporation of Pentecostal groups into the WCC was effected as all unions in the WCC, by requiring an affirmation of the Trinity. In view of the ways in which charismatic emphases reconfigured unity elsewhere, the WCC's approach is notable for the way in which it asks for holiness to be conceived of as a triune question first, before it is a matter of ecclesiological display. In this way, the WCC answered "Both" to what had elsewhere seemed an irresolvable either/or proposition. It brought in a form of holiness unknown to most of its members by emphasizing not *ecclesial* unity but *divine* unity as the basis for its inclusion: the same God who gives the church unity gives the church holiness in the same breath.

As we move forward, I will continue to sketch out four dimensions of church holiness that become contested in the twentieth century: (1) worship and liturgy, (2) political holiness, (3) bodily holiness, and (4) holiness across time. These four elements roughly correspond to the church's theological existence as (1) God's people in worship, (2) God's people before the world, (3) God's people individually, and (4) God's people through history. As we explore how the mark of holiness played out in ecclesiology, we will be able to see more clearly how practicing holiness and conveying it to creation remains a fraught enterprise. As I suggested at the onset, the stakes of holiness are not primarily individual but ecclesial, such that the church's pursuit of holiness has corporate implications not only for the church's conception of itself as a holy people but for its conception of the world as meant to bear God's holiness.

Holiness and Worship

As indicated already, with the construal of holiness during the Second Vatican Council, one of the subtexts of the twentieth century is the rise of populism, the emergence of "the people" as a major theme of politics, writing, and thus, for ecclesiology. Questions, already broached, of whether holiness is differentiated between laity and clergy will follow us here as well, but as an argument about what it means for the whole of God's people to be one people before God and whether the emergence of the laity ushered in a new day for church worship.

From the vantage point of the Orthodox, this concern for "the people" did not take the form of a vast movement to modernize the liturgy for the twentieth century, but of an impulse to ask more fully how the liturgy—the space in which the clergy and laity join together in worship—fully integrates theology and piety for all people. To quote Alexander Schmemann:

> The real problem ... is not of "liturgical reforms" but, first of all, of the much needed "reconciliation" and mutual reintegration of liturgy, theology and piety. Here, however, I must confess my pessimism. I do not see in Orthodox theology and in general the Orthodox Church even a recognition of that problem. ... It is my impression that with a few exceptions, the "patristic revival" remains locked within the old western approach to theology, is a return much more to patristic *texts* than to the *mind* of the Fathers, as if these patristic texts were self-sufficient and self-explanatory.[22]

During the twentieth century, as Schmemann notes, there was a great revival of interest—mirrored within Catholic circles of the *nouvelle theologie* movement—in the early church.[23] But Schmemann articulates an important concern here for this renewal: if this revival concerns only the priests, the divide between laity and clergy persists. Not only will the rise of "the people" be unacknowledged, but a distinction we saw at the opening of this chapter will be perpetuated: an expectation of holiness, but available for only a portion of the church.

While the research agenda of recovering the "mind of the Fathers" constituted one dimension of this liturgical retrieval, the rise of hesychastic prayer and the proliferation of rites within the church point to an approach to Orthodox liturgical renewal that simultaneously knits together laity and clergy and avoids the question of whether the liturgy itself needs to be addressed. Hesychastic prayer, a form of silent prayer articulated in the work of Gregory of Palamas in which Christ's presence to the soul is emphasized, became more popular across the century, spreading from the monasteries to private prayers beyond the Orthodox world.[24] The rise of hesychastic prayer, popularized

---

22. Alexander Schmemann, *Liturgy and Tradition: Theological Reflections of Alexander Schmemann*, ed. Thomas Fisch (Crestwood, NY: St. Vladimir's Seminary Press, 1990), 42.

23. It is no coincidence that this "revival" was accompanied by the founding of St. Vladimir's Seminary Press, St. Tikhon's Theological Institute, and many other research and publishing initiatives. See John Binnis, "Modern Spirituality and the Orthodox Church," in *The Cambridge History of Christianity*, ed. Michael Angold (Cambridge: Cambridge University Press, 2014), 5:587–90.

24. For this history, see Christopher D. L. Johnson, *The Globalization of Hesychasm and the Jesus Prayer: Contesting Contemplation* (London: Continuum, 2010).

by twentieth-century Orthodox luminaries such as Christos Yannaras and Kallistos Ware, helped to fulfill the need for the "mind of the Fathers" to be integrated into the lives of the laity.

But hesychastic prayer also, arguably, contributed to the political popularization that the Orthodox church struggled with. As Daniel Payne and others have argued, because hesychasm emphasizes the dignity of the person, its approach became the basis for a political platform; in Greece, Russia, and elsewhere, the Orthodox church's resurgence alongside nationalist movements was in part due to recovery of the dignity of the person found in hesychastic prayer.[25]

The proliferation of hesychastic prayer, along with its implications for expanded notions of holiness, with its assumptions of developing personal dignity for the one praying, ran into an unanticipated challenge: the diaspora of Orthodox Christians into the West. As the Orthodox world began to engage with Western countries, the populist promise of hesychastic prayer fit uneasily with a Western world in which individual dignity was more closely aligned with individualism.[26] Diaspora meant that the hesychastic prayer was now taking place no longer within a space of unified culture and peoplehood but in new pluralized spaces, with the danger of the people becoming corrupted by Western individualism.

The form of the Byzantine Rite, one of the most widely used liturgies, helps us to see the background tension that we have seen Schmemann identifying.[27] The rite consists of two areas that interlock—the prayers and devotions made by the clergy, on the one hand, and those made by the people, on the

---

25. See P. Daniel Payne, *The Revival of Political Hesychasm in Contemporary Orthodox Thought* (Lanham, MD: Lexington Books, 2011); Tone Svetelj, "Gregory Palamas and Political Hesychasm in the Fourteenth and Twentieth Centuries," *Analogia* 4 (2017): 61–79.

26. For the best known example here, see the history of the Russian Orthodox diaspora and the challenges this posed not only for Orthodox identity but for Orthodox notions of unity. This history is narrated in Sergei Hackel, "Diaspora Problems of the Russian Emigration," in Angold, *Cambridge History of Christianity*, 5:539–57.

27. The Byzantine Rite, for example, used by many of the autocephalous Orthodox churches, underwent few revisions during the twentieth century by comparison to other communions. Minor variations in practice, such as the use of local liturgical languages, became more common, but the Byzantine Rite remained in effect the same form that it had been since the fourteenth century. See Hugh Wybrew, *The Orthodox Liturgy: The Development of the Eucharistic Liturgy in the Byzantine Rite* (Crestwood, NY: St. Vladimir's Seminary Press, 1989), 173. For the complicated histories of the liturgy as Orthodox communities entered the Westernized world—along with the West's assumptions about lay participation and cultural integration—see the studies in Maria Hämmerli and Jean-François Mayer, *Orthodox Identities in Western Europe: Migration, Settlement and Innovation* (Surrey, UK: Ashgate, 2014).

other—but that remain distinct. Though the worshipers enter the church surrounded by the iconography of the saints, the prophets, the angels, and the heavenlies as they move toward their pews, the celebration of the liturgy takes place mainly apart from the worshipers in the pews. The priest, at the side altar, has been performing the rite of the prothesis (the preliminary preparation of the Eucharist), and many of the hymns are sung by the priest and not as congregational songs.[28]

As Elisabeth Behr-Sigel noted, the division present within the liturgy itself bears within it a different kind of division: of women from men, not in dignity but in their capacity to live into the fullness of holiness envisioned by the church. Pointing to the women behind the spirit of the liturgy—including the Holy Mother Mary, Macrina the Elder and other Cappadocian women, and other canonized saints, Behr-Sigel has made the case that the ordination of women falls within the purview of the liturgy as being a living tradition and that, by extension, the church can incorporate a more expansive notion of holiness.[29]

Behr-Sigel's question about women's ordination will be visited in a later chapter, but her work signals a standing question that Protestants and Catholics took up more directly: What does it mean to include all members of the church in holiness? One could argue that, by virtue of being Christ's body, all members, regardless of participation, are imbued with that holiness—that mode of participation and holiness are two different things. Would we say that if someone is incapable of attending weekly services, their participation in the holiness of the church is thereby in jeopardy? Anguish from not being present or a desire to participate more fully is different than participating in God's holiness, and yet, what is at stake in these questions of participation is how the church as a unified body—and not primarily its representative leaders—exhibits holiness.[30]

In this respect, Methodists tended to strike a middle ground between concerns for continuity with the past and concerns for including all members

---

28. Wybrew, *Orthodox Liturgy*, 4–5.

29. Elisabeth Behr-Sigel and Kallistos Ware, *The Ordination of Women in the Orthodox Church* (Geneva: World Council of Churches, 2000), 35.

30. That the Catholic and Orthodox churches envision unity as occurring through the unity of their leaders does not deflect this concern, insofar as lay participation is envisioned—as we have seen in both Catholic and Orthodox discussions—as key to the church's internal unity and holiness. Put differently, discussions of unity set the stage for questions about holiness to be asked in this way.

fully in the liturgy. Following the incorporation of various British Methodists into the Methodist Church in 1932, the *Book of Offices* and unified hymnals were soon published. Using extemporaneous prayers and often lay preachers, worship consisted of a recognizable set of events but no singular form. Communion was done, for example, at the discretion of the local minister, either as part of the worship or as a second event following worship.[31] By 1975, as Methodism grew globally, the more unified form present in the *Methodist Service Book* appeared, under the reasoning, as A. Raymond George puts it, that there needed to be more attention to the work of the people in the service.[32] The increased singing of hymns, the passing of the peace, lay participation in distributing Communion, and lay readings of Scripture all were meant to reinforce the role of the laity within the liturgy. New translations of older liturgies, beginning with the 1975 version, likewise emphasized inclusive language for men and women in instructions, including feminine biblical language in the celebration in 1984 and songs from the global reaches of Methodism in 1976.[33]

From the beginning, the Methodists positioned the denomination as one rooted in the Spirit's renewing work. Therefore, revisions to the liturgy reflected the larger ethos of church built upon Sunday school and lay formation: an ethos according to which all persons are called by God to be renewed by the Spirit.[34] Methodists, like many other denominations, endured the so-called worship wars of the latter twentieth century. But what became evident, according to Don Saliers, is that by foregrounding the work of the people in liturgy within what was done in the broader Methodist ethos of lay formation, Methodist churches could incorporate a plurality of worship styles insofar as the work of the people was a key concern to liturgical reforms.

Such developments were not simply confined to Methodists. Examples such as *Apostolicam Actuositatem* (a "decree on the apostolate of the laity" from Vatican II), the founding of Associated Parishes for Liturgy and Mission by the American Episcopalian Church, and the founding of the Church Service

---

31. A. Raymond George, "From *The Sunday Service* to 'The Sunday Service': Sunday Morning Worship in British Methodism," in *The Sunday Service of the Methodists: Twentieth-Century Worship in Worldwide Methodism; Studies in Honor of James F. White*, ed. Karen B. Westerfield Tucker (Nashville: Kingswood Books, 1996), 32–34.

32. George, "From *The Sunday Service* to 'The Sunday Service,'" 45.

33. Hoyt L. Hickman, "Word and Table: The Process of Liturgical Revision in the United Methodist Church, 1964–1992," in Tucker, *Sunday Service of the Methodists*, 123–30.

34. Don Saliers, "Divine Grace, Divine Means: Sunday Worship in United Methodist Congregations," in Tucker, ed. *Sunday Service of the Methodists*, 152–53.

Society by the Presbyterians all spoke to this elevation of the laity, but in a way that tied the elevation of the laity to a renewal in worship. Throughout the 1960s and 1970s, from Catholics to Evangelical Lutherans in Canada, liturgical updates and revised services were published, all with the intent of integrating the people into worship more fully.[35]

The winds of liturgical change began to blow within Catholicism in Belgium in 1909. First, a Benedictine monastery began to publish liturgical material, including a French-Latin missal, nearly sixty years before Vatican II's commendation of performing the Mass in local languages. During the era of Pius X—noted for his own liturgical reforms involving lowering the age of first Communion—the Belgians followed Pius's own lead and linked together the liturgy with the promulgation of the faith and the life of virtue. Lambert Beauduin, one of the key figures of the Belgian movement, ran alongside the vision of Pius X, whose 1903 declaration emphasized retrieving Gregorian chant and reforming the breviary.[36] Across Europe, this interest in connecting the congregation to the liturgy in a formative way began to develop, eventually moving to the United States through the work of Virgil Michel.[37]

One of the key concerns of Catholic liturgical reform, particularly among Michel and his later followers, was that church participation had become an increasingly privatized affair, with spirituality and holiness viewed as an individual concern. Accordingly, the liturgical renewal movements were invested in housing individual piety within the larger frame of corporate holiness.[38] With the promulgation of *Sacrosanctum Concilium* at Vatican II in 1963, the priestly heart of the liturgy, the "presentation of man's sanctification under the guise of signs perceptible to the senses,"[39] brought many of these liturgical insights into full practice. Emphasizing that the liturgy was centered in the unity of holiness, Pope Paul VI urged that the performance of the Mass be attentive to lay participation, education of the faithful, and the upbuilding

---

35. Mark A. Torgerson, *An Architecture of Immanence* (Grand Rapids: Eerdmans, 2007), 25–41.

36. Pius X, *Tra Le Sollecitudini* [Instruction on sacred music] (Vatican City: Holy See, 1903), https://www.papalencyclicals.net/pius10/tra-le-sollecitudini.htm.

37. Keith F. Pecklers, *Unread Vision: The Liturgical Movement in the United States, 1926–1955* (Collegeville, MN: Liturgical Press, 1998), 1–24.

38. Correcting course here did not mean becoming uniform in all things. Beauduin was among the first arguing for liturgy and liturgical publications to be made in local languages. See Pecklers, *Unread Vision*, 25–27.

39. Paul VI, *Sacrosanctum Concilium*, 6, in *Vatican II: The Conciliar and Post-Conciliar Documents*, ed. Austin Flannery, OP (Northport, NY: Costello Publishing, 1981).

of the church by using local languages.[40] As Paul VI writes, "The purpose of the sacraments is to sanctify men, to build up the Body of Christ and, finally, to give worship to God," an order that emphasizes the final ordering of the liturgy: the unity of humanity in worship.[41]

In American parishes, as well as in some European parishes, this emphasis on the local congregation raised the contextual question to new levels, as the cosmopolitan intent of the doctrine ran into practical tensions between White and Black parishioners, as seen in the rise of Black Catholic congregations in Chicago, in which Black Catholics fleeing the American South in the Great Migration of the 1920s–1970s began to emphasize practices of dance, shouting, and song in liturgy.[42] Whereas in a homogenous Austrian or German context, where Catholic liturgical renewal began, questions of race were not raised, the racially diverse context of America raised new questions about what liturgy did and how it did it. Even after the promulgation of *Sacrosanctum Concilium*, Pope Paul VI's recommendation to African bishops that they "give [their] gifts of Blackness to the whole Church" broached not just questions of liturgical uniformity but the question, In what way should the holiness cultivated and conveyed in the liturgy be interwoven with race and culture?[43]

This attention to context, as part of attending to holiness, was not unique to the American experience but had been seen in an offshoot movement designed to integrate the heart of the liturgy with the Belgian and French working classes, who felt alienated by the liturgy: the Worker-Priest Movement.[44] Started by Jacques Loew and Emmanuel Celestin Suhard, this movement involved priests beginning to abandon their traditional vestments and join with factory workers in their work, in order to join these laborers' labor with the life of the liturgy. Viewed by some as a secularizing of the liturgical work, the movement can be best summed up by Father Jean-Marie Lepetit, one of the original group: "The masses want their destinies regulated from the inside in their own natural communities. We must be like leaven in the lump."[45] In light of France's *laïcité* (secularism) policy, this approach to bridging an

---

40. Paul VI, *Sacrosanctum Concilium*, 26–36.
41. Paul VI, *Sacrosanctum Concilium*, 59.
42. Matthew J. Cressler, *Authentically Black and Truly Catholic: The Rise of Black Catholicism in the Great Migration* (New York: NYU Press, 2017).
43. Cressler, *Authentically Black and Truly Catholic*, 1.
44. Andreas Freund, "The Worker-Priest Movement in France Has Received New Papal Encouragement," *New York Times*, May 27, 1979, section E, p. 8.
45. Oscar Arnal, *Priests in Working-Class Blue: The History of the Worker-Priests, 1943–1954* (Mahwah, NJ: Paulist Press, 1986), 116.

institutionally rigid divide between church and civil society did not wait for factory workers to come to the liturgy, but brought the liturgical celebrants into the factories.

Holiness, insofar as it is a feature of the church, concerns how the people of God are invited to share in God's presence together. One of the questions that are raised as this is teased out ecumenically is not only *if* this is something to be done univocally but *in what ways* the common worship of the church should reflect that. The approaches of Catholics and Orthodox, in which laity and clergy share in this singular holiness differently, are built on the assumption that the divine life entails an analogy of hierarchy.[46] As *Lumen Gentium* puts it, the priests act in the Mass "in the person of Christ" to bring their congregations into common worship of God with all other congregations;[47] the holiness of the church works hierarchically because of the unity of the church is structured so.

Alongside this, however, emerged a new concern for holiness as encompassing the full life of all persons, whether in the factories of France, in the experience of American women Methodists, or in the lives of Black Catholics. This concern is not immediately at odds with a hierarchical arrangement: the most ardent supporters of hierarchy, as seen in *Lumen Gentium*, depict laity and clergy as one body together. But if the holiness of the church body is God's gift, given for the full lives of the members of the body, we can see how an affirmation of context began to entail a questioning of some of the distinctions between laity and clergy. If we affirm God's gift of holiness to all members of the body—in the full contours of their lives—the question could rightly be raised, Why are the roles of clergy and of laity still distinguished in the liturgy that joins all persons in the holiness of God?

The Visibility of Holiness: Two Forms of National Holiness

As we have seen, it is difficult to separate questions of how to elevate the people as partakers in God's holiness from larger questions of populism. In

---

46. *Lumen Gentium* makes this point explicit: "Priests, prudent cooperators with the Episcopal order, its aid and instrument, called to serve the people of God, constitute one priesthood. . . . They make [the bishop] present in a certain sense in the individual local congregations, and take upon themselves, as far as they are able, his duties and the burden of his care, and discharge them with a daily interest." Paul VI, *Lumen Gentium* (Vatican City: Holy See, 1964), 28, https://www.vatican.va/archive/hist_councils/ii_vatican_council/documents/vat-ii_const_19641121_lumen-gentium_en.html.

47. Paul VI, *Lumen Gentium*, 28.

a century characterized by populism, however, this question of public holiness became inflected into a new key: the relation between church holiness and political holiness. Here, we will briefly consider two areas of holiness implicated by these discussions that appeared dramatically: the holiness of the physical body and holiness of the social body. For in both instances, the holiness conveyed by Christ finds itself attested to not only in the gathered church—as seen most clearly in the questions surrounding liturgical renewal—but in what that holiness of the church means for the renewal of life both for the individual and for the surrounding world.

There are ample examples of the coincidence of church and nation within the twentieth century that are nefarious. But there are ample examples of this relation—particularly when viewed from a desire to offer the holiness of the church to the whole of creation—that do not warrant such easy dismissal. To illustrate this, let me briefly describe two Orthodox examples: from Russia and from Greece. As will be discussed shortly in relation to the Social Gospel, exhibiting the vision of the church in extra-ecclesial ways comes with its own set of difficulties, but perhaps the most complex vision of holiness in a broad social scale comes to us in the form of the *symphonia* of the Orthodox Churches.[48]

Orthodoxy and Political Renewal

One of the key challenges facing Orthodox churches in the twentieth century was the relation between the Eastern churches and Western culture, a challenge that included populist and nationalist movements, movements that alternately aided and used the Church. The Ukrainian Autocephalous Orthodox Church came into a fuller form at the end of the twentieth century after the collapse of the Soviet empire, alongside a renewed populism in Ukraine.[49] In Romania, the Orthodox Church property was nationalized and used in anti-Russian propaganda.[50] The Serbian Orthodox Church found itself caught between warring parties during the Yugoslavian war because of its deep connections to the populace.[51]

---

48. As discussed in the chapter on the church as one, the Orthodox notion of *symphonia* separates the Orthodox church from Protestant and most Catholic approaches to church by encouraging a geographical notion of the church's presence.
49. John Binnis, *An Introduction to the Christian Orthodox Churches* (Cambridge: Cambridge University Press, 2002), 187–88.
50. Sergei Hackel, "Diaspora Problems of the Russian Emigration," in Angold, *Cambridge History of Christianity*, 5:562–66.
51. Binnis, *Introduction to the Christian Orthodox Churches*, 190–92.

The story of the Russian Orthodox Church is in many ways the story of both sides of this relationship: both being used by and using political life in the pursuit of a nationalized holiness. It was not until the fifteenth century that the see of Moscow emerged as an equal to older sees of the church in Constantinople or the church in Alexandria, having been initially a mission province but becoming autocephalous in 1459.[52] But what rises with the people falls with the people as well. In 1917, with the Bolshevik Revolution, the church found itself in the place of having the national leadership actively opposed to its presence among the people, a situation that meant that the integration and cooperation between church and politburo was decidedly unidirectional: survival of the church meant accepting the limits placed on it by the state.[53] In the seventy years following the revolution, the church endured having liturgical objects sold for state benefit, having tens of thousands of clergy arrested, and having all religious activity limited to the church building.[54] By 1986, the nearly forty thousand parishes of the church had dwindled to less than seven thousand.

With relaxed laws of religious freedom passed in 1991, however, the Russian Orthodox Church was able to once again recover, though now with increased religious competition from outside churches such as the once prohibited Greek Catholic Church, evangelicals, and Baptist churches. But as the twentieth century came to a close, new restrictions by the government on non-Orthodox churches began to be enacted. The reasons for these restrictions on non-Orthodox churches are complex, but in any event, the 1990s represented an opportunity for the Orthodox Church to reclaim its role as the people's church over against non-Russian options. The Orthodox Church illustrates one way in which the holiness of the church and the flourishing of a people came together.[55] For the church to be a church of the people would necessarily involve suspicion of those who sought to alter the national character of the people.

52. Thomas Bremer, *Cross and Kremlin: A Brief History of the Orthodox Church in Russia* (Grand Rapids: Eerdmans, 2013), 16. For broad histories of the Russian Orthodox Church, see Nathaniel Davis, *A Long Walk to Church: A Contemporary History of Russian Orthodoxy* (Boulder, CO: Westview, 2003); and Irene Papkova, *The Orthodox Church and Russian Politics* (Oxford: Oxford University Press, 2011).

53. On Russian Orthodox ecumenical engagements, see also "Assessing Unity: The Eastern Orthodox Churches," in chap. 1.

54. Bremer, *Cross and Kremlin*, 81–82.

55. In the twenty-first century, many of these arrangements with the government have shifted to arguably create a much more full-blown vision of *symphonia*. See John Garrard and Carol Garrard, *Russian Orthodoxy Resurgent: Faith and Power in the New Russia* (Oxford: Oxford University Press, 2018).

But whereas the Russian Orthodox Church came into existence long before the nation of Russia, in Greece, the process of nationalization and church influence came about together. The Church of Greece came into existence in 1833 during the nationalist struggles of the nineteenth century that enveloped much of Europe, with the result that by the twentieth century, to be Greek was to be Orthodox. But whereas in Russia, the substrate of Russia's people remained Orthodox regardless of the official governmental positions, in Greece, official recognition by the government has meant a different road toward *symphonia* than what we see in Russia.[56]

With the Church of Greece, we find holiness embedded within and supported by broader governmental practice. Through taxation, then, the holiness of the church is supported materially by those who would otherwise find themselves outside the economy of the church's salvation. In participation in taxes, however, they are linked into the public work of the church—and indeed, into the public manifestation of the church's holiness—in ways that blur the distance between the church's distinct holiness (one of sacraments, prayer, and participation in the liturgy) and that in which all citizens participate by proxy.

At one level, this is a deeply scriptural image, for in the Gospels, we find Jesus eating and drinking in the houses of tax collectors and sinners, and thus supported in his ministry by those who are not disciples. The holiness of Christ (and by extension, of Christ's body, the church) thus is arguably seen in this intersection of Christ's presence and the world's participation. But the proliferation of holiness through the mechanism of taxation and governmental support forces us to ask what the relationship is between the holiness of the church and cultural integration. In both Greece and Russia, for example, deep-seated suspicion of cultural outsiders in the form of the Albanians and Muslims, respectively, points to the limits of a holiness linked with national identity, particularly when supported through governmental functions.[57] To help ourselves assess this further, let us leave behind the Orthodox engagements with political holiness and return to an American

---

56. Demetrios J. Constantelos, *The Greek Orthodox Church: Faith, History and Practice* (New York: Seabury, 1967).

57. The experience of the Orthodox Church in America highlights this point, in that America has never had this idea of *symphonia* in play for the Orthodox Church, because the United States had multiple ethnically rooted varieties of Orthodoxy in it during the whole of the twentieth century. See George C. Michalopulos and Herb Ham, *The American Orthodox Church: A History of Its Beginning* (Salisbury, MA: Regina Orthodox Press, 2003).

example, mentioned in chapter 1, for a different account of national holiness: the American Social Gospel.

As popularly depicted in the Social Gospel era bestseller *In His Steps*, pastors such as Walter Rauschenbusch and Josiah Strong emphasized partnership both in their social advocacy and in their preaching, bringing together preaching about God's kingdom with ecumenical action for the sake of the common good.[58] Building on the social-activism traditions of the late nineteenth-century revivalists, the Social Gospel preceded some of the later movements among their Catholic, working-class counterparts in Europe by nearly thirty years. As the movement developed in its advocacy of "Christianizing the social order,"[59] it became evident that not all of the social order was in view. Rauschenbusch, for example, spoke seldom about race, and when he did, he spoke in ways that reflected an unconscious affirmation of early twentieth-century American imperialism.[60] The parallel development of an African American Social Gospel movement, by contrast, viewed the implicit racism of Strong and Rauschenbusch as part of the problem and saw their combination of Manifest Destiny with the emergent kingdom of God in history as one of the very things that Christian political holiness needed to criticize most vocally.

For early Social Gospel figures such as Rauschenbusch and Strong, the kingdom of God—as a sociopolitical movement—is the fullness of Jesus's vision; the church should not restrict the holiness of God to the church. To restrict God's holiness is to misunderstand what that holiness is for and to repeat the sins of the Pharisees, Rauschenbusch argued.[61]

This understanding of the telos of the church's righteousness—public manifestation in social policy—would animate a number of Protestant movements, including the establishment of the National Council of Churches in the United States, and some of the discussions of the Life and Work division

---

58. Gary Dorrien, *Social Ethics in the Making: Interpreting an American Tradition* (Malden, MA: Wiley-Blackwell, 2009), 76ff.

59. The title of Rauschenbusch's most well-known (and bestselling) book.

60. See Ben Sanders, "Walter Rauschenbusch on Society," in *Beyond the Pale: Reading Ethics from the Margins*, ed. Stacey M. Floyd-Thomas and Miguel A. De La Torre (Louisville: Westminster John Knox, 2011), 111–18; and Miguel De La Torre, *Latina/o Social Ethics: Moving beyond Eurocentric Moral Thinking* (Waco: Baylor University Press, 2010), 6–13.

61. Walter Rauschenbusch, *A Theology for the Social Gospel* (Louisville: Westminster John Knox, 1997), 134: "The Church is primarily a fellowship for worship; the Kingdom is a fellowship of righteousness. . . . There are nations in which the ethical condition of the masses is the reverse of the frequency of the masses in the churches."

of the World Council of Churches.[62] Catholic analogues likewise began to emphasize the ways in which Catholic doctrine should animate public discussions.[63] The criticism of both Protestant and Catholic forms of this trajectory, as Stanley Hauerwas would put it much later, was that the real topic of theological ethics was consequently not God but America; these church leaders were preoccupied with political sacrality.[64] Hauerwas's critique is not without merit: despite their other divides on the nature of the liturgy, role of the laity, or other sacramental questions, it was this fundamental assumption of national holiness that drew together Protestants and Catholics.[65]

As I conclude discussion of these examples, it is important to note two things. First, we should note how holiness in a national key reconfigures church unity. Recall the ways that questions over charismatic gifts as the sign of holiness reconfigured ecclesial boundaries. Commitments to social holiness created new divisions and alliances as well. Here holiness produces unity, but unity with a broader population, prompting questions of what form that holiness should take. To put it sharply, the vision of political holiness that is obvious for Rauschenbusch is not the one that his African American contemporaries see as desirable, nor was it the one that the Orthodox pursued in Russia along with Russian Baptists or in Greece along with Greek evangelicals.

Second, we must ask whether this form of holiness reconfigures the church alone, or whether this reconfigured holiness is to be the form of the world as well. This second question is one of specificity: Does holiness take a specific form within the church? And, if it does, what is that form? Though the political ideals espoused in these examples differ, what draws them together is a common commitment to a union of church and world, with broader society sharing in the church's holiness in ways that, in more recent discourse, sound like "Christian nationalism," putting forth a broader social vision that is irreducibly tied to distinctly Christian doctrines. This argument as to whether there is a shared holiness between church and world is one that long precedes the twentieth century but is, in many ways, possible only in an increasingly

---

62. Melanie May, "The Kingdom of God, the Church, and the World: The Social Gospel and the Making of Theology in the Twentieth-Century Ecumenical Movement," in *The Social Gospel Today*, ed. Christopher H. Evans (Louisville: Westminster John Knox, 2001), 38–52.

63. On the impact of the Social Gospel beyond Protestants, see Roger Haight and John Langan, "Recent Catholic Social and Ethical Teaching in Light of the Social Gospel," *Journal of Religious Ethics* 18, no. 1 (1990): 103–28.

64. Stanley Hauerwas, "Christian Ethics in America (and the JRE): A Report on a Book I Will Not Write," *Journal of Religious Ethics* 25, no. 3 (1997): 57–76.

65. For these stories, see Dorrien, *Social Ethics in the Making*, 533–692.

Christian century when the social influence of churches is ascendant. It is no accident, for example, that one of the most frequently read works of the twentieth century in Christian ethics was H. Richard Niebuhr's *Christ and Culture*, which puts forward a vision of "Christ the Transformer of Society" as the paragon of Christian engagement.[66]

The Visibility of Holiness: Bodily Life

If the church's political holiness broaches the question of what it means for the church's holiness to be a property shared with the world, this must be paired with a more intimate question: What does the holiness of the church mean for the *bodies* of those gathered within it? If the twentieth century was one of various populisms and of the rise of the laity, this occurred in tandem with questions of how to preserve the particular person within groups. To offer a representation of these discussions, I will look at practices of healing as expressions of this concern of bodily holiness as an expansion of a commitment to the church's holiness.

The late nineteenth century was a hotbed of spiritual healing movements, both in the United States and across the Atlantic Ocean, with names like Mary Baker Eddy and George Muller coming to prominence.[67] A wide range of positions appeared among those that held that healing of the body's ailments is a sign of the Spirit's regenerative work, with Pentecostals and holiness movements as the best known. But healing movements were not the exclusive property of charismatic movements. The Emmanuel Movement, a pioneering effort to integrate psychological and spiritual well-being, was the work of Boston-based Episcopalians, and a revival of interest in anointing the sick took place among Catholics, Lutherans, and Episcopalians as well.[68]

It has been argued that such interest in bodily healing is the function of increased perfectionism of the body, or perhaps part of the proxy war between religion and science.[69] But the ecumenical pervasiveness of this link between bodies and holiness seems to offer a different possibility: that bodily healing was viewed as an expansive sign of ecclesial concerns, that the healing of

---

66. H. Richard Niebuhr, *Christ and Culture* (New York: Harper and Row, 1975).
67. For ancient and medieval roots of this, see Amanda Porterfield, *Healing in the History of Christianity* (Oxford: Oxford University Press, 2005), 21–92.
68. See Raymond J. Cunningham, "The Emmanuel Movement: A Variety of American Religious Experience," *American Quarterly* 14 (1962): 48–63.
69. Porterfield, *Healing in the History of Christianity*, 185.

the body makes sense if these bodies are part of the body of Christ. Let us consider two examples here: charismatic healings and the modern medical missions movement.

While an interest in healing did not begin with charismatic circles,[70] their vision frequently incorporated bodily healing as one of the marks of personal regeneration. Consider, for example, the way that the newly formed Christian and Missionary Alliance (CMA) incorporated bodily healing as one of the essential parts of the "fourfold gospel," alongside justification, sanctification, and the second coming of Christ.[71] Similar formulations are seen in the work of Aimee Semple McPherson, founder of the International Church of the Foursquare Gospel.[72] The more popularly known healing evangelists appeared alongside these movements, as messengers of a broader movement instead of individual entrepreneurs, with various denominations, including the Church of God, the Pentecostal Holiness Church, and the CMA including divine healing in their denominational bylaws.[73]

But the more charismatic expressions are but one form that this link between bodily healing and ecclesial holiness took. For the twentieth century was also the period in which medical missions became much more prominent. Medical care, as a facet of Christian commitments, dates back nearly to the beginning.[74] And though there was a distinction between healing and medical care, healing was viewed, as Helen Rhee notes, in the same breath as exorcisms and other charismatic gifts: known, but not commonly named as a gift of God.[75] But by the fourth century CE, it appears that institutionalized medical care had become the more regular form of attending to bodily ailments. Spiritual well-being remained the priority over physical health in these institutional arrangements, with medical care taking place as an extension of the work of churches and monasteries.[76]

---

70. See Nancy Hardesty, *Faith Cure: Divine Healing in the Holiness and Pentecostal Movements* (Peabody, MA: Hendrickson, 2003), 27–71, for the trans-Atlantic and ecumenical precedents to the Pentecostals.

71. Dora Dudley, *Beulah, or, Some of the Fruits of One Consecrated Life* (Grand Rapids, 1896), cited in Hardesty, *Faith Cure*, 92.

72. Edith Blumhofer, *Aimee Semple McPherson: Everybody's Sister* (Grand Rapids: Eerdmans, 1993), 190–93.

73. Hardesty, *Faith Cure*, 126–27.

74. As Helen Rhee observes, care is different from healing (the ministry of healing the sick supernaturally), the latter being more frequently associated with charismatic bodily healing. We will be following the first line, that of care. See Helen Rhee, *Illness, Pain, and Health Care in Early Christianity* (Grand Rapids: Eerdmans, 2022), 226–32.

75. Rhee, *Illness, Pain, and Health Care in Early Christianity*, 230–31.

76. Rhee, *Illness, Pain, and Health Care in Early Christianity*, 244.

As conceived early on, the term "medical missionary" seems to have been born of necessity; international mission work simply required this service, but it was not seen as the same thing as evangelism or church planting.[77] According to Samuel Marsden (the first person to use the term "medical missionary" in publication in English), medical care could bring "civilization," which could open the way for evangelism.[78] At the founding of one of the first medical missions societies, in Guangzhou, China, this basic thesis was affirmed, though not in "civilizing" terms: "The object of this Society is . . . to encourage the practice of Medicine among the Chinese, to extend to them some of the benefits, which science, patient investigation, and the very kindling light of discovery have conferred upon ourselves. . . . We have called ours a Missionary Society, because we trust it will advance the cause of missions, and because we want men to fill our institutions, who to requisite skill and experience add the self-denial and high moral qualities which are usually looked for in a missionary."[79]

The placement of the calling and gifts of physicians *parallel* to those of missionaries indicates an early willingness to think of medicine and evangelism not as the same task but as distinct and complementary ones. Medical care would, whether by "civilization" or by cultural benefit, open doors for evangelism—and, by extension, for expanding church holiness into the realm of the body.

Medical personnel were envisioned by their church-sending bodies not as pure technicians but as contributors to an integral work of *mission*, bringing health to the body while evangelists and ministers brought health to the soul. Consider, for example, the estimation of Pius XII in his *Evangelii Praecones*:

> We also wish at this point to pay the highest tribute of praise to the care taken of the sick, the infirm and afflicted of every kind; We mean hospitals, leprosaria, dispensaries and homes for the aged and for maternity cases, and orphanages. These are to Our eyes the fairest flowers of missionary endeavor; they give us as it were a vision of the Divine Redeemer Himself, who "went about doing good, and healing all that were oppressed." Such outstanding works of charity are undoubtedly of the highest efficacy in preparing the souls of non-Christians and in drawing them to the Faith and to the practice of Christianity; besides,

---

77. Christoffer H. Grundmann, *Sent to Heal! Emergence and Development of Medical Missions* (Lanham, MD: University Press of America, 2005), 2.

78. Grundmann, *Sent to Heal!*, 2–3.

79. *The Medical Missionary Society* (1838), as quoted in Grundmann, *Sent to Heal!*, 5.

Our Lord said to His Apostles: "Into what city soever you enter, and they receive you, . . . heal the sick that are therein, and say to them: the Kingdom of God is come nigh unto you.[80]

Critical assessments of twentieth-century international missions are right to point out the ways in which missions efforts were inattentive to cultural dynamics and to note that local attitudes and habits frequently conformed to the cultural expectations of the missionaries.[81] But medical missions, as a kind of sacramental enterprise—healing the body as an act of divine calling—offers an intriguing counterparadigm to the traditional narratives surrounding missions and imperialism, as well as an apt parallel to more charismatic accounts of healing.

As seen in the words of Pius XII, the work of the medical professional extends the kingdom of God, apart from any spiritual guidance the physicians might offer. In other words, medical missions offers a vision of medical care not as mercy but as *bodily holiness*: an indication that God's transforming work occurs in the body as a sign of God's presence.[82] Not only does such a vision decouple colonial influence from God's work—for it is, in this view, God who heals the patient and not ultimately the physician—but it imbues the patient with God's saving-work remainder: the kingdom of God and its holiness has included the patient in it, such that the patient's own body bears testimony. There is no need to adopt the physician's techniques since it is God's action that is efficacious through the physician.

Medical missions thus finds itself as a counterpart with charismatic commitments of healing movements, with both affirming that God might heal the sick as an extension of God's own holiness, and that such expectations should

---

80. Pius XII, *Evangelii Praecones* (Vatican City: Holy See, 1951), 45–46, https://www.vatican.va/content/pius-xii/en/encyclicals/documents/hf_p-xii_enc_02061951_evangelii-praecones.html.

81. See the various critiques levied in, among other works, Richard R. Cook and David W. Pao, *After Imperialism: Christian Identity in China and the Global Evangelical Movement* (Eugene, OR: Pickwick, 2011); Willie James Jennings, *The Christian Imagination: Theology and the Origins of Race* (New Haven: Yale University Press, 2010); and Michael W. Stroope, *Transcending Mission: The Eclipse of a Modern Tradition* (Downers Grove, IL: IVP Academic, 2017).

82. Pius XII's statement aligns with Fowler T. Franklin's assessment of the history of Southern Baptist medical missions when Franklin writes that "the growing concern of government authorities for the health of their own people is increasing, thus opening many doors to further undertakings. The opportunity for the medical missionary *to witness in healing* is thus brighter than ever before" (emphasis added) (Fowler T. Franklin, "The History of Southern Baptist Medical Missions," *Baptist History and Heritage* 10 [1975]: 194–203). Presbyterians, by contrast, experienced much more difficulty integrating spiritual and medical concerns, as Kristin L. Gleeson details in "The Stethoscope and the Gospel: Presbyterian Foreign Medical Missions, 1840–1990," *American Presbyterians* 71 (1993): 127–38.

be institutionalized as consistent with church visions of what God intends for the physical body. The difference comes in two aspects: (1) with naming what prerequisites there might be for such healing to happen in the form of appropriate technologies and pharmaceuticals and (2) with naming what normativity there is for the exercise of healing in this way.[83] We have seen already how holiness movements reconfigured institutional expectations or created their own institutional expectations, and healing is no different in that respect.

But as Pius XII points out, one might equally simply assume that God's work in healing bodies is first a work of God before it is a work of appropriate technologies. Christian traditions in which medical missions are more prominent, such as Methodism, Presbyterianism, Roman Catholicism, and the Baptist tradition, may see themselves far apart from more charismatic Christians. But healing movements and medical missions arguably represent two sides of the same concern—affirming that restoring bodily integrity is an integral aspect of bearing witness to God's holiness.

Those healed of their illness—whether through charismatic gifts or through physician skill—will die again, but in the midst of time, their healing is celebrated as a sign of future hope. Or more specifically, their bodily health is celebrated as a sign of how human bodies participate in the wholeness that God intends for all creation. To examine this question of bodily holiness opens the door to considering other events of the twentieth century and asking more broadly about what it means that the holiness of the church is extended into the bodies of its members. For alongside movements of healing, there also arose theologies of disability, ecclesial initiatives to provide health care on a broad scale, and globe-spanning controversies over issues of death and dying. These two examples open up broader questions, ones over which people are frequently divided politically, and often in stale and intractable ways. Asking these questions again as extensions of bodily holiness opens up new vistas.

Holiness: Redressing the Past

Thus far, we have examined in brief the ways that ecclesial holiness bore itself out in the life of the body, the nation, and the role of the laity in worship.

---

83. As Ivan Illich points out, the colonial assumptions of "Western medicine" may come sneaking back in at this point, assuming that God's saving activity is the result of certain medical techniques and sidelining traditional forms of medical care found in other cultures. See Ivan Illich, *Medical Nemesis: The Expropriation of Health* (New York: Random House, 1976), 108–15.

These dimensions roughly correspond to the various dimensions through which the church moves in the world: through particular lives of the faithful, among the nations, and as the whole people of God together. But there is a final dimension of movement that needs treatment: how the church—in its manifold witness to God's holiness—proceeds across time. Holiness is manifested in the church over time, a seed planted in a field that eventually yields its harvest.

Holiness is, thus, not only that which is immediately visible but also that which comes as a matter of patient retrospection and redress. As tides began to change for Christian dominance of the twentieth century, one of the unseen shoals that began to surface was what to make of the church's holiness, and particularly, what to make of sins past and present. That people were criticizing the church for its sins was nothing new, but with the decline of social power in Europe and secularization movements across the West, one of the unanticipated gifts that came was the opportunity for churches to make sense of past deeds that still had ongoing effects. The occasions for asking this question were legion, from the United Church's involvement in abuses against Canadian natives, to Catholic enslavement of Indians in Brazil, to clerical sexual abuse in nearly every denomination.[84] Corporate statements about past corporate sins of the church have been commented on copiously in other places, but for our purposes, three statements—from the Southern Baptist Convention of the United States, from the United Church of Canada, and from the International Theological Commission of the Catholic Church—will demonstrate how this pursuit of holiness, as a redress of the past, occurred.

Some articulations of the church's sins, most prevalent in traditions that emphasized the church as the mystical body of Christ, emphasized a distinction between the church, the chief sacrament of salvation, and the sins of those who made up the church.[85] But as Karl Rahner noted, if the church is composed of persons who make up the institution, there can be no other conclusion than to scandalously confess that "the Church is a sinful Church: it is part of her creed and no mere conclusion of experience."[86] Led by the Holy Spirit through time, the church shares in the eschatological holiness of God, even while it labors and sins, so that claims of "sinlessness" are

---

84. For documentation of the diversity of these apology movements, see Jeremy Bergen, *Ecclesial Repentance: The Churches Confront Their Sinful Pasts* (London: T&T Clark, 2011).
85. See Pius XII, *Mystici Corporis Christi*, which accomplishes this in part by distinguishing between juridical and organic elements of the church. See in particular sections 16–19.
86. Karl Rahner, "The Church of Sinners," *Cross Currents* 3 (1951): 64–74.

true in an eschatological sense but can obscure the way in which the church is always *in via* toward holiness. One of the ways in which the temporal dimensions of church holiness became most acute was in asking this simple question: Can the church repent? Breaking along the line of two different elements—of its faults of the past and of its official teachings—Christians of various tribes began to reckon with this overarching question across the twentieth century.

In Catholic discussions, the holiness of the church went hand in hand with the claim that the church was sinless, a claim that bears some unpacking. By making this claim to sinlessness, Catholicism did not (and does not) make the claim that Catholic Christians do not sin, but rather that if the church is the body of Christ, joined to the head that is Christ, then the church as a corporate body is given Christ's own holiness as its own essence. It remains holy by virtue of Christ, not by its own moral perfection.

The concept of "social sin"—established in the encyclicals of John Paul II[87]—complexifies this traditional notion of the impeccability of the church by asking whether there can be a history of the church in which the church is truthfully depicted as without sin. For as in the description that Rahner offers above, the distinction between the holiness conveyed by Christ to his body and the holiness that the church exhibits in its life can sometimes do too much work. As Rahner indicates, the past of a church is linked to the church's present not only in the church's witness to God's holiness but also in how the church inherits the benefits and liabilities of the church's past and in how the church's past might result in unacknowledged prejudices, biased teachings, and malformed theologies.

We will first return to the Southern Baptist Church to ask how this complex dynamic of holiness over time and penitence for the past occurs. Baptists, holding to a principle of congregational autonomy, struggle with the idea of transhistorical sin, for sins could take place in this manner only in particular places: in this congregation, but not across all congregations, such that logically there could be no such thing as a church that bears out sin or holiness over time. Here we will see that the Southern Baptist Church—in holding a very different doctrine of sin's presence in the church—found itself unable to confess both that the church sins (for only individuals truly sin) and that

---

87. See in particular Gregory Baum, "Structures of Sin," in *The Logic of Solidarity: Commentaries on Pope John Paul II's Encyclical on Social Concern*, ed. Gregory Baum and Robert Ellsberg (Maryknoll, NY: Orbis Books, 1989).

sins might be carried through time by institutions, practices, and doctrines (for there is only the local church).

The Southern Baptist Convention (SBC) was founded in 1845 in no small part over a disagreement over whether or not Christians who were slaveholders could have communion with non-slaveholding Christians.[88] In 1995, the Southern Baptists issued a resolution at the annual convention publicly acknowledging this historical link between racism, slavery, and the SBC's founding. In the document, a shift happens in discussing the effects of slavery on the denomination as a whole: in describing the denomination's lack of support for Civil Rights and support of slavery, the resolution pivots from *practices* of racism (which affected the material form of the denomination in the past) to racism as a kind of *idea* (a sin that a person could either hold or not hold).

The document begins by acknowledging practices of racism: "Many of our congregations have intentionally and/or unintentionally excluded African-Americans from worship, membership, and leadership; and . . . racism profoundly distorts our understanding of Christian morality, leading some Southern Baptists to believe that racial prejudice and discrimination are compatible with the Gospel."[89] But note how the emphasis shifts, in the present, to racism as an *idea*, using the language of "prejudice," "racism," and distorted understanding.[90] In other words, the document both acknowledges the historical sin of slavery by earlier Southern Baptists and maintains that, if the sin of racism has happened in the present, it has happened only through individual prejudices, with no structural implications for the present.

This duality has trouble holding, however. Even while trying to distinguish between *practices* of the past and *ideas* in the present, the resolution notes that the practices of the past are what make possible ideas in the present. In connecting practices of slavery to doctrinal malformations, we see that—though it tries to create distance between past and present—the resolution unwittingly acknowledges that ideas travel across churches and move over time, shaping the present even when the originating actions of slavery are

---

88. "Report on Slavery and Racism in the History of the Southern Baptist Theological Seminary," Southern Baptist Theological Seminary, December 12, 2018, https://cf.sbts.edu/sbts2023/uploads/2023/10/Racism-and-the-Legacy-of-Slavery-Report-v4.pdf.

89. "Resolution on Racial Reconciliation on the 150th Anniversary of the Southern Baptist Convention," Southern Baptist Convention, June 1, 1995, https://www.sbc.net/resource-library/resolutions/resolution-on-racial-reconciliation-on-the-150th-anniversary-of-the-southern-baptist-convention/.

90. "Resolution on Racial Reconciliation."

gone. Not only does the SBC statement fail to see how past actions affect present congregations, but it fails to recognize how *present* doctrines are the *result* of these past sins.

It is one thing for a distinct action or practice of one congregation to be disavowed as belonging only to that congregation—an entirely consistent position for Baptists to take!—but theologies (particularly within confessional entities like the Southern Baptist Convention) are arguably more transhistorical and transmutable than that. The holiness of the church over time is proposed in this way: past wrongs can be apologized for, but these wrongs are wrongs of *past actors* and do not affect what a people is over time.[91] Further, so long as people do not hold the ideas that went along with the practice, they are not culpable. For example, when the concept of systemic racism—deleterious effects on persons of particular races caused by ideas carried by systems—is raised, the resolution conspicuously limits the apology for it to that which is committed "in our lifetime"; it does not include those elements of present practice made possible by past sins.

This understanding of church holiness over time leaves aside the possibility that what has accrued over time might affect the holiness of the persons within these churches. For the SBC statement, only particular people can pursue holiness, and only within their own time. It is not that what is past is morally unimportant, but that what is past does not impeach or shape a particular person's (or church's) holiness.

For an example of church apology that connects the practices and theologies of past and present churches, and what it might mean for a church to pursue holiness over time, we turn to the 1986 statement by the United Church of Canada (UCC), "Apology to First Nations Peoples." In Canada, it was common practice for Aboriginal children to be sent to boarding schools to "reeducate" them in Western ways, colonizing their religious and cultural lives into the image of the British.[92] These schools were predominantly run by Catholics, but they were contributed to by other denominations, including

---

91. See also from "Resolution on Racial Reconciliation": "We commit ourselves to . . . racial reconciliation . . . to the end that our light would so shine before others, that they may see (our) good works and glorify (our) Father in heaven (Matthew 5:16); and Be it finally RESOLVED, That we pledge our commitment to the Great Commission task of making disciples of all people (Matthew 28:19), confessing that in the church God is calling together one people from every tribe and nation."

92. For a history of the actions of the British against the native populations in Canada, see Andrew Woolford, *This Benevolent Experiment: Indigenous Boarding Schools, Genocide, and Redress in Canada and the United States* (Lincoln: University of Nebraska Press, 2015).

the UCC. The UCC statement bears similarities to the SBC statement: both are dealing with questions of race-based exclusionary practices that are at the root of the church's history, and both are addressing populations whose identities and cultures were effaced by Christians.

But the UCC statement to First Nations goes beyond what is seen in the SBC statement, calling for internal work of repentance and change of practice, as well as taking ownership for past wrongs in ways that call for an alteration of both practice and present theology. Rather than distinguishing between past actions and present ideas, the UCC acknowledges that, in some cases, the ideas that made past sins possible continue in the present and need to be examined and dealt with. The UCC statement also goes further in acknowledging the spiritual damage that was caused by past actions and how those past actions shape the present reality that the UCC inhabits. The SBC statement, by contrast, makes no mention of the religiosity of slaves or of the ways in which Christianity was used as a tool for enslavement.[93]

The problem that is identified for holiness by the UCC statement differs in two ways from the SBC statement. First, in contrast to the SBC statement, the UCC's statement views the church's holiness as a matter not only of present practice but also of recognizing that the present is made possible—materially and spiritually—*by the work of* the past. Second, the UCC statement argues not just that the church failed in its vocation to be holy, but that the UCC forgot that the holiness they sought was shared in a differentiated way by the First Nations elders. The holiness of the church over time is thus a matter not of performance (as in the SBC statement) but of receiving that which only God can give, speculating that those beyond the church also share in this holiness in a measure. In acknowledging that holiness comes from God, the UCC statement opens the door to recognizing that their past failures have a long shadow, affecting not just practice but the theologies undergirding practice: in negating indigenous practice outright in the past, they have missed something of God's own holiness in both the past and the future.

For all their differences, these two statements are left with some intriguingly similar problems. Though going further than the SBC statement, the

---

93. From the UCC statement: "Long before my people journeyed to this land your people were here, and you received from your Elders an understanding of creation and of the Mystery that surrounds all that was deep, and rich, and to be treasured. We did not hear you when you shared your vision. In our zeal to tell you of the good news of Jesus Christ we were closed to the value of your spirituality." "Apology to First Nations Peoples (1986)," quoted in Bergen, *Ecclesial Repentance*, 59.

UCC statement (like the SBC statement) still leaves the relationship between past failure and present holiness unclarified, particularly with respect to what repair entails. For both the UCC and the SBC, then, repentance involves, primarily, apologizing for past failures in church holiness and for how the holiness of the church did not bear out in political holiness, even if they diverge on what the past's effect on the present is. The complex problem of how to account for the failures of the past remains a live one, even if we recognize that past failures affect the present.

As the century closed, the Catholic Church—building on the work of the International Theological Commission—issued a statement, *Memory and Reconciliation: The Church and the Faults of the Past*, that placed the issue of the past in the center of the question of church repentance. Building on the work of *Gaudium et Spes*, which repented for the science-faith opposition that had been rampant in Catholic circles in the early twentieth century, *Memory and Reconciliation* distinguished between the intrinsic holiness of the Church as the bride of Christ (Eph. 5:27) and the penitent members of the church, who are always in need of repentance. At this juncture, it is analogous in structure to the SBC statement, pointing to a pure originating source (Christ's own work, witnessed to through the Scriptures and history) that must be distinguished from the actions of the present members. To quote from *Memory and Reconciliation*: "One can only speak of social sin by way of analogy. It emerges from this that the imputability of a fault cannot properly be extended beyond the group of persons who had consented to it voluntarily, by means of acts or omissions, or through negligence."[94]

Though the Catholic document has a decidedly different vision of transhistorical peoplehood than the Baptists or the UCC—that the past and present are caught up together as one body—a distinction between past and present exists in *Memory and Reconciliation* just as it does in the statements of those other communions. The refutation of "social sin" as a concept limits any culpability of the present for the past, for reconciliation is described in the document as done by an active participant for acts that would impugn their worship.[95] This is not to say, however, that past actions do not linger in the present; the baptized, being made aware

94. International Theological Commission, *Memory and Reconciliation: The Church and the Faults of the Past*, December 1999 (Vatican City: Holy See, 1999), http://www.vatican.va/roman_curia/congregations/cfaith/cti_documents/rc_con_cfaith_doc_20000307_memory-reconc-itc_en.html.
95. International Theological Commission, *Memory and Reconciliation*, 2.2.

of the past, are called to let the "holiness in the Church . . . correspond to the holiness of the Church."[96]

While one generation is not another, the document does note that there is a way in which the past and present are bound together not simply genealogically but theologically:

> The bond between past and present is not motivated only by the current interest and by the common belonging of every human being to history and its expressive meditations, but is based also on the unifying action of the Spirit of God and on the permanent identity of the constitutive principle of the communion of the faithful, which is revelation. . . . Communion in the one Holy Spirit also establishes a communion of "saints" in a diachronic sense, by virtue of which the baptized of today feel connected to the baptized of yesterday and—*as they benefit from their merits and are nourished by their witness of holiness*—so likewise they feel the obligation to assume any current burden from their faults, after having discerned these by attentive historical and theological study.[97]

For all of their theological distinctions, then, Baptist, UCC, and Catholic statements regarding past wrongs end in remarkably similar places. The past remains a wound that informs the present, but without providing clarity on what to do in the present. This much is clear: the past remains as a wound of one's founding (the SBC), within one's present theology (the UCC), or within the family of the baptized that one cannot disavow (the RCC). What remains less clear is how to move forward penitently in a way that offers the past up to God while yet being thankful to God that the past made the present possible.

To say that the present church remains sinless by virtue of the work of Christ is a claim that could be made of all churches, irrespective of other ecclesiological commitments. But while such a claim helps a present church (whether Baptist, UCC, or Catholic) distance itself from guilt for the wrongs committed by its forebears, it does not keep that church from being *responsible* for those wrongs. The past participation of its churches in the forcible reeducation of First Nations children helped to establish the UCC as the thoroughly Canadian church it is today.

The second, and more difficult, dimension to church holiness raised by the past is that raised by the UCC statement but rejected by the Catholic and

---

96. International Theological Commission, *Memory and Reconciliation*, 3.2.
97. International Theological Commission, *Memory and Reconciliation*, 4.2 (emphasis added).

Baptist statements: that the animating doctrines that allowed for past sins are *themselves* part of what inhibits the present practice of holiness. As wave after wave of accusations began to break in the final years of the twentieth century, with thousands of Catholic clergy accused of sexual misconduct, doctrines of celibacy, of hierarchical order, and of intrinsic evil came under scrutiny as intrinsically bound up with the abuses.[98] My intent here is not to name a specific site of doctrinal responsibility so much as to name that doctrines—communicated over time—must be part of what is held up to scrutiny. For if the holiness of the present church is to be performed in a manner in keeping with its founding, then doctrinal contributions to moral failure inevitably come into view.

The mark of holiness, in this way, is a haunting mark, for it lingers over the present both as a reminder of the past and as a sign of hope that even in past failure, God sustains the church, the body of Christ. But these comparative statements also push us to consider the mark of holiness as the occasion for ongoing repair with our neighbors. For if the church is that body of Christ which is embedded in time, it will never be free of the wounds of time, for better or worse; no amount of doctrinal scrutiny might make the church pure, for the wounds of the past are part of what the Spirit has worked through to make the present church what it is. Repair is part of that endless work of time, with the work of internal interrogation being part of what is appropriate to being a living sacrifice.

Conclusion

Tracing the mark of holiness in the churches is a fraught enterprise, for multiple reasons. Our present holiness establishes what the future church will see as faithful, as well as obscure its possibilities for holiness. God's holiness is for the whole church to enjoy, and through the church, it is God's gift to the world, but taking up holiness on these terms involves instability: holiness creates its own new connections that outstrip established ones. Attending to the corporate shape of holiness has meant that, at times, churches have been uncertain as to how to attend to the particular bodies in them. And yet, over time, churches find ways to repent of their failings and expand how the

---

98. For one of the earliest works on the still-unfolding abuse scandal, see Frank Bruni, *A Gospel of Shame: Children, Sexual Abuse, and the Catholic Church* (New York: HarperCollins, 2002).

holiness of God is shared with their neighbors. Such is the lifeblood of any church, that by attending to the Spirit's gift of God's holiness, the church remains penitent and brave, seeking renewal and faithfulness.

Our engagement with various church traditions draws out surprising overlaps, with respect to both their appropriation of this gift of holiness and their all-too-common failures of holiness. It is not realistic to hope that we will not fail again, but we may hope to fail in new ways, attentive to wisdom and prompted by courage. The struggle of how to—as a people—live into the holiness of God stays with our own century, but only because what we see in the twentieth century is part of an ongoing story of holiness and its struggles. Such is what we learn from the past, that we might rest in God's manifold gifts to God's body and not fear, because of past failures, to live into the future. For we will sin, yet God remains faithful.

3

In All Times and All Places

The Church as Catholic

The questions of the previous chapters have been undergirded by a particular claim made in the introduction of this book: the Holy Spirit gives life to the church, and does so in the particularities of the body of Christ as it appears in the world. These are not competitive features. Divine agency is not the same as human agency, and so God's sustaining work of the Spirit is not the same as human faithfulness. Unity, in other words, is that which is true of the body of Christ because it is true of God and made possible in us by God; the holiness that the church has is first a gift of God before it is a performance of the church.

Our present chapter—on catholicity—takes us deeper into that mystery. Catholicity, roughly, refers to the universality of the faith. And catholicity, like the previous marks, is both a gift of God and an invitation to action. By the Spirit, we belong to the same universal calling to salvation, to receiving the mystery of God in its fullness. And churches work out this calling in their particular times and places, working out the fullness of what Christians confess to be true of God and God's works, by attending to the Spirit and to how God has guided the body of Christ over time. Catholicity is a complex mark in this way. It ties together that which is universal (God's work in Christ by the Spirit) and the church's time-bound particularity—that is, the church's effort to be faithful in the specifics of its life to that which is universally given.

The church's catholicity, as we will see, involves questions of what it means to confess the full range of Christian belief, not shrinking it down or cutting off parts of it. But it also involves how that faith, "once for all entrusted to the saints" (Jude 3), is confessed in ways that draw the particular lives and fullness of the churches confessing that faith to God. Catholic confession draws the confessors into the fullness of the Spirit's work in time and space.

Thus, catholicity has multiple—and frequently competing—dimensions, which will frame this chapter. When we say that catholicity means universality, are we speaking of a faith that is believed in its expansiveness of confession, even if it doesn't achieve geographic universality? When we say that the church is catholic, does this also mean something with respect to the fullness of the *lived* faith? And what do we do with something that builds out the full confession and texture of what a church is, even if some of those particularities are not shared by all churches?

Catholicity: Unity by Another Name?

By way of a brief definition of catholicity, consider this statement of Saint Vincent of Lérins:

> But the Church of Christ, the careful and watchful guardian of the doctrines deposited in her charge, never changes anything in them, never diminishes, never adds, does not cut off what is necessary, does not add what is superfluous, does not lose her own, does not appropriate what is another's, but while dealing faithfully and judiciously with ancient doctrine, keeps this one object carefully in view, if there be anything which antiquity has left shapeless and rudimentary, to fashion and polish it, if anything already reduced to shape and developed, to consolidate and strengthen it, if any already ratified and defined to keep and guard it.[1]

This definition, better than his more well-known formula of "that which has been believed everywhere, always, in all places," captures the complexity of catholicity. Here Vincent speaks as if Christian confession has a future and

---

1. From Saint Vincent of Lérins, "Commonitorium," in vol. 11 of *The Nicene and Post-Nicene Fathers*, Series 2, ed. Philip Schaff (1886–89; repr., Peabody, MA: Hendrickson, 1994), 148–49.

places, areas or aspects of confession, that are left inchoate by the earliest Christians and so fall to later generations to unpack while remaining faithful to the original deposit of the faith.

In this way, catholicity, existing as a property of the church, is fundamentally a confession about whose church the church is: a confession that catholicity, in referring to the fullness of God's work, first refers to the work of Christ, but that this work of God immediately catches up creation in it. As Saint Paul reminds us, "in [Christ] all things hold together" (Col. 1:17), or as John puts it, "Through him all things were made; without him nothing was made that has been made" (John 1:3 NIV).

Because catholicity is associated with, and often seen as derivative of, another mark of the church, sorting out—and allowing for—the pluriform dimensions of catholicity to appear can be a challenge. Mediating the different accounts of catholicity can be an exercise in interlocutors talking past one another. Seeing the full range of this mark as I have laid it out thus far is partly a problem of semantics. When most students are taught church history, the history of the church is divided into three main branches: Roman Catholic, Orthodox, and Protestant. While this organization is somewhat helpful as a pedagogical tool, catholicity becomes immediately associated with one, but not all, divisions of the Christian church.[2] Because the church exists in a divided state, then, catholicity is colloquially treated as belonging to one branch of the divided church, as existing within a unified Roman Catholic church.

This means, in turn, that catholicity becomes annexed to another mark—namely, unity. To quote from Gustav Aulén's midcentury reflections on the topic: "Perhaps it could be said that the meaning of catholicity does not appear as immediately as that of unity, holiness, and apostolicity. . . . But two fundamental aspects inevitably come to the fore: *universality* and *continuity*. The two are closely related and cannot be separated. The church could not be the universal church if it did not through the ages stand in unbroken relationship with the original church which had its origin in Christ, the church of Easter and Pentecost."[3]

The comments of Aulén, a Lutheran bishop, are representative of many others. *Catholicity* does not refer simply to what is confessed; it refers to what is

---

2. This is further complicated by an acknowledgment of the Old Catholic Church, a communion of formerly Roman Catholic churches based in Utrecht. For an introduction, see Jan Visser, "The Old Catholic Churches of the Union of Utrecht," *International Journal for the Study of the Christian Church* 3 (2003): 68–84.

3. Gustav Aulén, *Reformation and Catholicity* (Westport, CT: Greenwood, 1961), 182–83.

confessed *in continuity with all churches*. A church can claim catholicity only if (1) it is unified and (2) it can reach back to the apostles. Consider also the account from the Catholic theologian Avery Cardinal Dulles: "Catholicity always implies, in principle, adherence to the fullness of God's gift in Christ. Christianity is inclusive not by reason of latitudinarian permissiveness or syncretistic promiscuity, but because it has received from God a message and a gift for people of every time and place, so that all can find in it the fulfillment of their highest selves."[4]

Dulles, like Aulén, holds that catholicity does not have to do with how many believe the gospel message or where they are believing it, but rather with the original content of that message and whether one's present confession coheres with that articulation. For Dulles, a church is catholic because it is faithful to the original deposit. Thus, catholicity does not depend on the church being universal in the sense of incorporating into it all that is on offer in the world. Because the church's "wholeness" depends on this original gift, it would seem that catholicity is simply rehearsing the oldest confessions of the church, adhering to the earliest and original faith confessions. Such a claim privileges not simply God's original work in Christ but the church's articulation of that work from the patristic era, meaning that the church's catholicity depends on its adherence to earlier doctrine.

But the end of Dulles's statement opens a dimension of catholicity that is very different than merely rehearsing the doctrine of an earlier era: catholicity is a gift for "people of every time and place" for "the fulfillment of their highest selves." Such a claim is not about the message itself but about catholicity involving *implementation* and *reception*, ubiquity and intensity. Here Dulles acknowledges that our Christian faithfulness, dependent on Christ's work, takes place in different times and places than the original. And so, the "fullness of God's gift in Christ," as Dulles notes, does depend on its geographical expansiveness and operates against the backdrop of cultural plurality. This dual tension is expressed elsewhere and will shape the remainder of this chapter, as it shaped twentieth-century discussions.

Consider an Anglican example that makes this tension more explicit: a report presented at the 1947 Lambeth Conference of the Anglican Communion. Before discussing the concept of what counts as "wholeness," the report opens with a lengthy discussion of "the primitive unity" of the church.[5] Thus, from

---

4. Avery Dulles, *The Catholicity of the Church* (Oxford: Clarendon, 1985), 9.
5. E. S. Abbot et al., *Catholicity: A Study in the Conflict of Christian Traditions in the West* (London: Dacre, 1947), 11.

Lambeth's perspective, discussions of the church's unity and of its catholicity, while distinct, cannot be ultimately separated. As the document argues, "The 'wholeness' of the visible Church manifests itself in its outward order," so that when churches engage in divided worship, they evince disagreement over catholicity.[6]

This joint consideration of unity and catholicity assumes that catholicity is most visible in the teaching and practice of the earliest Christians, granting priority to the early church in considerations of what counts as catholic. But this seems to conflate the issues significantly. A 1950 Anglican report, taking issue with the earlier 1947 report, questions just this elision of catholicity with "primitive unity." The later, 1950, report argues that, in the Reformation, the Reformers were not subtracting from the faith but filling out contours of the faith that had been minimized or neglected in previous eras.[7] The issue was not whether Protestants had the fullness of faith as given by God but what kind of unity this faith produced.[8]

For the later report, in other words, catholicity takes time. The work of Christ by the Spirit is to draw in all that has been given to the Church. And it is possible (as we saw in the previous chapter) that some things have not been given yet, or that they were misunderstood when they were given in the past. One need not hold a progressivist vision of history to believe, with the author of Hebrews, that there were things not beheld in the past so that they might be perfected together with the saints in the future (Heb. 11:40).

Catholicity: Universality without Immediate Unity

This argument among midcentury Anglicans opens up important areas for thinking about the church's catholicity, areas that appear as afterthoughts or are foreclosed by Dulles and Aulén. First, these Anglican statements broach the

---

6. Abbot et al., *Catholicity*, 13. The work of the Holy Spirit, while formative in the present, is for this document retrospective, referring the people back to the work of the apostles (15). Thus catholicity, while temporally performed, is not temporally unfolding or expanding but is instead a conservationist work. The final chapter, "The Anglican Communion," holds out hope for synthesis of diverse theological opinions, but given that catholicity resides in the past work of the Spirit, and not in a present work of the Spirit, it appears that catholicity is ultimately a return to a past unity, not a presently enacted fullness.

7. R. Newton Flew and Rupert E. Davies, eds., *The Catholicity of Protestantism: Being a Report Presented to His Grace the Archbishop of Canterbury by a Group of Free Churchmen* (London: Lutterworth, 1952), 28.

8. Flew and Davies, *Catholicity of Protestantism*, 30.

question of the relationship between historical change and fullness of faith: Does catholicity require restricting articulations of the faith to a certain era? The earlier, 1947, report assumes that catholicity—a gift of God—is something that, while contextualized or unfolded, does not substantively change over time, for if it did, it would divide the church.

Earlier Protestants, working out what catholicity consisted of, opened the possibility that catholicity entailed not only unity but *ubiquity*, that which is believed universally, so that unity could not foreclose catholicity's expansion into new times and places. Martin Luther, for example, chose to substitute the term "Christian" for "Catholic" to indicate the ways in which the Roman tradition's claim to catholicity was, ironically, sectarian by excluding other Christian performances.[9] In Calvin's Geneva, children were taught that catholicity referred to a normativity of being Christian reflected in all churches, but also that it "is extended throughout the world."[10] These dimensions of catholicity—both its historical connection and its geographical breadth—would resurface more distinctly in the twentieth century, not just to encompass the future but to bring the fullness of the faith together with the expansiveness of creation.

Such an inclusion of geographic ubiquity is more than tokenism and different from subjecting the majority to a tyranny of the minority. It is, instead, asking *how* the historic claims of the faith find new articulation and expansion over time, not *whether* they do. What edges, as the faith is lived out across centuries, become blunted? And how might these lost edges resurface? And does catholicity mean having to account for that which was not seen by the first generations of Christians, but not incompatible with them?

If the first aspect of catholicity opened by this intra-Anglican debate concerns whether or not time and place affect what is meant by "fullness of the faith," the second question that quickly emerges is this: Can a church be "catholic" by exhibiting the fullness of faith in its own context, even if such performance *temporally* divides it from other Christians? If catholicity

---

9. David Yeago helpfully draws out Luther's struggle with catholicity, how he insisted that it was a quality that must diverge from particular manifestations of the faith while he simultaneously affirmed the God who is spoken of by the Roman Catholic Church. This struggle, Yeago notes, does not disavow church, but—in the wake of doctrinal divergence—must yield a performance that builds out from Roman Catholicism. See David Yeago, "The Catholic Luther," in *The Catholicity of the Reformation*, ed. Carl E. Braaten and Robert W. Jenson (Grand Rapids: Eerdmans, 1996), 13–34.

10. John T. McNeill, *Unitive Protestantism: The Ecumenical Spirit and Its Persistent Expression* (Louisville: John Knox, 1964), 69.

belongs as tightly together with unity as Dulles and Aulén suppose, one cannot claim fullness of the faith apart from being united *in office* with other churches. Others (including the 1952 Anglican rebuttal) will argue that these terms need to be separately considered, that a movement toward the fullness of the faith will inevitably involve challenges to historical structures, such that the pursuit of fullness cannot be linked to the historical accident of structural unification.

This argument over the relationship between the catholicity of the church and the unity of the church broadly separates Catholic and many Protestant conceptions of catholicity, but it also is a question raised by the rise of global Christianity. For much of Christian tradition that depicts the fullness of what Christians confess—Catholic, Protestant, and Orthodox—depends on certain material, cultural, or metaphysical assumptions not shared by all corners of the church, or all corners of the world. In the early twentieth century, for example, the theological metaphysics articulated by Thomas Aquinas were said by Pius X to be inseparable from the faith itself, a judgment rearticulated in Vatican II.[11] If the Christian faith proceeds into a culture that is not wedded to the assumptions of Thomas Aquinas,[12] catholicity runs headlong into the question of historical continuity: Does having the fullness of faith mean remaking every context according to the metaphysical assumptions of a different era? Or can the fullness of the faith be confessed in a way that is fitting to the world it is confessed in? Must one choose between these?

Put differently, catholicity draws in concerns for *contextualization*. Contextuality can be used cheaply, valued as a way to *not* have to embrace the substance of faith from the past, but this is not what is meant here. The concern for contextuality, as the material conditions in which Christians seek to confess the fullness of the Christian faith, is consistent with what Dulles has articulated. Likewise, taking up context as a feature of catholicity exposes at times the ways in which Christians have seen discussions over what counts as a full confession of the faith as derivative of concern for unity with the past,

---

11. Pius X, *Doctoris Angelici* (June 29, 1914); and Paul VI, *Optatam Totius* (Vatican City: Holy See, 1965), 15, https://www.vatican.va/archive/hist_councils/ii_vatican_council/documents/vat-ii_decree_19651028_optatam-totius_en.html.

12. The articulations of Thomas Aquinas's work in the twentieth century are variegated and beyond the scope of this book. See Fergus Kerr, *After Aquinas: Versions of Thomism* (Malden, MA: Wiley-Blackwell, 2002); Mark D. Jordan, *Rewritten Theology: Aquinas after His Readers* (Madlen, MA: Wiley-Blackwell, 2008), for introductions to these varieties.

instead of allowing the act of confession to be a provocation to the kind of unity made possible by a metaphysically unified culture.

This being said, this warning from Aulén seems apt: "Universality and continuity are inseparably connected. Without this union with continuity, boundary-transgressing universality would run the risk of becoming an undefined spiritualism. The continuity which characterizes the church of Christ ... derived primarily from the fact that Christ and his Spirit unchangeably use the same means for the realization of salvation in the church, namely, the means of grace, the Word and the sacraments."[13]

Aulén's concern that "undefined spiritualism" would reign absent a prior concern for continuity asks us to hold concern for how a particular people confess the fullness of the faith loosely, our concern that what is considered sacrosanct by culture may in fact be that which Christian faith needs to contest. At the same time, his formula makes little room for the Anglican concerns that, for example, catholicity expands, and often into new places that knew not Aquinas. We will try to hold these two tracks together.

Catholicity and Context: A Limit Case

Catholicity, for it to be a description of a church's faith and practice in all times and places within creation, depends on God's first being present to creation. Framed this way, the question of catholicity—how the triune God is known and worshiped fully—stands behind some of the biggest debates in twentieth-century theology, such as the debates over the relationship between nature and grace.[14] The technical arguments surrounding the relationship between nature and grace would be most contested ecclesiologically as they concerned this question of what it means to faithfully name *context* as intrinsic to faithful practice. For if faithful catholicity involves attention to time and place, a question appears: Are there limits to what counts as faithful?

In this light, let us consider the example of twentieth-century Germany. The struggle of how to name the fullness of God's presence can be seen in the rise of the German National Church during the era of the Third Reich in Germany. In 1933, the introduction of the "Aryan paragraph" was, at one

---

13. Aulén, *Reformation and Catholicity*, 183.
14. For a contemporary overview of the debates and their aftermath, see Thomas Joseph White, OP, ed., *The Analogy of Being: Invention of the Antichrist or the Wisdom of God?* (Grand Rapids: Eerdmans, 2010).

level, a procedural intrusion by the state upon the church's ability to organize itself, banning anyone of non-Aryan descent from church leadership. But theologically, the Aryan paragraph connected Christ to the world by equating Christ's work with the historical rise of the Nazis, seeing in the rise of the Nazi party the renewing work of God in Germany.[15]

The rise of the Reich church was, thus, a perverse form of catholicity in that it proposed to deepen the relation between Christ's work, the church, and the world, but at the expense of Christ's covenant people, the Jews. It is, in other words, allowing context to *undermine* scripturally nonnegotiable features of what the faith is, losing a baseline of catholic confession: that Jesus is Jewish and that the Jews are God's covenant people. Defenders of the paragraph, such as Emanuel Hirsch, well-known Lutheran pastor and dean of the theology faculty at the University of Göttingen, linked together Christ's work in the German nation in a way that demonstrates just this transgression: "The question regarding those among us who are not German Christians by blood is just a part of a far deeper and more urgent question. It follows from the obligation of Protestant Christianity to be a church of the people that in a German Protestant church Germanness and Christianity must encounter each other in a deep intimacy that will determine the historical shape of both."[16]

For Hirsch, if the church is to be named catholic—confessed in all times and places—the church must risk being shaped by its history and culture. For Hirsch and defenders of the German National Church, confessing Christ's fullness involves linking historical developments together with church confessions as two parts of the same work of Christ. But here the German martyr Dietrich Bonhoeffer rises in protest. For Bonhoeffer's defense of the Jews contests the German National Church on precisely this point: that a contextual work of Christ must be a catholic work as well—that is, a work that pertains to all persons. By working to sustain a Lutheran church that could be fully German and fully for all those in Germany, Bonhoeffer offered a witness that displayed the costliness and difficulty of this truth.[17]

15. For the text of the paragraph and the initial responses by German theological faculties, see Mary M. Solberg, ed., *A Church Undone: Documents from the German Christian Faith Movement* (Minneapolis: Fortress, 2015), 53–81.

16. Solberg, *Church Undone*, 111.

17. For a detailed account of Bonhoeffer's advocacy for the Jews, see Ruth Zerner, "Dietrich Bonhoeffer and the Jews: Thoughts and Actions, 1933–1945," *Jewish Social Studies* 37 (1975): 235–50; and Zerner, "Church, State and the Jewish Question," in *The Cambridge Companion to Dietrich Bonhoeffer*, ed. John de Gruchy (Cambridge: Cambridge University Press, 1999). For

The struggle for the soul of the German church opens wide the question of contextualization, and particularly the importance of how we name how contextualization is working. For though most questions of theological contextualization begin from a desire for political and theological *fidelity*, whereas the Nazi question began from a desire for *restriction*, the animating question of how to name God's fullness in history is the same. Beginning most stridently with the New Delhi Assembly of 1961, the World Council of Churches discussions began to emphasize contextuality as significant features of their discussions, as with the demise of colonialism, churches outside Europe could no longer be assumed to simply reflect Western Christian theology and practice.[18]

The experience of 1930s Germany indicates that (at the risk of a vast understatement) incorporating context into our conceptions of catholicity is easier said than done. For not all Christians join in using context in this way. John Meyendorff, in summarizing the Orthodox position on catholicity, notes that alteration of the original deposit constitutes a divergence from catholicity.[19] This is not to say that there is no concern for geographical expansions of the church, but these expansions occur as an *outworking* of catholicity, not as an *intrinsic* quality in the way that the Protestant Reformers framed the question.[20]

As we move forward, the case of the Nazis serves as an instructive point on catholicity's limits. God's work in creation is indeed expansive and does account for new historical moments and new twists in human lives. But when

---

the question of whether Bonhoeffer was anti-Judaic without being anti-Semitic, see Timothy Stanley, "Bonhoeffer's Anti-Judaism," *Political Theology* 17 (2016): 297–305.

18. These conversations happened throughout the assemblies of the WCC, predating the first assembly meeting in 1948. But it would not be until the New Delhi meeting—the first of the WCC assemblies taking place outside of Europe (after Amsterdam [1948] and Evanston, IL [1954]) that considerations of non-Western contexts came to the forefront.

19. John Meyendorff, *Catholicity and the Church* (Crestwood, NY: St. Vladimir's Seminary Press, 1983), 11.

20. This is not to say that Orthodox churches rejected the notion of context, but that their sensibilities tended to work in the opposite direction: transforming the local setting into an Orthodox one. See Nektarios Hatzimichalis, *Orthodox Ecumenism and External Mission: Towards a Theology of the Catholicity of the External Mission* (Athens: Zeno Booksellers, 1974), 55. Throughout the work, Hatzimichalis uses "ecumenicity" as the backdrop for—and at times, as interchangeable with—"catholicity." A similar sentiment is found in Vatican II's decree on missionary activity: "Missionary activity wells up from the Chruch's inner nature and spreads abroad her saving Faith. It perfects her Catholic unity by this expansion." Paul VI, *Ad Gentes* (Vatican City: Holy See, 1965), 6, https://www.vatican.va/archive/hist_councils/ii_vatican_council/documents/vat-ii_decree_19651207_ad-gentes_en.html. For further work on Orthodoxy, mission, and context, see Petros Vassiliadis, *Eucharist and Witness: Orthodox Perspectives on the Unity and Mission of the Church* (Geneva: WCC Publications, 1998).

our account of the Christian faith becomes that which (1) undermines basic scriptural presumptions concerning God's universal work or (2) seeks to emphasize context at the expense of the universal nature of God's gospel, claims for catholicity have gone sour. This important caveat—as we see with the Orthodox position summed up by Meyendorff—does not resolve all issues, but it gives us ways to have a good disagreement.

Catholicity without History: Twentieth-Century Renewal and Restoration

Thus far, we have seen how discussions in the twentieth century surrounding catholicity tied together—in one way or another—the need for the historic faith to be confessed in our time and place. For some approaches, such confession meant emphasizing the faith as expressed in the idioms and material forms of the earliest Christians, and for some, it meant emphasizing how Christ mediates God's presence in our own time, in ways dissimilar from the first centuries. But great divergence happened as to what weight to give to context. More modest affirmations of the weight of context, such as those expressed by the mid-century Anglicans, should not be equated with extreme affirmations of context such as those of the Nazis. And yet, the example of the Nazis raises the question in this way: In what way does *context* matter for confessing the fullness of the faith?

If one of the major questions that emerge for catholicity is how God's fullness has been present in contextual ways in history, various restoration and renewal movements of the twentieth century offered an alternative approach: that being fully the people of God meant abandoning contextualization as a primary concern. What was needed was to return to the practice of the earliest church, to move beyond questions of contextualization and embrace early church practice as most indicative of what it means to fully receive Christ's presence and embody the fullness of the Christian faith.

As discussed previously, the Pentecostals who participated in the Azusa Street revivals emphasized a unity of the Spirit that moved behind the historically nuanced—and predicated—divisions of Christian history.[21] In doing so, these Christians named catholicity as an indwelling of the Holy Spirit that involves a return to the practices of the New Testament. William Seymour,

---

21. See chapter 2, above, for criticisms of this appeal to invisible unity.

cofounder of the original Pentecostal movement, in describing the work of the Holy Spirit, puts it this way: "Many people today are sanctified, cleansed from all sin and perfectly consecrated to God, but they have never obeyed the Lord according to Acts 1:4–8 and Luke 24:39, for their real personal Pentecost, the endowment of power for service and work and for sealing unto the day of redemption."[22] Put differently, the Pentecostal emphasis on the originalism of speaking in tongues was not simply about restoring the ways of the New Testament, but about the fullness of the presence of God, and with that, a fullness of Christian practice and confession that *transcends* time or context. Whether a form of Christianity had been carried forth in this way over time, or whether it had contextual resonance, were relatively less important in light of the work of the Spirit, who alone brought fullness of the Christian life.

The Restorationist Movement, born in the nineteenth century, likewise exhibited this spirit in the twentieth century. This Christian unity movement, through the efforts of Barton W. Stone and Alexander Campbell, drew from former Baptists, Presbyterians, Methodists, and others, preferring the name "Christian" to any other designation. Rather than moving through the divisions of churches to arrive at this place, though, the movement arrived there by seeking to restore original church practice as indicated by Scripture.[23] The movement toward unity through elimination of certain practices and doctrines brought with it its own form of catholicity: the fullness of the faith realized by returning to a reconstructed apostolic form of church life.[24] That the Restorationist Movement did this by division from other Christian groups is not in and of itself a reason to discount it; annexing catholicity to unity is a problem for reasons already laid out. But it is worth asking how this kind of catholicity might look if it once again sought to make use of the history prior to this movement's arrival in the world.

When looked at from this vantage point—that historical development is not a dominant concern for a church desiring to be catholic in its confession—what the Pentecostals and Restorationists offer is not entirely dissimilar from

---

22. William J. Seymour, "Receive Ye the Holy Ghost," in *World Christianity in the Twentieth Century*, ed. Noel Davies and Martin Conway (London: SCM, 2008), 79.

23. For the hermeneutics of the Stone-Campbell movement, see Gary Holloway and Douglas A. Foster, *Renewing God's People: A Concise History of Churches of Christ* (Abilene, TX: Abilene Christian University Press, 2006), 73–81.

24. The famous prohibition on musical instruments by many Churches of Christ stems from this commitment to the fullness of the Christian faith, omitting that which cannot be found to have clear scriptural precedent.

Orthodox articulations of the relation between the fullness of Christ and Christ's presence in history, in that both traditions emphasize the unity of participation in Christ, which looks first to the original deposit of Christ and not first to the historical moment in which a particular church appears. In seeking to mirror the original Christian deposit, groups like the Pentecostals and Restorationists are not lacking in concerns for catholicity; rather, they open up more fully the question as to whether or not catholicity requires historical mediation or just recovery of the original.

Catholicity: Expansion and Confession of the People

In the previous sections, we have seen a developing cluster of concerns: catholicity is about confessing the fullness of the content of the Christian faith, doing so in ways that do justice to the original deposit of the faith, but bearing that out in a particular context. For some, this involves returning to the original deposit, restoring what has been obscured by history. But what of the possibility of catholicity expanding to incorporate that which was never lost—because it was never incorporated to begin with?

In theory, this is what both Protestant and Catholic accounts of catholicity suppose. But it is unclear as to whether this expansion—on both Protestant and Catholic grounds—is about more than *philosophical and political* developments. In what follows, we will see that catholicity became additionally about what we might call "lived religion." For if the fullness of doctrine is confessed in particular times and places, then arguably, the content of the faith must bear itself out not just in persons generally but among people particularly.

To explore this, let us consider the example of Black Catholics in the twentieth century.[25] First organized in 1917 by Thomas Wyatt Turner, American Black Catholic laity began to meet and advocate for a fuller inclusion of Black Catholics into the structures of the Church. Other denominations globally had been created to provide Christians of color a space to freely practice, but Catholics sought neither to divide the church nor to leave it for one of these

---

25. Black Americans belonged to nearly every denomination, with few exceptions. Our focus here on the experience of Black Catholics is for the sake of sharpening the exploration of catholicity and time. For an overview that focuses on distinctly Black denominations, see Anne H. Pinn and Anthony B. Pinn, *Fortress Introduction to Black Church History* (Minneapolis: Fortress, 2002).

denominations.[26] By the end of the twentieth century, there would be more Catholics of color in the Western hemisphere than White Catholics. And yet, the Catholic hierarchy was slow to respond to issues of racism that hounded Black Catholics throughout the century.[27]

As has been noted, following the Second Vatican Council, global, non-White Catholics began to receive far more attention than before, which came together with the movement to recognize more saints of color. As Katie Walker Grimes has argued, however, the canonization of saints such as Martin de Porres has served not to trouble the legacy of racism but to codify it into Catholic hagiography; canonizing saints such as Porres as exemplars of antiracism has, Grimes contends, not only ignored their historical record but spiritualized racism so as to quiet Black Catholic concerns.[28]

The challenge of catholicity present in the story of Black Catholics is whether catholicity can be understood as an unfolding of the fullness of Christ's presence in a straightforward manner, in which *future* iterations of faithfulness can be narrated in continuity with the *past*, or if catholicity requires openness to expansions that trouble the way in which catholicity has been understood. The example of Black Catholics surfaces unspoken assumptions both about what it means to confess the fullness of the faith in context and also about whether catholicity can be conceived of apart from attention to particulars of race.[29] Race has appeared already as a factor in our consideration of the mark of the church's oneness, but it appears again here to question whether the contexts that racial identity produces are those contexts that open up new dimensions in what a universal Christian confession looks like.

One way forward, as the previous examples of the Restorationists and the Pentecostals indicated, is to negate questions of historical precedent: perhaps problematic articulations of the faith after Scripture need not be taken into

---

26. M. Shawn Copeland, ed., *Uncommon Faithfulness: The Black Catholic Experience* (Maryknoll, NY: Orbis Books, 2009), 17. The legacy of Black Catholics in the United States is traced back to the beginnings of slaves in the United States, including the formation of a religious order, the Sisters of the Holy Family (57). For a comprehensive overview of African American Catholics, see Matthew J. Cressler, *Authentically Black and Truly Catholic: The Rise of Black Catholicism in the Great Migration* (New York: NYU Press, 2017).

27. The decisive statement on racism was issued in 1979: "Brothers and Sisters to Us," United States Conference of Catholic Bishops, 1979, http://www.usccb.org/issues-and-action/cultural-diversity/african-american/brothers-and-sisters-to-us.cfm.

28. Katie Walker Grimes, *Fugitive Saints: Catholicism and the Politics of Slavery* (Minneapolis: Fortress, 2017).

29. See the ethnographic work of Danny Duncan Collum, *Black and Catholic in the Jim Crow South: The Stuff That Makes Community* (Mahwah, NJ: Paulist Press, 2006).

account. But another way, seen above, is that we recognize that catholicity means incorporating modes of practice that are possible only *now* that embracing the fullness of faith requires us to ask questions of what a new confession of the old faith might look like.

It is here that the example of Black Catholics finds overlap with a very different partner: twentieth-century evangelicalism.[30] Consider here the formulation of Harold John Ockenga, cofounder of American evangelical institutions such as Fuller Theological Seminary, the National Association and Evangelicals, Gordon-Conwell Theological Seminary, and *Christianity Today*, who described the marks of the church in this way: "[The church's] purity must be derived from its faithfulness to the Word and its practice of the Sacraments. Its universality must include all believers. Its apostolicity must be derived from *direct* connection with the Holy Spirit called and anointed by the apostles. Its unity must be by relation to and submission to the Lord Jesus Christ."[31]

The universality, or catholicity, of the church does not require repetition of the early church, Ockenga argues. Catholicity is given by the Holy Spirit primarily in the form of incorporating all believers and secondarily in the content of the apostolic preaching. Accordingly, the first measure of catholicity is experience with God in the present, not whether that experience strictly conforms to received traditions of the church apart from Scripture.

In the teaching and work of Ockenga's better-known associate, Billy Graham, this presupposition shaped the crusade movement. For in the preaching crusades, what mattered most was the experience of conversion, the universal experience of the Holy Spirit, not the ecclesial articulation of it. Drawing from a wide range of churches, ethnicities, and backgrounds, Graham's crusades deemphasized the particularist context and traditions of, for example, the AME or Southern Baptist churches that would join together during a local crusade, and the crusades emphasized the Spirit-enabled conversion that rose above denominational divides and controversies.[32] Like the example of Black Catholics, we find here a similar case of seeking the fullness of faith, but in

---

30. Garth M. Rosell, *The Surprising Work of God: Harold John Ockenga, Billy Graham, and the Rebirth of Evangelicalism* (Grand Rapids: Baker Academic, 2008), 22.

31. Harold John Ockenga, "The Unique and Unparalleled Position of Park Street Church in Boston's Religious History," cited in Rosell, *Surprising Work of God*, 81 (emphasis added).

32. Prayer gatherings and youth movements that preceded and accompanied these crusade revivals were accidentally ecumenical. Recounting one such revival in Los Angeles led by Ockenga, a pastor commented that "it was a time of the heavenlies . . . with not a breath of controversy or theological argument" (Rosell, *Surprising Work of God*, 129).

a way that could not have been seen prior to that era. For in setting aside denominational controversies in order to have a unified preaching and evangelism event, the crusade offered a new approach to confessing the fullness of the faith for a world tired of denominational divides and exhibiting a desire for partnerships after decades of division.

One could read evangelicalism as a rejection of catholicity, but it seems more appropriate to read it as a *reorientation* of catholicity, asserting that whatever else catholicity means vis-à-vis formal confessions, it must first be about a form of faith once delivered for all that is also marked by accessibility for all persons regardless of theological knowledge.[33] What emerged in the wake of these crusades was, arguably, as Ockenga put it, a kind of catholicity that would "include all believers" in a necessarily populist way, with the authenticity and fullness of the Christian faith determined solely by the experience of the decision to follow Christ.[34]

If the evangelical crusades emphasized catholicity as a kind of universality of experience, it is not surprising that the crusades gave birth not to new denominations but to a companion movement designed to give durable shape and form to this kind of ubiquitous, nondenominational confession of the church's faith: parachurch organizations. The origin of the parachurch movement was not a twentieth-century phenomenon, but the rise of evangelicalism and its populist catholicity fit well with interdenominational organizations such as the recently established InterVarsity Christian Fellowship, Youth for Christ, and Campus Crusade for Christ. Even when the crusades of Graham began to wane in popularity, these movements continued this ethos of the fullness of Christ's presence occurring in the present moment, expanding into new arenas, unconditioned by tradition.[35] The burgeoning parachurch

---

33. This is contra R. David Rightmire's "Subordination of Ecclesiology and Sacramental Theology to Pneumatology in the Nineteenth-Century Holiness Movement," *Wesleyan Theological Journal* 47 (2012): 27–35.

34. For analysis of the structure of Graham's crusades, see Grant Wacker, *America's Pastor: Billy Graham and the Shaping of a Nation* (Cambridge, MA: Harvard University Press, 2014), 255–65. This is not to say that such populist retrievals of catholicity were without problems: over time, the populist approach to conversion inevitably broached further questions that encouraged more theological specificity than the crusades were able to provide. For one case study illuminating the practical difficulty of this form of catholicity, see Nathan A. Finn, "John B. Rice, Billy Graham, and the Dilemma of Ecclesiastical Separation," *American Baptist Quarterly* 33 (2014): 229–52.

35. See John G. Turner, *Bill Bright & Campus Crusade for Christ: The Renewal of Evangelicalism in Postwar America* (Chapel Hill: University of North Carolina Press, 2008), for example, on how Campus Crusade specifically proliferated the revivalist evangelical ethos into the subcultures of college campuses.

movement of the twentieth century continued the work of nineteenth-century luminaries such as the YMCA but also saw the emergence of new ventures, such as the Fellowship of Christian Athletes and Bible Study Fellowship, which, while not seeing themselves as churches, amplified and extended the implications of the revivals' catholicity.

For all of the overlap between evangelicals and Black Catholics, it is here that we begin to see a parting of the ways from the Black Catholic experience. By bringing together interest groups from across ecclesiological backgrounds (athletes, college students, women), these parachurch ministries became more particularly focused, in contrast to their Catholic peers. In the Catholic parish, Black Catholic concerns were liturgically drawn together (not without friction) with those parishes not immediately sharing the context or concerns of Black Catholics. But particular parachurch understandings of catholicity took on the textures peculiar to those groups, from the youthfulness of the college-driven groups to the "muscular Christianity" emphasis of groups such as the Fellowship of Christian Athletes.[36] In other words, in one way catholicity in the parachurch model became intensified—a person's particularity was taken up into the universal experience of Christ—while in another way it became more limited, in that each subgroup had unclear institutional or cultural connections to other subgroups. In deepening catholicity in the lived sense, parachurch organizations tended to downplay the universal-confession aspect of catholicity.

This impulse to draw the fullness of the people's experience into the confession of the faith is not simply a phenomenon of the Western hemisphere; it can be seen in one of the most well-studied religious events in twentieth-century Africa: the "East African Revival," a revival encompassing parts of Uganda, Congo, Kenya, and Rwanda.[37] The revival began in earnest in 1929 through the work of Simeon Nsibambi and his brother, Blasio Kigozi, and—as opposed to other revivals—did not emphasize miraculous works so much as the public confession of sin.[38] The Church of Uganda, which had been established in

---

36. For one midcentury critique of the practical ecclesiology of Campus Crusade, see Clyde R. McCormack, "Campus Crusade for Christ: A Crisis for Lutheran Theology and Practice," *Lutheran Quarterly* 21 (1969): 263–73. For analysis of the Fellowship of Christian Athletes and other sport-based parachurch groups, see Tony Ladd and James A. Mathisen, *Muscular Christianity: Evangelical Protestants and the Development of American Sport* (Grand Rapids: Baker Books, 1999); and Tom Krattenmaker, *Onward Christian Athletes: Turning Ballparks into Pulpits and Players into Preachers* (Lanham, MD: Rowman and Littlefield, 2009).

37. I use the present-day names of the territories to orient the reader.

38. Other iterations of the revival would proceed differently. In Mark Shaw's interpretation, the Rwandan wing, which emphasized dreams and visions, worked more collaboratively

1877, was perceived as too intertwined with social status and its relation to the colonial authorities and as less interested in a life of holiness.[39]

The perception of revivalists in Uganda was that the Church of Uganda had become complacent and, in adopting the ways of the colonizers, it had become less *Balokole* ("the saved ones"). Anglican officials were initially criticized for their complacency, for their adoption of modern principles of biblical interpretation, and in the 1960s, for their being on the side of the colonizers in the midst of the nationalization of Uganda. In this way, the beginning of a new Uganda and the revivalist movement of the *Balokole* became partners: the creation of a new nation fueled by a revivalist movement that saw the need to remove itself from its originating past.

Unintentionally, being truly Ugandan and truly Christian became close partners, with public confession of sin the mark of the faith all people were expected to have. As seen in the rise of revivals, both in America and in East Africa, the presence of Christ in populist forms creates a form of catholicity that is intensively particular, taking up the fullness of what the confessing Christian is culturally and historically, but which is in practice restricted to national Ugandans. In each of these examples, universality is translated to a universally available experience, but in a way that is connected to a kind of populism: having an intensively particular catholicity—connecting the universal faith with a particular people—yielded a kind of depth that struggled in turn to create new forms of unity *across* those particularities.

Catholicity and Context: The Challenge of Having a Supporting Culture

To call the church the catholic body of Christ already involves us in the difficulties that the previous section opened up: time, context, history. As Henri de Lubac reminds us, the "body of Christ" is both a universal and particular body of believers, variegated in time and place yet knit together by this one

---

with the Anglican church than its Ugandan partners (*Global Awakenings: How 20th-Century Revivals Triggered a Christian Revolution* [Downers Grove, IL: IVP Academic, 2010], 104–6). For introductions to the East African Revival, see Jason Bruner, *Living Salvation in the East African Revival in Uganda* (Melton, UK: Boydell and Brewer, 2017); and Kevin Ward, *The East African Revival: History and Legacies* (Surrey, UK: Ashgate, 2012).

39. The degree to which politics and social influence shape the movement is debated by its interpreters. For a reading that emphasizes these dimensions, see Derek R. Peterson, *Ethnic Patriotism and the East African Revival: A History of Dissent, c. 1935–1972* (Cambridge: Cambridge University Press, 2012).

particular body of Jesus of Nazareth, through a common meal, the body and blood of Jesus. To name the church as "the body of Christ" thus is already to acknowledge the interrelation between particularities of this one human life and those of the diverse bodies in which the Spirit sent by Christ dwells.[40] Attending to the particular gathered members of the church thus is one facet of deepening our attention to a church's catholicity.

What we saw in our exploration of holiness is true also with respect to catholicity: to understand this mark of the church, we must ask what it means for the church to be a body in the world and how the church is in fact embedded in the world. We turn first to the Orthodox notion of *sobornost*. As noted briefly already, Orthodox thought about context does not hold that Christian doctrines must be contextualized but aims for the integration of faith and time in a different way, through an organic union of church and society. Naming the communions of the Orthodox Church according to nationality (Serbian, Syrian, Greek, etc.) is not only a matter of administrative accuracy but indicative of the way in which the church is to be the church of a people, building up that locale into a symphonic relationship.[41] *Sobornost*, the Russian analogue for "conciliarity" or "catholicity," means not only that the whole of the church is involved in the search for the truth but that the good and development of the individual are bound up with the whole—the whole church and, importantly, the whole culture.[42]

As such, catholicity, as a kind of full participation in the faith, cannot be simply individuals seeking the fullness of faith, or even individual congregations pushing one another in a contested fashion; to live the fullness of the faith is to do so in concert with the whole of the church, in unity with the *culture*.[43] The Russian Orthodox Church found itself struggling with the implications of *sobornost* as both tsars and Communist regimes attempted to utilize the church for their own ends. By theologically connecting itself so deeply with its culture, Russian Orthodoxy avoided a dualist "church versus culture" motif,

---

40. Henri de Lubac, *Corpus Mysticum: The Eucharist and the Church in the Middle Ages* (Notre Dame, IN: University of Notre Dame Press, 2007).

41. As John Meyendorff observes, this "symphonic" relationship is a best-case scenario, often requiring intensive negotiation to prevent the state from absorbing religious functions entirely. See Meyendorff, "Russian Bishops and Church Reform in 1905," in *Russian Orthodoxy under the Old Regime*, ed. Robert L. Nichols and Theofanis George Stavrou (St. Paul: University of Minnesota Press, 1978), 170.

42. Thomas Bremer, *Cross and Kremlin: A Brief History of the Orthodox Church in Russia* (Grand Rapids: Eerdmans, 2013), 101.

43. Bremer, *Cross and Kremlin*, 102.

but it found itself striving with how to maintain independence of practice in the face of imperial power. Put differently, the Russian Orthodox concept of *sobornost* sidesteps the Protestant problems of "translating" the faith, but it trades these for the problem of church independence from powers that seek to co-opt its influence.

The spread of Christianity into Communist cultures likewise posed profound challenges for catholicity: Does a society that is Communist produce a *different* faith, or can a universally recognizable faith be preserved in a society that embraces Communism? In one way, taking the latter road is an uphill struggle: theological denunciations of Communism date back to the mid-nineteenth century, when Pius IX named it as "a doctrine most opposed to the very natural law."[44] Likewise, Pius XI, in his 1937 encyclical *Divini Redemptoris*, charges Communism with "aim[ing] at upsetting the social order and at undermining the very foundations of Christian civilization."[45] Lest we think this is simply a rhetorical flourish, Pius XI uses this term "Christian civilization" as a way of describing the relation between the natural and the supernatural—of saying that the Church's faith is developed not in the abstract but against the backdrop of a society in which "natural" conditions operate in conjunction with grace.

Pius XI goes on to argue that because the church exists as God's divine instrument in creation, the material conditions of a society are not accidental to the reception of doctrine. Thus, the notion of a Christian civilization, far from being a rhetorical flourish, is a real concern as to whether the faith catholic is being passed on.[46] This is not to say that the faith rises or falls on whether societies cooperate with churches, but the question is indeed raised as to whether Communism's culture represents a threat not simply to societies but to the reception of the faith.[47] Undoubtedly, papal teaching preceding Pius XI had its qualms with capitalist societies as well, but it detects in them continuity with Catholic teachings on the dignity of the human individual and on property.[48]

---

44. Pius IX, *Qui Pluribus* (Vatican City: Holy See, 1846), 16, available at Papal Encyclicals Online, https://www.papalencyclicals.net/pius09/p9quiplu.htm.

45. Pius XI, *Divini Redemptoris* (Vatican City: Holy See, 1937), 3, available at Papal Encyclicals Online, https://www.papalencyclicals.net/pius11/p11divin.htm.

46. Pius XI, *Divini Redemptoris*, 29: "God has likewise destined man for civil society according to the dictates of his very nature. In the plan of the Creator, society is a natural means which man can and must use to reach his destined end."

47. Pius XI, *Divini Redemptoris*, 19–20.

48. Pius XI, *Divini Redemptoris*, 31. Here, Pius XI specifically refers to Leo XIII's *Rerum Novarum*, the modern genesis of Catholic social teaching, which famously criticizes capitalist

The Catholic Church was not alone in asking this question about culture and catholicity. In the wake of the Velvet Revolution, Bulgarian Orthodoxy faced a very different set of challenges from a post-Communist culture. With the demise of a Communist regime in Bulgaria, charges were made against the Bulgarian Orthodox Church that they had been collaborators with the Communist regime.[49] The desire to be present to a post-Communist society led to a split in the church, including a duplication of the synods and governing organs of the church. While the new democratic government did not recognize the schismatic group, it did place pressure on the Orthodox Church to support political slogans, attend political meetings, and otherwise support the new government.[50]

The charge—leveled against Orthodox churches in other contexts—that the church routinely engages in theocratic machinations, collaborating with whomever is in power for its own sake, simply does not hold up universally in this light. By articulating the church's catholic vocation as the church's transmission of the whole faith to the whole world and partnering with the Communist government, the church's catholicity came into conflict with its unity. Though not unique to Bulgaria, this facet of catholicity, as an intensive relation to human culture, bears with it a certain risk: to be catholic in this way—embracing without division the full anthropological range of God's work—will bear itself out in political risk and misunderstanding.[51] From an Orthodox perspective, such an approach was preferable to those that treated the substance of the faith as abstract principles requiring translation.[52]

---

cultures for not respecting the dignity of laborers. See Leo XIII, *Rerum Novarum* (Vatican City: Holy See, 1891), available at Papal Encyclicals Online, https://www.papalencyclicals.net/leo13/l13rerum.htm.

49. Ivan Zhelev-Dimitrov, "The Orthodox Church in Bulgaria Today," *Greek Orthodox Review* 45 (2000): 504.

50. Zhelev-Dimitrov, "Orthodox Church in Bulgaria Today," 504.

51. See also the case of the Kenyan Orthodox Church, which was likewise suspected as a quasi-protest movement, in John N. Njoroge, "The Orthodox Church in Africa and the Quest for Enculturation: A Challenging Mission Paradigm in Today's Orthodoxy," *St. Vladmir's Theological Quarterly* 55 (2011): 405–38.

52. See Petros Vassiliades, "Contextuality and Catholicity: The Task of Orthodox Theology in Ecumenical Theological Education," *International Review of Mission* 98 (2009): 37–48. Orthodox theology in the twentieth century was in part a reaction to the "Westernization" of Orthodoxy seen by seminal figures such as Georges Florovsky and a return to the patristic era instead of chasing the contemporary context. See Brandon Gallaher, "'Waiting for the Barbarians': Identity and Polemicism in the Neo-Patristic Synthesis of Georges Florovsky," *Modern Theology* 27 (2011): 659–91. Florovsky was an observer at the 1948 Amsterdam meeting of the World Council of Churches and leveled many of these criticisms there, as noted in the discussions

Challenges to Catholicity and Context: Economics

I have named some of the difficulties of this variety of catholicity, which seeks "wholeness" not just in terms of the doctrine delivered but in terms of how this connects to the whole of the people. But this concern for bringing the whole faith to the whole people was certainly not an Orthodox concern alone; it was a recurring theme in the WCC, beginning most explicitly with the New Delhi Assembly in 1961. There, in the opening document on the nature of witness, the WCC noted that "solidarity with all men of every nation, class, colour and faith without distinction in our common manhood is a starting point of the renewal of the life and witness of our churches by the Holy Spirit."[53] The opening statement is deeply characterized by attention to how social conditions undermined the propagation of the faith, forecasting the prominence of this theme for years to come.

Put differently, confessing the fullness of the faith as a lived reality could not be divorced from attention to those aspects of culture—politics, language, economics—that affected Christians' ability to live the gospel fully. The 1968 Uppsala Assembly of the WCC qualifies this motif, describing catholicity as having less to do with geographical ubiquity and more to do with "spirit and quality of life—fullness of life in fellowship with God," attending to the human concerns entailed in various global churches, without becoming simply "pan-humanism."[54]

The 1975 Nairobi Assembly returned these themes of social conditions to the forefront of discussions of catholicity, emphasizing the various ways in which economic privation, nationalism, and human suffering undermined the lived nature of catholicity.[55] But the notion that catholicity, the fullness of Christ, implicates all of human life is best represented by the presentation "Life in Its Fullness" at the 1983 Vancouver Assembly of the WCC. As we have seen in previous WCC meetings, catholicity was discussed predominately

---

around Amsterdam's statement on the doctrine of the church. See Georges Florovsky, "The Church: Her Nature and Task," in *Man's Disorder and God's Design: The Amsterdam Assembly Series* (New York: Harper and Brothers, n.d.), 43–59.

53. *The New Delhi Report: The Third Assembly of the World Council of Churches* (New York: Association Press), 80.

54. "The Holy Spirit and the Catholicity of the Church: Introduction to the Theme," in *The Uppsala Report 1968: Official Report of the Fourth Assembly of the World Council of Churches Uppsala July 4-20, 1968* (Geneva: World Council of Churches, 1968), 7–9.

55. *Breaking Barriers: Nairobi 1975; The Official Report of the Fifth Assembly of the World Council of Churches, Naibroi, 23 November–10 December, 1975* (Geneva: World Council of Churches, 1975), 46–48.

as it pertained to doctrine, but in Vancouver this theme took an explicitly economic turn:

> Christ promises life in its fullness—life new and eternal. Sharing here and now in the risen life of Christ, the Church is called to proclaim and embody this gospel of full life for all the world. This entails, among other things, challenging false gospels and their illusory promises. For Dr. Dorothee Sölle, the great illusion of our age finds expression in the materialism of the affluent nations. . . . By participating in structures that impoverish millions of people, the world's wealthy not only make fullness of life impossible for themselves; they also strip the poor of life's goodness.[56]

This account of Christianity vis-à-vis economic concerns was not at odds with Christian approaches. The Second Vatican Council (1962–65) had likewise addressed issues of global poverty and economic injustice, with the Conference of Latin American Bishops meeting in Medellín, Columbia, in 1968 applying the teachings of the council more directly to issues of poverty.

But in these broadly Protestant conversations at the WCC, the effect of poverty on ecclesial catholicity stretched to ask broader questions about humanity as such: that which is true in church conversations is applicable beyond the church, for the fullness that God brings to the church is the fullness God desires for humanity as well. Throughout the Vancouver WCC meeting, the question of economics appeared not only in doctrinal discussions of the nature of Christian witness, of church unity, and of the building up of pastoral communities but also in the church's witness to peace and justice more broadly.[57]

It is fair to ask why economics is identified so frequently in these conversations of how a faithful Christian confession is enacted. Some see this as a degradation of ecclesiological questions, a distraction from specifically ecclesial concerns. But if catholicity is concerned with how the church is united to the depths of human life, then attending to concerns of labor and economy are significant. The challenge of economics posed by the WCC was not unique. In the late nineteenth century, beginning with *Rerum Novarum*, papal encyclicals had addressed labor and economic concerns as significant moral questions facing Catholic piety. But as Ross Emmett argues, the twentieth century was

---

56. David Gill, ed., *Gathered for Life: Official Report of the 6th Assembly of the World Council of Churches, Vancouver, Canada, 24 July–10 August 1983* (Geneva: World Council of Churches, 1983), 24–25.

57. Gill, *Gathered for Life*, 37–39, 45, 68–69, 74–75.

a time when economic concerns were separated from theological ones, or at least when the ways theology interacted with economics were modified. This meant that connections between material worlds and theological ones—which would have been intuitive in the latter part of the nineteenth century—now had to be interrogated once again.[58]

By one argument, attention to economics offered a vantage point to deepen the catholicity of the church, by recognizing additional and previously neglected virtues. As Latin American bishops began to take up the teachings of Vatican II, the council's naming of the "preferential option for the poor" received great attention, not only with respect to issues of justice but with respect to how this renewed focus on the poor would reorder Latin American ecclesiology.

In the 1979 WCC assembly at Puebla, Mexico, we see most clearly one example of this.[59] In outlining the significance of Vatican II's call for Latin American ecclesiology, the authors of the Puebla documents note that "commitment to the poor and oppressed and the rise of grassroots communities have helped the Church to discover the evangelizing potential of the poor. For the poor challenge the Church constantly, summoning it to conversion; and many of the poor incarnate in their lives the evangelical values of solidarity, service, simplicity, and openness to accepting the gift of God."[60]

That the authors of the document do not name the traditional virtues of faith, hope, and love could be read as a capitulation to economic determinism. Or it could be read, as the WCC indicates, as *expanding* the central concerns of catholicity as well as the vision of what virtues are needed amid privation. As the authors note, this commendation of the virtues of the poor builds on the prior example of Christ himself and was "demanded by the scandalous reality of economic imbalances in Latin America."[61] The document does not

---

58. For these histories, see Paul Oslington, ed., *The Oxford Handbook of Christianity and Economics* (Oxford: Oxford University Press, 2014), particularly 135–50. As Ross B. Emmett describes it, the late nineteenth and early twentieth centuries saw the emergence of "non-overlapping magisterial" analysis, which divided economic process from moral valuation. Their unity in pre-twentieth-century Christendom began to come apart by the early twentieth century, culminating in their effectual division as separate disciplines. See Oslington, *Oxford Handbook of Christianity and Economics*, 136–37.

59. Latin American liberation theologians had been writing on the ecclesiological ramifications of poverty for quite some time prior to this meeting. See in particular Gustavo Gutiérrez, *A Theology of Liberation* (Maryknoll, NY: Orbis Books, 1973), 143–62.

60. John Eagleson and Philip Scharper, eds., *Puebla and Beyond* (Maryknoll, NY: Orbis Books, 1979), 265–66.

61. Eagleson and Scharper, *Puebla and Beyond*, 266.

abandon the need for proclamation, Eucharist, and liturgy, but all of these things are informed by the prior assumption that the poor are expanding the range of virtues that are to be commended and amplified by the church.

The attention to economic conditions, in order to cultivate a deeper connection between the church's professed faith and the human condition, does not cut in only one direction. Consider, as counterexample, the prosperity gospel. Is it simply an accident of history that prosperity teaching emerged during the same era in which catholicity was becoming intertwined with discussions about economics? While the roots of prosperity preaching in the United States predated the 1960s by several decades, it was during this time—when global economic conditions were being pressed by the Vatican, the World Council of Churches, and liberation theologians—that prosperity teaching began to find global expressions as well. The question prosperity preaching pressed, in contrast to Medellín and Puebla, can be put this way: If the presence of God comes to us in material ways, why should we assume that God is most present in poverty? Why should we not think of the fullness of God's presence in terms of material *abundance*? And how does such abundance cultivate the possibility for a full implementation of the Christian faith?

The roots of prosperity gospel teaching are complex and lie in a complex seedbed of Holiness traditions, Pentecostals, spiritualists, and Baptists.[62] Far from being simply the possession of charismatics, the prosperity gospel appeared as an ecumenical swath of ministers sought to understand the relationship between the material goods of life—such as health, financial prosperity, and flourishing interpersonal relationships—and the full presence of God. Whereas early social responses to poverty, as seen in Walter Rauschenbusch's Social Gospel, William and Catherine Booth's Salvation Army, or Catholic social teaching, emphasized God's specific care and attention for the poor as an outworking of Christian faith, the prosperity gospel emphasized that true gospel occasioned results such as wealth and freedom from sickness.[63]

As prosperity preaching became a global phenomenon in the twentieth century,[64] megachurches around the world, which explicitly center on this

---

62. Kate Bowler, *Blessed: A History of the American Prosperity Gospel* (Oxford: Oxford University Press, 2013), 11–40.

63. Bowler, *Blessed*, 31.

64. The international genealogy of this is contested. In his *The New Faces of Christianity: Believing the Bible in the Global South* (Oxford: Oxford University Press, 2006), 103–6, Philip Jenkins links its prominence to early Pentecostal missionaries to the African continent following the Azuza Street Revivals of 1906. For a more variegated approach to global origins of prosperity

connection between the fullness of God's Spirit and the abundance of material blessing, offered a counter vision for how economic prosperity's effect on catholicity should be understood. While the connection between material blessing and God's presence is less prevalent in Scripture, the connection between the fullness of God's Spirit and material wealth is, by all accounts, one that comes about by asking about what conditions prevent the fullness of the Christian faith from being connected to the full lives of the people. In this sense, the prosperity gospel is born out of the same attention to contextual dynamics—economic privation—and attempts to answer that question in a different way.

If pre-twentieth-century accounts of catholicity attend to catholicity as having to do either with the original deposit or with ubiquity, but not the material conditions affecting how the Christian faith is confessed, the various movements I have described here offer a different way forward: that the church cannot know the fullness of Christ except by attending to cultural dynamics of wealth, poverty, politics, and other social dynamics that affect the church. What becomes clear in these two different trajectories is not whether catholicity involves attention to culture, history, and time, but in what way.

Once this question is opened, what it means for the fullness of the Christian faith to be lived by the fullness of people opens up into new vistas but, as I proposed in the introduction, not in a way that requires us to provisionally refrain from judgment. To be sure, great bias against prosperity teaching was voiced by critics globally, both for its uses of Scripture and for the moral behavior of some of its proponents, but any critique of prosperity teaching—by the lights of this discussion—cannot proceed by pulling theology and money apart. Rather, the question must be asked in this way: Does prosperity teaching stretch catholicity's concern for context to the breaking point by beginning with wealth as the measure of whether or not God's fullness is present?

Challenges for Catholicity: Globalization

In the previous section, attention was given to how the church's faith could be deeply connected to various times and places. In these discussions of

---

teachings, see the studies in Steve Brouwer, Paul Gifford, and Susan D. Rose, *Exporting the American Gospel: Global Christian Fundamentalism* (New York: Routledge, 1996). For a map of these theologies in an African context, see Andreas Heuser, "Charting African Prosperity Gospel Economies," *HTS Teologiese Studies* 72 (2016): 1–9.

catholicity, a more qualitative form of discussion took place: disagreements among these movements was not on whether a movement could lay claim to the fullness of faith, but on what material conditions affected the whole faith being known by the whole people.

But in contrast to these discussions, we can also speak of "quantitative catholicity," which emphasizes the geographic expanse of the faith, calling forth a much older definition of catholicity from the early Protestants: *ubiquity*. In each of the Gospels, the vision of Christ's work is not that it remain within the house of Israel, but that, in one way or another, it will proceed throughout the world. As we saw with our discussion of twentieth-century ecumenism, it was this very missionary impulse and the challenges of missions in a divided church that spurred on the early ecumenical movement. It is to these challenges of ubiquity, of global breadth, that we now turn.

By comparison with the questions treated in previous sections, ubiquity seems a much more manageable question; unless one envisions missions activity as requiring extraterrestrial travel, there is only so much world to travel.[65] But catholicity is not the same as geographical extension. One can point to the ancient presence, but present diminishment, of Christian churches in certain corners of China, India, North Africa, or Denmark to see that ubiquity is an ongoing concern for catholicity; the faith of a place may yet be reversed and need to be planted again.

The question that the global expansion of Christianity raises for catholicity is how local contexts receive and transmit the fullness of the faith. The twentieth century was an age of missions expansion, with denominations and independent missions organizations fanning out across the world. But no story of Christianity's spread in the twentieth century can be told without addressing colonialism.[66] In this story, though, a complex rendering appears. According to some recent studies, the suggestion that religious missionaries

---

65. This is, in and of itself, a fascinating question, but beyond the purview of this work. See Andrew Davison's *Astrobiology and Christian Doctrine: Exploring the Implications of Life in the Universe* (Cambridge: Cambridge University Press, 2023).

66. What is meant by this claim is not that colonial practices were benign but that the relationship between Christian faith and colonial populations is not a straightforward one. While it is without question that the histories of modern missions and colonization are intertwined, mapping all of these lineages would take us beyond the intent of this study. For introductions to these discussions of colonialism and Christian missions, see, among other excellent analyses, Hilary M. Carey, *God's Empire: Religion and Colonialism in the British World, c. 1801–1908* (New York: Cambridge University Press, 2011); and Dana L. Robert, ed., *Converting Colonialism: Visions and Realities in Mission History* (Grand Rapids: Eerdmans, 2008). For a dissent, challenging the view that the study of missions has been too conditioned by colonial studies,

were simply encoded functionaries of colonialization—stamping the colonizing religion onto the colony—tells a true, but only partial, story.[67] At times, missions contexts were rich and experimental sites in which Christianity itself entered and was changed as a consequence.[68]

One example, from El Salvador, will help illustrate this. Throughout the twentieth century, local dynamics changed the face of Christianity, as countries throughout Central and South America began to leave their Catholic roots for increasingly charismatic expressions. In modern El Salvador, the Tabernáculo Bíblico Bautista, led by Edgar López Bertrand, boasts over four hundred satellite congregations and nearly eighty thousand members.[69] But the shift from Catholic to Protestant was in some ways an internal development, not entirely the result of one imported version of Christianity displacing another.

As Timothy Wadkins argues, this transformation of El Salvador into an increasingly Protestant country was due, in part, to the very economic and political dynamics that brought colonial Christianity into El Salvador. As El Salvador shifted away from a hierarchal conception of governance following the civil war of the 1980s, so too it began to shift away from forms of Christianity that mirrored the assumptions of that old world.[70] Liberation-inspired churchmen such as Óscar Romero saw themselves as taking the social teachings of the church to their logical conclusion, siding with the people of El Salvador over against the oppressive regime, in the spirit of the second Episcopal Council of Latin America (CELAM) and Vatican II. The ironic outworking of this was that these Catholic church leaders portended a shift toward a more democratic, populist variety of Christianity—or, as we have been tracing this story, a shift from one version of catholicity to another, paving the way out of Catholicism and into a more democratized charismatic Christianity.

---

see Jane Samson, "The Problem of Colonialism in the Western Historiography of Christian Missions," *Religious Studies and Theology* 23 (2004): 3–25.

67. Lamin Sanneh, "The Yogi and the Commissar: Christian Missions and the African Response," *International Bulletin of Missionary Research* 15 (1991): 9.

68. Norman Etherington, *Missions and Empire* (Oxford: Oxford University Press, 2005), offers a variety of studies on this point, viewing colonialism both in terms of its propagation of Western forms of Christianity and in terms of its experimental nature.

69. Timothy H. Wadkins, *The Rise of Pentecostalism in Modern El Salvador: From the Blood of the Martyrs to the Baptism of the Spirit* (Waco: Baylor University Press, 2017), 17.

70. Wadkins, *Rise of Pentecostalism in Modern El Salvador*, 58–65. For more on this point, see Donald E. Miller and Tetunao Yamamori, *Global Pentecostalism: The New Face of Christian Social Engagement* (Berkley: University of California Press, 2007), 160–83.

Similar stories radiating from South Africa, India, and China across the century echoed the Salvadoran case.[71] Whether the instruction was delivered by White Europeans, African associates of the missionaries, or Black American missionaries, the story remained remarkably similar: Christian practice and place were inseparable partners in producing inextricably local forms of Christianity and, in the process, expanding the breadth of the faith.[72]

If globalization poses one challenge to catholicity by undermining the ability of a culture to be stabilized long enough for the faith to take root deeply, migration poses a similar kind of challenge to how we conceive of catholicity. Migration's role in shaping this question of the relationship between culture and the practice of the Christian faith by a people is not new; migration has shaped the faith and practice of churches since the beginning.[73] As we see in the example of early Pentecostalism, fluid borders between Mexico and the United States in the early twentieth century not only brought new dimensions to the phenomenon of "speaking in many tongues" but also helped Pentecostalism spread rapidly throughout Latin America, posing challenges to Catholicism's prevalence.[74]

But during the twentieth century, increased possibilities for mobility, both through migration and through refugee resettlement, pulled the question of catholicity more clearly into focus.[75] Beginning in the mid-nineteenth century,

---

71. See Robert J. Houle, *Making African Christianity: Africans Reimagining Their Faith in Colonial South Africa* (Bethlehem, PA: Lehigh University Press, 2011); Selva J. Raj and Corrine G. Dempsey, eds., *Popular Christianity in India: Riting between the Lines* (Albany: SUNY Press, 2002); and Ziming Wu, *Chinese Christianity: An Interplay between Global and Local Perspectives* (Leiden: Brill, 2012).

72. For two accounts of non-White missions movements, whose work accelerated noncolonial forms of Christianity, see Edward Andrews, *Native Apostles: Black and Indian Missionaries in the British Atlantic World* (Cambridge, MA: Harvard University Press, 2013); and Andrew E. Barnes, *Global Christianity and the Black Atlantic: Tuskegee, Colonialism, and the Shaping of African Industrial Education* (Waco: Baylor University Press, 2017).

73. See here the narration of Jehu J. Hanciles, *Migration and the Making of Global Christianity* (Grand Rapids: Eerdmans, 2021).

74. For this story, see Daniel Ramirez, *Migrating Faith: Pentecostalism in the United States and Mexico in the Twentieth Century* (Chapel Hill: University of North Carolina Press, 2015).

75. As interrelated, yet distinct, phenomena, migration and refugeeism have become the unspoken forces influencing reflection on the questions of who counts as belonging to a people and what it means to belong to a place. For theological and ethical introductions to migration and refugeeism, including their differences, see Joseph Carens, *The Ethics of Immigration* (Oxford: Oxford University Press, 2015); Elena Fiddian-Qasmiyeh et al., eds., *The Oxford Handbook of Refugee and Forced Migration Studies* (Oxford: Oxford University Press, 2016); and Susann Snyder et al., eds., *Church in an Age of Global Migration: A Moving Body* (New York: Palgrave Macmillan, 2016).

the first waves of modern mass migration began to alter the shape of Christianity in Europe, as Orthodox Christian peasants from Russia fled from Ottoman troops in 1854. The Orthodox migrations to Europe and America likewise dislocated Orthodox Christians, who were used to thinking about the scope of a church in terms of territory. That there can exist, within America, for example, Armenian, Russian, and Greek Orthodox congregations exemplifies this challenge to Orthodox ecclesiology presented by migration.[76] For during these migrations, the previous way of thinking about the church, as national in scope and as belonging to a place, gave way, in part, to transnational thinking about what "place" is and what it means for a church to confess the full faith in that place.[77] Orthodox ecclesiology, trading on a concept of integration between the people of a land and the church, found itself in a unique situation in diaspora, with the traditional configuration of catholicity put in question.[78]

A different example from South Africa will help illuminate these dynamics of how migration alters how Christian confession occurs.[79] During the time of apartheid, various forms of Christianity developed alongside the predominantly Dutch Reformed White churches, including Pentecostal, African Independent, and evangelical congregations. Despite the well-known *ubuntu* theology articulated by Desmond Tutu during this period—a theology that emphasized the common humanity of all persons—the South African churches struggled to integrate various migrant outsiders working in Johannesburg, including Zimbabweans.[80]

As researcher Elina Hankela describes it, this critical gaze toward outsiders is understandable, but it created a crisis for the *ubuntu* elements of churches,

---

76. Maria Hämmerli and Jean-François Mayer, *Orthodox Identities in Western Europe: Migration, Settlement and Innovation* (Surry, UK: Ashgate, 2014). The example of the American Orthodox church is a unique one, but in some ways indicative of the challenge that migration poses for Orthodox ecclesiology elsewhere.

77. Victor Roudometof, "Transnationalism and Globalization: The Greek Orthodox Diaspora between Orthodox Universalism and Transnational Nationalism," *Diaspora: A Journal of Transitional Studies* 9 (2000): 361–97.

78. As Berit Thorbjørnsrud has argued, this occurs when one's new homeland is infused with influences from one's former homeland. See Berit Thorbjørnsrud, "'The Problem of the Orthodox Diaspora': The Orthodox Church between Nationalism, Transnationalism, and Universality," *Numen* 62 (2015): 568–95.

79. For an overview, see Kevin Roy, *The Story of the Church in South Africa* (Carlisle, UK: Langham Global Library, 2017).

80. Elina Hankela, *Ubuntu, Migration and Ministry: Being Human in a Johannesburg Church* (Leiden: Brill, 2014), 1.

as churches struggled to incorporate Zimbabwean temporary workers.[81] Over time, however, as Zimbabwean teens began to attend a "teen church," it offered a point of encounter between Zimbabweans and Black South Africans. As the attitudes of the South African teens toward the Zimbabweans changed over time, it was not because *ubuntu* ceased to be a significant part of the theological teachings, but because the presence of the migrants in the context of worship opened up new dimensions of *ubuntu* that had not been emphasized.[82] The material alteration of place, in other words, opened up the theological concepts to include those present in the liturgical space.

Squaring the Circle: Local Christianity, Catholicity of Confession

As William Cavanaugh has argued, because of the incarnation of Christ, locality is the essence of catholicity. The dynamics of globalization create an account of the church that loses the value of local texture, whereas catholicity offers a vision in which Christ is present in each location without requiring the homogeneity of globalized corporations.[83] Vincent Miller identifies the specter of renewed tribalism on the horizon in this proposal: if locality is celebrated at the expense of a recognition of the same Spirit and same Christ being celebrated in "all places and by all people," the virtues of localism become a new and more pernicious vice, with localism a defense against that which is new, against having local customs and presumptions troubled.[84] If catholicity means attending more intensively to local forms of faithfulness, this could mean becoming so inwardly focused that one becomes immune to critiques from the outside; it could lead to becoming so contextualized that one cannot be broached by outsiders. How can this tension be resolved? How can the faith be at the same time catholic and local, universal and particular, "the fullness of faith" and also a work in progress?

One answer, voiced by both Protestants and Catholics, is that of mission: that the mission of God is to encompass the whole world in that which the church proclaims, and thus, to be a truly catholic church is to be a church

81. Hankela, *Ubuntu, Migration and Ministry*, 250–54.
82. Hankela, *Ubuntu, Migration and Ministry*, 338.
83. William T. Cavanaugh, "The World in a Wafer: A Geography of the Eucharist as Resistance to Globalization," *Modern Theology* 15 (1999): 181–96.
84. Vincent J. Miller, "Where Is the Church? Globalization and Catholicity," *Theological Studies* 69 (2008): 412–32.

engaged in mission, drawing in that which is not already present, so that the church might be composed of localities united in a common faith.[85] The Protestant voices on this are ample and have been explored at length elsewhere. But consider how one way in which this is addressed is seen in the Vatican II document *Ad Gentes*, which explores the missionary nature of the church. The document opens with a simple claim, which ties together mission and catholicity: "Divinely sent to the nations of the world to be unto them 'a universal sacrament of salvation,' the Church, driven by the inner necessity of her own catholicity and obeying the mandate of her Founder . . . strives ever to proclaim the Gospel to all men."[86]

The definition of the church as "missionary by her very nature, since it is from the mission of the Son and the mission of the Holy Spirit that she draws her origin,"[87] clarifies catholicity as *missionally* inflected, as always in search of what has not been drawn into the church yet. In this document, diverse activities such as preparation of ministers, missions organizations, and lay bodies all serve the divine mission, which unfolds in the course of history as the church offers itself to the world in witness.[88] As mission takes place and as Christian influence grows, the church "thus take[s] them up into full catholicity," so that the whole of the church shares in the fullness of the faith as all its members share in the one mission of God to the nations.[89]

Missions activity presumes that what the church is in possession of is the fullness that creation needs, and thus its internal activities are ordered toward the growth of the visible mystical body of Christ, a work that results in "the whole human race . . . form[ing] one people of God."[90] Each of the various congregations of the faithful, which belong to this singular people of God, is "endowed with the riches of its nation's culture [and] should be deeply rooted in the people," a vision that includes the flourishing of intermediary associations, schools, social apparatuses, and family arrangements.[91]

---

85. Proponents of "missional theology" differ on this point, proposing that theology is best done by identifying what God is doing apart from the church and asking how the church might join in that. See, for example, John Franke, *Missional Theology: An Introduction* (Grand Rapids: Baker Academic, 2020).
86. Paul VI, *Ad Gentes* (Vatican City: Holy See, 1965), 1, https://www.vatican.va/archive/hist_councils/ii_vatican_council/documents/vat-ii_decree_19651207_ad-gentes_en.html.
87. Paul VI, *Ad Gentes*, 2.
88. Paul VI, *Ad Gentes*, 5.
89. Paul VI, *Ad Gentes*, 6.
90. Paul VI, *Ad Gentes*, 8.
91. Paul VI, *Ad Gentes*, 15.

But despite their overlap, it is here that the Catholic and Protestant accounts also begin to diverge. In *Ad Gentes*, outward-facing activities such as attending local religious customs and dialoguing with neighbors are commended,[92] but in the document, the inner fullness of the church is *not* at risk if the church does not fully take root. This is important to signal because it reveals, as we have seen, a deeper divide between Catholics and Protestants about what constitutes catholicity: Is it a fullness of faith linked to the original deposit—a deposit that cannot be lost—or are there additional dimensions, including the whole of the faith coming to bear on the whole of who a people is?

Moving Forward

Catholicity in the last century remained one of the most difficult marks of the church, but not because conceiving of the universality of the church is a totalizing claim. The difficulty came in naming how catholicity involves not simply confessing in a full-throated way what Christians have confessed in the past, but doing this in a way that knits together time, space, cultural depth, and geographical expanse. Catholicity runs into a particular problem that we did not see with the church's oneness—for example, the plurality of dimensions of catholicity resulting in, at times, competing notions of whether catholicity's range prevented it from being united with the mark of oneness.

Though some assume that catholicity depends on the church's unity, what I have marked out here suggests that catholicity frequently exists in tension with the church's unity and that any sense of unity must not override the already existing dimensions of catholicity: that the goods of the church be known in all times and all places. This is not to render unity impossible, but to say that if unity is possible, it must refrain from treating catholicity as a derivation of unity and must affirm it as a related-yet-distinct mark.

Catholicity, among the four marks, is perhaps the most complex and the most difficult to describe. This is because it invites us to ask not only what the church's faith has been historically but how this faith is related to living it virtuously, with prudence, judgment, and attention to our neighbors. Insofar as catholicity relates to all people at all times, it seems there is no other way than to journey with God's people by the power of the Spirit through time, asking questions about next steps as they come.

92. Paul VI, *Ad Gentes*, 16.

Navigating such terrain is difficult, but it is difficult only because a doctrine of the church is already difficult. For ecclesiology requires us to ask not only what it means for God's Spirit to be operative in creation but what it means for that juncture to occur over time and in various spaces. Catholicity, thus, invites us to draw in questions of context, material conditions in which confession occurs, and the dynamics that cause the church to pause in *how* it articulates the faith, without ceasing from speaking entirely. It is appropriate that, after speaking of mission, we turn then to the final mark: apostolicity. For apostolicity requires us to consider not only how the materiality of the church affects its confessions in our time but what it means for the church to have a witness *across* time.

4

In the Past, the Present, and the Future

The Church as Apostolic

Relative to other marks—particularly the challenge of being "one"—apostolicity received less explicit treatment and incited fewer discussions. By the twentieth century, many of the questions associated with apostolicity—namely, how continuity between the past and present operate and who are to be the bearers of that continuity—were largely moot. If there were to be a time to forestall the multiplicity of apostolicity (and with it, questions about what continuity of past and present means), it would have been the sixteenth century (or the eleventh, or the fourth perhaps). Apostolicity became the necessary mark, but one nearly impossible to adjudicate, if only because the past and present could be connected in multiple ways.

Additionally, as we have seen with the other marks, by the twentieth century, many of the presumptions surrounding apostolicity had become functions of other discussions. If one were to discuss the validity of a new form of Christianity, one would do so in terms of whether it moved the faithful toward piety (the mark of holiness) or whether it divided the church (the mark of unity).

If a new expression of Christianity was gaining traction, discussions of its connection to the apostles were frequently subordinated to other concerns.

In this chapter, we will follow the pattern of the previous chapters, teasing out the variegated strands that compose the argument about what it means for churches not only to be in continuity with the apostles and to name themselves as apostolic but also for that authority to be a property of the church. In previous chapters, I have brought up the ways in which doctrine is altered not only by the internal discussions but by the moral questions that wove themselves into the doctrine's performance. Apostolicity's challenges are more subtle: various questions emerge concerning who bears the authority of the church, including material questions about what it means to transmit a faith well.

To sort out the ways in which apostolicity was contested across the century, I will draw out the two key questions of apostolicity in this way. First, I examine the question of *continuity*: In what ways does having a church that is connected to the first generation in visible, institutional, or methodological ways matter? Asking this question will take us into questions of what kinds of materiality matter for apostolicity, for connections between past and present involve some kind of common medium. To press beyond this, we must ask a second question, one about *authority*: What kind of pressure does the past exert on the present church, and why does that pressure matter?

How Should We Define "Apostolicity"?

"Apostolicity" is not merely how churches are contiguous over time, but how their continuity is *apostolic* and what bearing this out means for all the church's members. One of the lingering suspicions over this term is that it bundles all these other aspects under a more stultified institutionalism: to be "apostolic" primarily means to be a part of an institutional form that originated in the apostolic age. The basic complaint, echoing back to at least Adolf von Harnack, was that whatever was meant by "apostolicity" was quickly swallowed up by episcopal authority: an institution retained the charisma of the original authority, eclipsing the meaning of the original office.[1] Thus, a

---

1. See Adolf von Harnack, *History of Dogma*, vol. 2 (New York: Columbia University Press, 1895), 67: "It is not sufficient to prove that the rule of faith was of apostolic origin, i.e. that the Apostles had set up a rule of faith. It had further to be shown that, up to the present, the Church had always maintained it unchanged. This demonstration was all the more necessary because the

suspicion arose in the late nineteenth century that appeals to the apostolic nature of the church were largely coded appeals to "institutional authority" rather than to theological fidelity or to spiritual maturity and insight.

Protestants freely speculated and improvised on what it meant for the laity to live in continuity with the apostles, but they also did not uniformly reject the need for institutional continuity. Instead, new forms of authority emerged: presbyteries, ordination councils, "spiritual fathers," and other configurations. John Williamson Nevin, cofounder of the nineteenth-century Mercersberg Theology movement, sums up such a middle ground: though the church exists in divided form, this does not negate the need for the handing on of the faith to be "kept up in some way within the bosom of the institution itself."[2] What would become more common in the twentieth century—an appeal to the unity of the Spirit absent other physical features—was less prominent here.[3]

As John J. Burkhard describes, apostolicity is the last of the notes of the creed to be included, though this does not mean that apostolicity is the least of the notes: a church may very well be unified with itself and committed to holiness and to an expansive notion of the gospel, but much turns on whether what it names as "gospel" would be connected to that preached and assumed *by the apostles*.[4] In these conversations surrounding apostolicity, Burkhard identifies four distinct aspects:

1. *Apostolicity of Origin*. A church is named apostolic because it is connected to the apostles in its founding and in its message. What a community professes is related to whom it learned the faith from. This emphasizes the continuity of the church with Christ and the apostles.

---

heretics also claimed an apostolic origin for their *regulae*, and in different ways tried to adduce proof that they alone possessed a guarantee of inheriting the Apostles' doctrine in all its purity."

2. John Williamson Nevin, *One, Holy, Catholic, and Apostolic*, vol. 2, *John Nevin's Writings on Ecclesiology (1851–1858)* (Eugene, OR: Wipf & Stock, 2017), 48. For Nevin, the division of the church renders apostolicity questionable, as "the office itself could be of force only as it retained always the character of a single body bound together, and in union with itself" (47).

3. William Thompson-Uberuaga posits that the "ordinary-extraordinary" form of continuity by which Catholic conversations frame the Protestant/Catholic divide should be thought of as universally extraordinary, that the Spirit makes good of the extraordinary situation of post-Reformation division in a way that relativizes concerns for apostolic succession. Thompson-Uberuaga, "Continuity amidst Disruption: The Spirit and Apostolic Succession at the Reformation," *Horizons* 29 (2002): 290–98.

4. John J. Burkhard, *Apostolicity Then and Now: An Ecumenical Church in a Postmodern World* (Collegeville, MN: Liturgical Press, 2004), 25.

2. *Apostolicity of Doctrine.* A church is named apostolic not because of who its founders were, but because the contents of its beliefs are consistent with the apostolic deposit of the faith. This emphasizes the content of teaching and held doctrines.
3. *Apostolicity of Life.* A church is named apostolic because the expressed culture of the church is in union with the qualitative life of the church. This emphasizes not simply the doctrines, but patterns of leadership, moral principles, exercise of charity, and so forth—that which contributes to the overall culture of a church over time.
4. *Apostolic Succession.* A church is named apostolic because of the integrity of ordination, and most specifically, because the church exists in communion with other churches. This emphasizes not simply contiguous lines of ordination, but that the ordination occurring in a particular church is in concert with the judgment of the wider church.[5]

In these four dimensions, we can detect fault lines similar to those we have followed thus far. For if apostolicity is not just about institutional continuity but about how the teachings of the apostles bear themselves out in the lives of the laity, we can see how our discussion of apostolicity parallels conversations already rehearsed concerning the three other marks.

If we look for apostolicity as fundamentally a matter of life, as defined above, this allows us to identify ways in which the lives of the church's members have guidelines and guardrails; we can see that what counts as apostolic must at minimum have resonance with the apostles and not be speaking of a "different gospel." If we look for apostolicity as primarily a matter of doctrinal cohesiveness, this allows us to identify the ways in which various arguments emphasize one dimension (perhaps to the exclusion of others).[6] If we look to apostolicity in terms of succession alone, then questions of institutional validity become paramount, insofar as the faith is handed on across time as more than an intellectual proposition. These divergent definitions, however,

---

5. Burkhard, *Apostolicity Then and Now*, 26–39.
6. Burkhard, *Apostolicity Then and Now*, 15–18. What makes apostolicity complicated, even if one looks to a sense of historical continuity, is that Scripture itself does not name one discrete group in the early church as "the apostles"; rather, it attributes this name to persons who would have had very loose connections to the Twelve, nothing approaching firsthand knowledge of their teaching. Burkhard persuasively argues that "apostles" in New Testament usage is less a protoepiscopacy than it is an office with flexible dimensions. Apostles represented churches, and in their representation of churches, they taught and witnessed authoritatively.

assume that each is not complete: an institution's doctrinal precision can be falsified by its unwillingness to repent, and a church may imitate the deeds of Jesus while denying the substance of his person.

Continuity: A Question of the Medium

Let us begin by looking at one of the major aspects of apostolicity: continuity with the apostles. From the Roman Catholic perspective, von Harnack's criticism rings hollow: the original apostles, while *sui generis*, were not swallowed up by the institution; without the persons of the apostles, there could be no institution called "church" at all.[7] While order and institutional form are intrinsic to apostolicity, contra von Harnack, the institutional form bears not a bureaucratic face but a personal one, mediated by bishops and priests. The salient point here is that churches must not only have connection with religious ideals but be in relation to these original apostles; the faith must be handed down in relational as well as institutional form. But as we shall see, this concern for continuity was shared across many Christian bodies, though perhaps not in the same form as is expressed by Catholics.[8]

A case in point is the ongoing dispute between Orthodox and Catholic over the role that the papacy plays in how to name that continuity. Early discussions of the papacy seemed to indicate that the "honor" attributed to Rome was one of piety and service, recognizing that Rome, unlike Constantinople, had links to the sacrifice and service of Peter and Paul.[9] But this historiographical note does not in and of itself necessitate a papacy. As Kallistos Ware puts it, "It is simply

---

7. "It was Jesus Christ in person who called the apostles to be the leaders of his infant Church, the organized assembly, or community, of his followers." Kenneth D. Whitehead, *One, Holy, Catholic, and Apostolic: The Early Church Was the Catholic Church* (San Fransisco: Ignatius, 2000), 24.

8. Alongside these concerns with the *form* of continuity came questions over what authority the continuity entails. In *Unitatis Redintegratio*, as discussed in the chapter on unity, the Second Vatican Council describes the issue of division between East and West as one in which "the heritage handed down by the apostles was received with differences of form and manner" (Paul VI, *Unitatis Redintegratio* [Vatican City: Holy See, 1964], 14, https://www.vatican.va/archive/hist_councils/ii_vatican_council/documents/vat-ii_decree_19641121_unitatis-redintegratio_en.html). This is a true historical statement as far as it goes. Theological and liturgical developments across the Roman Empire were not uniform and were frequently subject to misunderstandings between East and West.

9. Brian E. Daley, SJ, "The Meaning and Exercise of 'Primacies of Honor' in the Early Church," in *Primacy in the Church: The Office of Primate and the Authority of Councils*, vol. 1, ed. John Chryssavgis (Yonkers, NY: St. Vladimir's Seminary Press, 2016), 35–50. Kallistos Ware, Metropolitan of Diokleia, echoes this reading of the papacy in his essay "Primacy, Collegiality, and the People of God," in Chryssavgis, *Primacy in the Church*, 1:93–108.

not possible to lay down a set of external criteria, such as will automatically *guarantee* that the pope (or anybody else) will speak infallibly in the name of the whole Church. We Orthodox cannot believe that this is the way in which the Spirit works."[10] This is not to say that the bishop at Rome does not lead faithfully as God's servant, but that the papacy—independent of the other bishops of the church of the East—lacks the ability to speak with authority for all of the church, and thus cannot be the singular measure of how continuity of the faith occurs.

But even the more expanded form of continuity that Ware proposes is not so easily maintained, particularly in a technological age. The twentieth century brought an explosion of new technologies into the orbit of ecclesiology; long before the Internet explosion of the late twentieth century, radio broadcasts and televangelism opened up the channels of transmission of church services and teaching in ways that complexified the question of continuity in defined traditions. It was not as if, prior to the twentieth century, the proliferation of pamphlets, circuit preachers, tent revivals, and printed sermons had not already contributed to this situation.[11] As I discussed earlier, the rise of evangelicalism—and the forms of ecumenical convergence that came with it—had already broached the question of whether denominational particularities were significant factors in the traditioning process.

Television, in its translocal reach, created a new kind of question for how church authority operated in practice, particularly for traditions that had a more explicit notion of apostolicity as deriving from magisterial authority. The ways in which televangelism created new vistas for religious authority in Protestant circles are more well known.[12] But the challenges created for apostolic authority by media are a Catholic story as well. By the 1950s, Bishop Fulton Sheen was one of the most recognizable figures on television, with his landmark show *Life Is Worth Living* carried across the English-speaking world and winning an Emmy in 1952.[13]

---

10. Ware, "Primacy, Collegiality, and the People of God," 102.

11. On these intertwined legacies, see Jeffrey K. Hadden and Anson Shupe, *Televangelism: Power and Politics on God's Frontier* (New York: Henry Holt, 1988), 43–54.

12. Quentin J. Schultze, *Televangelism and American Culture: The Business of Popular Religion* (Grand Rapids: Baker, 1991); Razelle Frankl, *Televangelism: The Marketing of Popular Religion* (Carbondale: Southern Illinois University Press, 1987); Carolyn Rouse Moxley, John L. Jackson Jr., and Marla F. Frederick, eds., *Televised Redemption: Black Religious Media and Racial Empowerment* (New York: NYU Press, 2016).

13. Marck G. McGowan, "The Fulton Sheen Affair: Religious Controversy, Nationalism, and Commercialism in the Early Years of Canadian Television, 1952–1958," *Historical Studies* 75 (2009): 21–38.

During this period, Sheen's program was restricted on Canadian public television because of its overt religious content and concerns that the Canadian Broadcasting Corporation (CBC) might not appear neutral on the program's religious content. Sheen's defenders, such as Father Eugene Cullinane, appealed to Sheen's role in "defend[ing] the spiritual and moral values that make democracy and democratic ideals possible."[14] But more important than Cullinane's worry about democratic values is the ecclesial question it raises: Sheen's popularity raises the question of whether not just Canadian broadcast authorities but Canadian *parish authorities* were being superseded in practice by Sheen's virtual authority.[15]

The challenge that mass communication presented can be posed in the following way: Sheen's radio broadcast presented Christian teaching as a communication from nowhere in particular. This can be framed, as it often is, as justifiable because it increases the impact of evangelism by modern means. But from the vantage point of apostolicity, the question of mass media broaches a question of what kind of authority and continuity is present in the teaching. Open access means not only *increased* access but *undifferentiated* access. Following the Second World War, a variety of Christian thinkers began to be concerned about what Spanish philosopher José Ortega y Gasset would name as "the mass man," humanity without differentiations, which created a crisis of how authority (apostolic or otherwise) worked.[16]

This is an important feature for us to note in the conversations around apostolicity, but the question of the medium of Christian transmission vis-à-vis

---

14. McGowan, "Fulton Sheen Affair," 28.

15. McGowan, "Fulton Sheen Affair," 34. Though Sheen's popularity in Canada would wane by 1957, the effects of his show on Canadian religious life would endure, not least in prompting Toronto-based clergy to coordinate and cooperate among themselves in broadcasting efforts, realizing the promise that the medium held for evangelization of the country (38). The translocal diffusion of religious authority after Sheen remains largely unstudied.

16. José Ortega y Gasset, *The Revolt of the Masses* (New York: Norton, 1994). In the wake of the Second World War's defeat of European fascism, an increasing tendency emerged in Europe and the United States (and their allies and colonies) toward technocratic solutions, to facilitate democratic processes over against the autocratic politics of the Axis powers. For the details of these figures, see Alan Jacobs, *Year of Our Lord 1943: Christian Humanism in an Age of Crisis* (Oxford: Oxford University Press, 2018). Tim Wu's *The Curse of Bigness: Antitrust in the New Gilded Age* (New York: Columbia University Press, 2018) draws parallels between the antitrust period of the early twentieth century and the late twentieth century's shift back toward large-scale, managerial solutions to social problems. Innumerable examinations of these effects across the globe during the century exist, but our focus will be on the religious effects of this phenomenon.

authority is not a novel one.[17] Questions regarding the appropriateness of translating Greek texts into Latin, of using the printing press, and of the technology of the open-air revival all serve as pre-twentieth-century precedents for the challenge of how a new technological advancement evokes questions of who counts as an authoritative interpreter of the Christian tradition, and how continuity functions for church authority.

The implications of this history are well documented with respect to the rise of managerial culture in the late twentieth century and the companion phenomenon of the rise of mass culture, in which local traditions became subsumed by more homogenizing forces. Religious media is an important part of this story, particularly because of the intrinsic link between *what* content is communicated and *how* that content is communicated. The assumption that televangelism and a local parish sermon constitute equivalent forms of communication would have been curious to earlier decades, and would accordingly evoke questions as to what changes are made by televangelism's modality, establishing religious authority outside established traditional modes of transmission.

That both Catholics and Protestants adopted these modes of communication does not mean they struggled with this challenge in the same way. Rather, it indicates how both Catholics and Protestants, in applying the principle of apostolicity in their respective contexts, came to terms with electronic media, not just as expedient ways of communicating the faith but as means that complicated what counts as faithful communication of the faith and, in particular, to what they should accord authority. To turn to a figure like Aimee Semple McPherson—founder of the Foursquare Church and for a time the most widely publicized Protestant radio evangelist[18]—as a supplemental or devotional authority was one thing; to look to such figures as the bearers of the apostolic message was another.

---

17. For a more recent iteration of these concerns, see *The New Evangelization for the Transmission of the Christian Faith*, in which the synod of Catholic bishops took up the question of evangelization amid an influx of new technologies relating to the Internet and digital media. Synod of Bishops, *The New Evangelization for the Transmission of the Christian Faith*, instrumentum laboris for 2012 (Vatican City: General Secretariat of the Synod of Bishops; Libreria Editrice Vaticana, 2012), 59–60, https://www.vatican.va/roman_curia/synod/documents/rc_synod_doc_20120619_instrumentum-xiii_en.html.

18. McPherson was pioneering in multiple ways, but relevant to this story is her status as the second woman in the United States to own a radio broadcasting license, significant for expanding her ministry reach. See Edith L. Blumhofer, *Aimee Semple McPherson: Everybody's Sister* (Grand Rapids: Eerdmans, 1993), 183.

Who Is a Bearer of the Apostolic Faith?

The proliferation of religious mass media was one of the key ways in which questions of apostolicity and authority began to expand beyond the official organs of the church, but in the twentieth century, the questions of who counted as bearers of apostolic authority continued to expand as well.[19]

Pope Paul VI's decree on the apostolate of the laity, *Apostolicam Actuositatem*, describes how "the areas for the lay apostolate have been immensely widened particularly in fields that have been for the most part open to the laity alone," naming the emergence of Catholic lay advocacy and instruction groups that have expanded Catholic influence into various corners of the world.[20] But the decree explicitly names the way this plays out among the ordained and the laity differently, with the expectation of unity: "In the Church there is a diversity of ministry but a oneness of mission. Christ conferred on the Apostles and their successors the duty of teaching, sanctifying, and ruling in His name and power. But the laity likewise share in the priestly, prophetic, and royal office of Christ and therefore have their own share in the mission of the whole people of God in the Church and in the world."[21] As we saw in the discussion of holiness (chap. 2), this configuration creates a unified mission and calling, but not one in which notions of holiness can be maximally shared between laity and clergy. Here, the text differentiates between the life situations of laity and clergy, indicating that authority is not shared equally between them, though apostolicity belongs to both.

If holiness raises a question about this arrangement with respect to what counts as a full expression of the church's holiness, apostolicity raises this question in Catholicism with respect to *gender* as well. For in Catholicism, and several other traditions, the clergy were composed only of men, meaning that apostolicity, while shared between laity and clergy, was not shared in this

---

19. This is one of the many ways in which the marks of the church are unified—the stresses of one mark become shared stresses. Therefore, it is not surprising that, if the marks are unified, we should find the questions of the church's unity echoed here, this time under the auspices of authority. Questions of church unity have frequently involved questions of in whom the church is visibly unified. Accordingly, a crisis of church unity involved a crisis of who the bearers of that unity are.

20. Paul VI, *Apostolicam Actuositatem* (Vatican City: Holy See, 1965), 1, https://www.vatican.va/archive/hist_councils/ii_vatican_council/documents/vat-ii_decree_19651118_apostolicam-actuositatem_en.html#.

21. Paul VI, *Apostolicam Actuositatem*, 2.

differentiated way between men and women. Depictions of women leading in worship date back to the earliest centuries, and these accounts dovetail with sporadic evidence in the New Testament to create a picture that, while not the norm across Christendom, opens the question of the relationship between gender and the mediation of Christ's presence and authority across time.[22] Ordination of women among Pentecostals occurred with regularity, as an extension of their commitments to the gifts of the Spirit being distributed in an egalitarian fashion.[23]

But among other Christian traditions, the links between apostolic succession and gender became more ambiguous. Baptists, for example, have had long traditions of commissioning women for ministry in international missions. Among Southern Baptists, two of the annual missions offerings are in the names of Annie Armstrong and Lottie Moon, nineteenth-century missionaries whose duties regularly involved preaching and teaching, though their legacies are generally not described in the categories of the handing on of the historic Christian faith. And yet, the 1984 Southern Baptist Convention, in a special statement on women's ordination, denies that women could be engaged in a "role of authority over men," on the basis of preserving "a submission God requires" because of Eve's role in the fall.[24] The question of authority resurfaced, as the 1983 statement on this topic had opened the door for future discussion, but the 1984 follow-up statement sidestepped the discussion of ecclesial authority by emphasizing the ministry role of women in "building godly homes."[25]

In other words, it is not so much that apostolicity is not open to women in this tradition, but that their mode of apostolicity is envisioned by the

---

22. On the evidence for women's leadership in churches from the earliest era, see Caroll D. Osburn, ed., *Essays on Women in Earliest Christianity* (Eugene, OR: Wipf & Stock, 2007).

23. As Joy Langford argues in "Feminism and Leadership in the Pentecostal Movement," *Feminist Theology* 26 (2017): 69–79, because Pentecostal leadership initially was intrinsically related to a display of the spiritual gifts, the barriers to recognizing women as church leaders remained historically lower. On this question historically in Pentecostalism, see Margaret English de Alminana and Lois E. Olena, *Women in Pentecostal and Charismatic Ministry: Informing a Dialogue on Gender, Church, and Ministry* (Leiden: Brill, 2016). The early Pentecostal narrative "The Apostolic Faith Restored" likewise emphasizes the ways in which women served as justifying exemplars of the Pentecostal emphasis on speaking in tongues and are frequently named as taking leadership in international missions. See "The Apostolic Faith Restored," in *Three Early Pentecostal Tracts*, ed. Donald W. Dayton (New York: Garland, 1985).

24. J. Gordon Melton, ed., *Women's Ordination: Official Statements from Religious Bodies and Ecumenical Organizations* (Detroit: Gale Research, 1991), 236.

25. Melton, *Women's Ordination*, 236.

Southern Baptists as *pre-ecclesial* or *extra-ecclesial*, limited to private authority that provides the basis for public authority or in the extraordinary space of international missions. Similar acknowledgments regarding the de facto religious authority of women can be found among American Lutherans in 1973, though with the opposite outcome: the Lutheran statement advocating for women's ordination rests upon the free movement of the Spirit, who has liberated women in society, in the home, and now in the church.[26] The Lutheran statement says out loud what the Baptist statements seem to be unable to say: the practice of women's authority already occurs (both in the extraordinary conditions of the mission field and in ordinary church life), with ordination making official what has always been the case.[27]

If gender is one face of the question of who the bearers of apostolic authority are, much later in the twentieth century, the issues of ordination of gay and lesbian ministers began to emerge in denominations, precisely as questions of apostolicity. By the 1960s, gay and lesbian ministers were more visible in the United States, culminating with the establishment of the Metropolitan Community Church in 1972. Beginning as a single congregation in San Francisco, the MCC began to emerge as a denominational home for gay and lesbian Christians from within previous institutional bodies.[28] Debates in Episcopal and Presbyterian bodies were soon to follow, broaching the question of whether noncelibate gay and lesbian persons could be bearers of apostolic authority.[29]

Unlike the question of women's ordination, where those in opposition had offered various answers across time,[30] opposition to the ordination of noncelibate gay and lesbian Christians rested upon the link of behavior, authority, and sexual identity: In what ways did same-sex relations offer a different account

---

26. Melton, *Women's Ordination*, 119: The document *Can Women Serve in the Ordained Ministry?* flatly declares, "The times have changed. Women have taken their place with men in our society" (119), then offers its exegetical and theological arguments for the change.

27. Melton, *Women's Ordination*, 124. To the question, "Does the ordination of women make any practical difference," the document reads, "Yes and no. It is difficult to be so certain. Already women are ministering in ways that cover every function of the ordained ministry. They teach, lead in worship, counsel, organize, and administer, baptize. . . . And they preach—regularly on the missions fields. . . . Yet they do not preach in our pulpits!"

28. For the broader contours of this movement, see Brian Stanley, *Christianity in the Twentieth Century: A World History* (Princeton: Princeton University Press, 2018), 277–87.

29. Stanley, *Christianity in the Twentieth Century*, 285.

30. See William Witt, *Icons of Christ: A Biblical and Systematic Theology for Women's Ordination* (Waco: Baylor University Press, 2020), 51–74, 189–270, for the historically shifting arguments against women's ordination.

of apostolic authority? Seeing changing attitudes with regard to sexual identity as a divine opportunity, the Episcopal study on "changing patterns of sexuality and family life" contends that gay ordinands need to be brought in because to discount gay ordinands would be to ignore the work of the Spirit, the one who gives continuity to the church over time.[31]

The questions of noncelibate gay and lesbian ordination and women's ordination are frequently treated as companion issues of equity and justice in ordination practices, but from the vantage point of apostolicity, the question of the relation of sexual practice to apostolicity becomes salient. The arguments against the ordination of women, as improper bearers of church authority across time, shift to maintain women's de facto spiritual authority limited to non-ecclesial spheres, whereas the arguments against noncelibate gay and lesbian ordination rest upon the need to maintain historical continuity amid new cultural conditions.

One way to frame this issue is to say that the issue is not solely whether Scripture forbids or permits particular persons to be leaders but whether, as Joseph Ratzinger wrote in 1986, this ordination retains the figural significance of Christ before the congregation.[32] If apostolicity is, in part, a question of how Christ is known in and through a church—how the era of the apostles connects to our own age—then from Ratzinger's vantage point, the signifier of Christ's presence matters. This is where the two issues, appearing together historically, begin to diverge. It is not clear, as we have seen, that

---

31. "The challenge to the Church to respond creatively to changing patterns of sexuality and family life in America must be seen as an instance of the Holy Spirit leading us to respond to the blessing and claim of the Realm of God foreshadowed and made continually present in the life of Jesus Christ" (Task Force on Changing Patterns of Sexuality and Family Life, *Report of the Task Force on Changing Patterns of Sexuality and Family Life* [Newark, NJ: Episcopal Church, Diocese of Newark, 1987), 4, https://www.episcopalarchives.org/sites/default/files/sclm-c056/diocesan/031_Newark_1987.pdf). One counterargument deployed here is that ordination in this way immanentizes eschatological realities, conflating the newness of the eschaton with the present injunctions against same-sex behavior in the New Testament; in doing so, such ordination abolishes any sense of historical continuity in favor of apocalyptic novelty. Simon Vibert, "Divine Order and Sexual Conduct," in *The Way Forward? Christian Voices on Homosexuality and the Church*, ed. Timothy Bradshaw (Grand Rapids: Eerdmans, 2003), 113–27.

32. "To chose [sic] someone of the same sex for one's sexual activity is to annul the rich symbolism and meaning, not to mention the goals, of the Creator's sexual design. Homosexual activity is not a complementary union, able to transmit life; and so it thwarts the call to a life of that form of self-giving which the Gospel says is the essence of Christian living." Joseph Ratzinger, "Letter to the Bishops of the Catholic Church on the Pastoral Care of Homosexual Persons" (Rome: Congregation for the Doctrine of the Faith, 1986), 7, https://www.vatican.va/roman_curia/congregations/cfaith/documents/rc_con_cfaith_doc_19861001_homosexual-persons_en.html.

gender qualifications bear out in any of the most significant elements of apostolicity, whether with respect to doctrine, origins of the church, or the qualitative life of the church.[33] Gay and lesbian ordination is differentiated here, not for reasons of gender, but according to how sexual activity affects the ability of the ordained to be an icon of Christ for the congregation. Tying these ordination questions together under the rubric of justice highlights one important dynamic in the ordination question but misses the relevant distinction apostolicity wants to name: that LGBTQ+ ordination is one that turns on a different axis than women's ordination with respect to what it means to be a figure of Christ for the congregation.

Continuity of History: The Question of Episcopal Succession

Episcopal succession remained one of the live questions, particularly as reunion movements among Protestant branches and between Catholics and the Orthodox burgeoned. But the question of episcopal succession was not simply a question of establishing an unsplintered family tree that could trace its roots back to the apostles themselves. The question of episcopal succession—of how figures of authority were authorized through their connection to the apostles—mattered because it signified the degree to which a church's worship and faith was universal and not parochial.

Reunion efforts between the Orthodox and Roman Catholic churches will help illustrate this. The Joint International Commission for Theological Dialogue between the two churches proposed a series of working statements between 1982 and 1988, with the goal of common worship. Other issues were involved here, such as what the Eucharist is and how baptism is related to it. But, at the bottom, a common worship necessitated a common understanding of presidency, of who was qualified to celebrate the Eucharist—that is, a common understanding of apostolic succession. Succession here is not an abstract doctrine so much as a necessary condition for unified worship.[34] That these talks would be suspended in the early 1990s after the resurgence of the Catholic Eastern Churches—churches who recognized the authority of

---

33. The one possible objection that could be raised to apostolicity on the question of gender is that it is not recognized across the broader church body. But at that point, it seems we are approaching an impossibly high bar, higher than that of the ordination of gentiles.

34. Paul McPartlan, "Primacy and Eucharist: Recent Catholic Perspectives," in Chryssavgis, *Primacy in the Church*, 219.

the papacy but wished to retain separate governance and liturgy—underscores the seriousness with which these questions of authority and worship were connected.[35]

In view of the stakes for the liturgy, questions of *primacy* within apostolicity became significant. Primacy, for both East and West, names the one capable of commissioning the church to be this body sent into the world and to carry out its vocation of being a community. If the church's existence in the world mirrors God's own nature as the One who sends into the world, this needs to be mirrored not only in the body but in the temporal head of the body.[36] It is this figure, bearing specific pastoral responsibilities for the *shape* of the communion, who, Ware notes, is part of how the churches bear out apostolicity together. And thus, it is of great concern who these persons are!

From the perspective of the Orthodox churches, the Roman emphasis on the pope as the head of the apostolic communion overreaches to establish the papacy over against other patriarchs. The pope has long been described as the "first among equals," but such a posture does not guarantee infallibility. To quote Ware again:

> Christ has assured us that he will be present in the Church to the end of the world . . . and that the Spirit of truth will guide her into all truth. . . . But exactly how Christ's presence will be manifested, in what specific manner the guidance of the Paraclete will become apparent, who will be the spokesman of God's truth—this we cannot know in advance. . . . It is only in the continuing life of the Church that it becomes apparent whether the Spirit of God has spoken through the assembled bishops or not.[37]

Ware's comments here highlight that the form of apostolicity—to have a pope or not—is not incidental. Distinguishing between juridical concerns and concerns for the quality of the church's life, Ware suggests, is a false distinction, as the two are mutually confirming.

The interrelationship between apostolic content and apostolic structure traveled together in Protestant circles as well, underscoring this concern that

35. McPartlan, "Primacy and Eucharist," 220.
36. The impression by outsiders that these structures simply exist for institutional maintenance is not lost on the participants of these discussions. As the late Kallistos Ware put it, synods, councils, and administrative structures are more dynamic than their critics give them credit for, but they still must answer the question as to whether they exist by convention or by *jure divino* (divine right). See Kallistos Ware, foreword to Chryssavgis, *Primacy in the Church*, 7–8.
37. Ware, "Primacy, Collegiality, and the People of God," 102–3.

apostolicity—as structured as it was formally—made sense only when it was qualitatively present. This dual set of concerns complicated constructive discussions among churches—and not just along the Protestant/Catholic divide.

Consider here the 1989 Porvoo Common Statement (1989), a document that came about from discussions between the Church of England and various Scandinavian Lutheran churches. The churches had generally maintained friendly relations, but a 1968 report raised the question as to whether there could be full communion between the Church of England and other nearly identical churches in Scandinavia that were divided from the Church of England on the question of the historic episcopate.[38] Over the next thirty years, various reports and dialogues were held between Anglican and Lutheran bodies. What was at issue was the way in which certain Lutheran communions no longer retained historical episcopal succession; their bishops had no connection to an unbroken episcopate in the way that Anglicans claimed to have.

The union among these churches in terms of their theological views carried similar apostolic content, in other words, but the question of form remained a dividing line. The 1987 document "Episcopé in Relation to the Mission of the Church Today" proposed keeping commitments to full fellowship on a more ad hoc basis because of this impasse. While acknowledging the historical reasons for abandoning a contiguous connection to the past—that church leaders had been corrupt, and that juridicism had been the excuse to squelch faithful risks in the present—the 1987 document names the episcopate as the way in which ministry gained both coherence and supervision.[39]

Porvoo resolves this material difference of apostolicity by writing that because apostolic continuity "is carried by more than one means," churches may continue to honor one another's formal processes out of deference to the historical ways in which those churches have developed. This may seem like a theological punt, an indifference to how apostolic continuity is maintained, but what it conveys, rather, is a respect for how a church embodies this connection and an acknowledgment that this embodiment is not simply a matter of present choice but of

---

38. Ola Tjørhom, ed., *Apostolicity and Unity: Essays on the Porvoo Common Statement* (Grand Rapids: Eerdmans, 2002), 3. The conversations among these groups that dated back to 1909 likewise centered on this question. Swedish churches held that "no particular organization of the church and of its ministry is instituted *jure divino*" while insisting that it was not indifferent to the question of historic episcopal succession (Tjørhom, *Apostolicity and Unity*, 17). Following the mergers of churches in Southern India in the 1950s and 1960s, the question of intercommunion became more pressing globally for other Lutherans.

39. Anglican-Lutheran Consultation, "Episcopé in Relation to the Mission of the Church Today," para. 20, cited in Tjørhom, *Apostolicity and Unity*, 26.

how a church has carried forth that embodiment over time. The histories that make the present possible are valued by God, it seems; therefore, to renounce the histories would be to disavow the good God had done in that divided history.[40]

In the end, Porvoo became part of the way that Anglicans and Lutherans were able to fully recognize one another's ordinations and enter into full communion. Couching the question of apostolicity as a concern relative to the heritage of the past could be read as a disregard for apostolic order, but what surfaces here is rather a recognition that apostolicity is not merely a matter of the present deposit of faith but of continuity with a *broken* past. Whatever present faithfulness a church has—and however it faithfully transmits the faith in the present—depends on it not writing off its past, not disavowing the broken past God has worked through to make its present faithfulness what it is.

Apostolicity and Its Cultural Challenges

Thus far, we have been haunted by the question of materiality when it comes to the apostolic nature of the church: for the church to convey the same faith, it cannot do so simply by relaying the same idea but must bear some kind of continuity with the beginning. But if the question here is not simply one of continuity through the ordained but of continuity as a property of the church as a whole, the question of materiality becomes more complex. For churches are composed not only of the ordained but of the laity.

Thus, apostolicity becomes a question not only of theological transmission but of culture, not only of speaking but of hearing. Ghanian theologian Kwame Bediako, in reflecting on what a Greco-Roman heritage might mean for twentieth-century Ghana, writes, "With the exception of the dominant role of Latin in the European phase of Christianity and in some sectors of Roman Catholicism, Christianity has developed as a 'vernacular' faith. The significance of this has been most marked in Africa, where the early possession of the Scripture in mother-tongue meant that African peoples had access to the original sources of Christian teaching. . . . Each of us with the Bible in our mother-tongue can truly claim to hear God speaking to us in our own language."[41] Bediako's point is this: the intercultural development of Christianity has been obscured to the degree that African lay theology appears to

---

40. Tjørhom, *Apostolicity and Unity*, 29.
41. Kwame Bediako, "Jesus in African Culture: A Ghanian Perspective," in *Jesus and the Gospel in Africa: History and Experience* (Maryknoll, NY: Orbis Books, 2004), 32.

be a bridge too far, but only because of the historical staying power of Latin. But in a post–Vatican II world, which emphasized not only the need for the faith to be communicated in local languages but also the reception of the faith by the laity, the materiality of apostolicity began to emerge more clearly.

The question behind Bediako's argument is this: In the era prior to the twentieth century, was apostolicity made possible by colonialism? The answer seems to be that, at the minimum, colonialism played a material role, though it remains debated whether it is the substrate upon which a global unity of faith is built. But even setting aside the role of colonialism specifically (discussed in the previous chapter), questions began to be raised about the role of material cultures more broadly in how apostolicity had functioned. Particularly, it raised questions about whether the collapse of those cultures meant needing to reconceive how apostolicity could function in the future.

Turning briefly to two very different examples—apostolic continuity in Catholic and evangelical church spaces in China—will help highlight the role that *non-ecclesial* elements play in sustaining apostolic continuity. Like Ghana, China had a lengthy history of imperialism, followed by the twentieth century's anti-imperialist and anticolonialist turn.[42] Despite these similarities, the status of Catholicism in China is distinct, in that (as discussed in chap. 1) 1958 marked the separation of Chinese Catholicism from Roman jurisdiction. Beginning in 1949, with the founding of the People's Republic of China under Mao Zedong, Chinese Catholics came under greater scrutiny, as their transnational governance made Catholicism more difficult to discourage than Protestant groups that had emphasized local leadership and a more decentralized polity. The papal nuncio of China was expelled in 1951. In response, the pope warned that a national church would be detrimental to Chinese Catholicism. In 1958, Chinese bishops took over dioceses in Hankau and Wuchang, and the bishops they were replacing were jailed, with their representatives.

In his 1958 *Ad Apostolorum Principis*, Pius XII outlines the problem of apostolicity occasioned by these events in this way:

> Assuming false and unjust premises, [those suspicious of the Apostolic See] are not afraid to take a position which would confine within a narrow scope

---

42. There are innumerable excellent studies on Chinese Christianity. For histories on China's relationship to Christianity and the effects of colonialism on that relationship, see in particular Brian Stanley, *The Bible and the Flag: Protestant Missions and British Imperialism in the Nineteenth and Twentieth Centuries* (Leicester, UK: Apollos, 1990); and Ralph R. Covell, *Confucius, the Buddha, and Christ: A History of the Gospel in Chinese* (Maryknoll, NY: Orbis Books, 1986).

the supreme teaching authority of the Church, claiming that there are certain questions—such as those which concern social and economic matters—in which Catholics may ignore the teachings and the directives of this Apostolic See. This opinion—it seems entirely unnecessary to demonstrate its existence—is utterly false and full of error because, as We declared a few years ago to a special meeting of Our Venerable Brethren in the episcopacy: "The power of the Church is in no sense limited to so-called 'strictly religious matters'"; but the whole matter of the natural law, its institution, interpretation and application, in so far as the moral aspect is concerned, are within its power.[43]

The questions of governance laid the groundwork for a separation of the church's influence—for limiting the church to governing purely invisible and immaterial things. Doing so, however, had consequences for viewing how apostolicity operated. If questions such as material distribution and economics were not within the church's jurisdiction, then neither were material questions about how its continuity happened:

> For it has been clearly and expressly laid down in the canons that it pertains to the one Apostolic See to judge whether a person is fit for the dignity and burden of the episcopacy, and that complete freedom in the nomination of bishops is the right of the Roman Pontiff. But if, as happens at times, some persons or groups are permitted to participate in the selection of an episcopal candidate, this is lawful only if the Apostolic See has allowed it in express terms and in each particular case for clearly defined persons or groups, the conditions and circumstances being very plainly determined.[44]

In 1958, when pressed to answer the question of whether material conditions and apostolicity have anything to do with one another, the Vatican forcefully issued a rejoinder that the two questions of church and of the material conditions in which the church persists are of a piece.

From the vantage point of the West, the material dynamics affecting apostolicity in China bore a particular name: Communism. Though Chinese Marxism was distinct from other forms of Marxism globally,[45] the "Three Self"

---

43. Pius XII, *Ad Apostolorum Principis* (Vatican City: Holy See, 1958), 30–32, https://www.vatican.va/content/pius-xii/en/encyclicals/documents/hf_p-xii_enc_29061958_ad-apostolorum-principis.html.

44. Pius XII, *Ad Apostolorum Principis*, 38.

45. The intricacies of Chinese Marxism with respect to Christianity are parsed in numerous places. See Denis R. Janz, *World Christianity and Marxism* (Oxford: Oxford University Press,

movement complicated the question of what relationship Chinese Catholicism had to its European counterparts. A 1960 document from Archbishop Pi Shu-shih, chair of the National Patriotic Catholic Association, indicates that over four hundred bishops, priests, and laypersons were serving in government positions, though by 1966, all churches in China were closed.[46] By 1972, churches were reopening, and by the 1980s, Catholic church facilities were opened (including seminaries) under the jurisdiction of the National Patriotic Catholic Association.[47]

The position of underground Catholic leaders remains difficult to know, but what appears via official communications indicates that the relationship between China and Rome was significantly altered. As articulated by Bishop Tu Shihua, the bishop and the local church "possess the right of independent self-rule and self-management in line with the apostolic tradition of collective leadership and democratic administration. No other bishop is allowed to interfere, to restrict, still less to deprive a bishop of this ordinary, immediate, proper power awarded by God. On the contrary, it must be respected."[48]

In this way, the perfect form of apostolicity, as articulated by Tu, hews close to many charismatic notions: that apostolic power comes from God and cannot be abrogated, even by another bishop. Consider, for example, the Latter Rain Pentecostal movement. In 1910, D. Wesley Myland articulated a form of Pentecostalism that emphasized increased pneumatological signs prior to the end of the world, with "latter rain" being the outpouring of God's Spirit after the dry period of medieval Christianity. In 1947, the Latter Rain movement gained momentum following a series of Canadian revivals that drew together leaders from the Independent Assemblies of God, charismatic churches, and numerous free churches.[49] For these leaders, apostolicity was a function of God's action evident in the manifestation of various spiritual signs and wonders. Apostolicity was not guaranteed by denominational structures

---

1998), esp. 123–49; Yiwu Liao, *God Is Red: The Secret Story of How Christianity Survived and Flourished in Communist China* (New York: HarperOne Books, 2011); Khio-Khng Yeo, *Chairman Mao Meets the Apostle Paul: Christianity, Communism, and the Hope of China* (Grand Rapids: Brazos, 2002); Huilin Yang, *China, Christianity, and the Question of Culture* (Waco: Baylor University Press, 2010); and Zheng Yangwen, ed. *Sinicizing Christianity* (Leiden: Brill, 2017).

46. Janz, *World Christianity and Marxism*, 135–36.
47. Janz, *World Christianity and Marxism*, 142–43.
48. Janz, *World Christianity and Marxism*, 144.
49. John Weaver, *The New Apostolic Reformation: History of Modern Charismatic Reformation* (Jefferson, NC: McFarland and Company, 2016), 28–29.

or by contiguous leadership, but by a gifted apostle who then forged networks with other gifted apostles.[50] Future leaders came into being through their association with present apostles, much like Timothy came to be a leader through his relationship to the apostle Paul.

In both the example of Tu and in the Latter Rain movement, we find a suspicion about the imposition of external measures to name whether the faith transmitted is valid. Whatever else we might make of the integration between patriotism and Catholicism in the Chinese Church, the Chinese bishops were not alone in identifying the increasing role that non-European cultures were wanting to play in ascertaining what faithful apostolicity looked like.

To see this further, consider Latin America's reaction to Vatican II. Much has been written on the ways in which the council was received by the Catholic global communion, particularly with respect to the second Episcopal Council of Latin America (CELAM) in Medellín, Colombia, in 1968. The work of Vatican II was taken up there, but through a particular lens that emphasized "a preferential option for the poor" and an approval of Christian base communities, both of which open up the way in which apostolicity is intertwined with material conditions in which the church finds itself. In responding to the sixteen documents of the Second Vatican Council, the Medellín Statement of the Latin American bishops begins by documenting the material plight of their dioceses.

The documents of CELAM 1968 were unambiguous that the poverty and violence of the land created a different kind of condition for how the church could continue into the future. In the words of Jon Sobrino, reflecting on the commitment of Vatican II to the people, "The term *people* has a historical, social, economic, dialectical and confrontational reality and so does this people's destiny: *crucifixion*. Crucified people and people of God may converge in reality. In the Council *texts* the term *people* is less historic, whereas in the texts cited above [letters of Óscar Romero and Ignacio Ellacuría], it is radically historical. The *crucified people* points to Jesus crucified, and thus christologizes the people, taking a further leap than that taken by the Council when it ecclesiologized them."[51] As in the preface to CELAM 1968, Sobrino points to the historical dynamic that reconfigures what counts as authentic authority: the experience of having suffered with the people.

50. Weaver, *New Apostolic Reformation*, 29.
51. Jon Sobrino, "The 'Church of the Poor' Did Not Prosper at Vatican II," in "Vatican II," ed. Silvia Scatena et al., special issue, *Concilium* 3 (2012): 82.

This assessment that the rubric of apostolicity needed to be expanded was not limited to Latin American Catholics. Kathleen Holscher, in her examination of New Mexican parishes after the council, observes a similar dynamic in the rural towns around Santa Fe, in which less than 25 percent of parishes had a resident priest.[52] What followed Vatican II was, Holscher observes, the emergence not just of laity performing the work of ordinary ministry, but of the laity initially providing nonsacramental leadership. Over time, however, the divide between lay service and ministry grew thin: "Listening to their accounts means acknowledging that the Second Vatican Council, and its emphasis on the immediacy of God's presence in the lives of ordinary Catholics, helped reorient lay spirituality. Developments in Catholic life in the half century since the Council have done the same. Today Catholic spirituality in New Mexico includes an evangelical strain, one that refuses to be summed up as the product of external intermediaries, whether they are the rules and leaders of a diocese or the customs of a region."[53]

If apostolicity (as we saw in the discussions surrounding the various forms of lay Catholicism earlier in this chapter) entails new forms of authorization, then the role of material scarcity reframes the nature of apostolicity in ways that could not have been anticipated by the framers of the documents of Vatican II. To name the argument between Europe and Latin America as one of liberation theology versus European theology is to miss seeing that liberation theology grew out of a broader concern: the question of how material conditions shape what the possibilities of apostolicity are.[54]

The fields of moral theology and ethics likewise found themselves shifting in significant ways, as analogous questions were being asked by Protestants and Catholics about how the moral life should be transmitted, and what it meant for the authority of the church to have salience in the modern world. For both Catholic and Protestant moral theology, the century offered titanic

---

52. Kathleen Holscher, "Lay Workers in the Rural Churches of New Mexico: Vatican II, Memory, and Ministry," in *Catholics in the Vatican II Era: Local Histories of a Global Event*, ed. K. Cummings, T. Matovina, and R. Orsi (Cambridge: Cambridge University Press, 2017), 110–34.

53. Holscher, "Lay Workers in the Rural Churches," 128.

54. Teodoro C. Bacani's analysis of the reaction in the Philippines to the council mirrors the Latin American response in similar ways, emphasizing that any future church there would likewise be a church of the poor, a church in which the laity took more of a direct role in the future of faithfulness there. See "Church of the Poor: The Church in the Philippines' Reception of Vatican II," *East Asian Pastoral Review* 42 (2005): 147–64.

shifts, not only with respect to the sources of moral wisdom but with respect to what was being offered to Christian congregations broadly.

As the twentieth century opened, Catholic moral theologians remained deeply indebted to the manualist tradition, which broadly treated moral questions according to defined traditions from the received tradition and applied them according to the particulars of a situation. This was also reflected in the reception of the "Angelic Doctor," Thomas Aquinas. Aquinas's work had received increased attention in the late nineteenth century,[55] but in the first half of the century, his treatment of sin was published independent from the other dimensions of the *Summa Theologica* that would have emphasized not only the avoidance of vice but the cultivation of virtue.[56]

Over the course of the twentieth century, the manualist tradition of the early twentieth century was challenged in three ways, and with it, its salience for communicating the shape of the moral life in the twentieth century. First, the role of integrative psychology in pastoral care became more emphasized, that persons are moved by more than reason in their moral deliberations, and that these dynamics should be given more weight. Second, the increased attention to social questions as opposed to questions of personal vice made some of the material of the manuals less immediately applicable to questions being asked by Catholics of the middle to late century; increasingly, papal encyclicals leading up to the Second Vatican Council addressed not only birth control but war, poverty, economic injustice, and relations with non-Christian religions. Third, while the manuals addressed predominantly vice and duty, virtue was often left undertheorized, or at the end of the manual treatments.[57]

As the Second Vatican Council approached, increased attention to the cultivation of virtue and to the close reading of Scripture displaced the manualist tradition, both in the formation of priests and in pastoral practice. As *Optatam Totius* (the conciliar document concerning the formation of priests) reads, "Special care must be given to the perfecting of moral theology. Its scientific exposition, nourished more on the teaching of the Bible, should shed light on the loftiness of the calling of the faithful in Christ and the obligation that is

---

55. See Leo XIII, *Aeterni Patris* (1879); and Pius X, *Doctoris Angelici* (1914), which argued that the received tradition could not be understood from the work of Aquinas.

56. James F. Keenan, *A History of Catholic Moral Theology in the Twentieth Century: From Confessing Sins to Liberating Consciences* (London: Continuum, 2010).

57. Keenan, *History of Catholic Moral Theology*, 26–30.

theirs of bearing fruit in charity for the life of the world."[58] Attention to the personal development of the Christian became more emphasized than it had been in the manualist specification of penance. The challenge in this shift, as exemplified by the incorporation of attention to the psychological strata of the moral life, is that one could reach conclusions that diverged dramatically from those of previous generations, all while reading the same texts. Speaking authoritatively could no longer proceed as it had in the past. It had to attend to new dynamics in the lives of the faithful.

This shift toward social ethics and virtues was matched in many ways by developments in Protestant life as well. As Catholic moral theology broadly began in the parish context and grew outward to embrace questions of the common good, Protestant moral theology—at least in the American context—began as a question of the public good. As Gary Dorrien explains, in both sides of the segregated American church, the question of what the moral life entailed was, from its roots, already intertwined with a renewed public life.[59] Whether located in the originating work of W. E. B. Dubois or in the largely Anglo-American traditions of the Social Gospel, the moral life of the Protestant Christian was intertwined with facing down social questions affecting the country, be they questions about Darwinism, poverty, alcoholism, war, or racism. Both Protestants and Catholics thus were navigating how to speak authoritatively of the Christian moral life and were coming to similar conclusions: however the moral life is passed on, it can no longer avoid the individual (and sometimes inaccessible) dimensions of conscience, psychology, and material conditions, in the process altering questions of how apostolic authority functioned in the moral life of the believer.

Who Gets to Be Apostolic? Catholic and Evangelical Lay Options

If the question of institutional continuity is one of the most obvious aspects of apostolicity, the other is lay practice. The division here lies not at the level of "experience" versus "institution," as if one were possible apart from the other, but rather between one experience and another—specifically, between the different ways in which these groups embodied apostolic teaching and practice.

58. Paul VI, *Optatam Totius* (Vatican City: Holy See, 1965), quoted in Keenan, *History of Catholic Moral Theology*, 95.
59. Gary Dorrien, *Social Ethics in the Making: Interpreting an American Tradition* (Malden, MA: Wiley-Blackwell, 2009), 6.

In his *Christifideles Laici*, John Paul II lays out criteria that historian Massimo Faggioli finds useful for evaluating the perplexing field of lay Catholic movements: (1) apostolic aim, (2) cooperation with the hierarchy, (3) unity of the lay apostolate, and (4) mandate of the church hierarchy.[60] There have always been Christian lay associations, but what makes the movements in Catholicism from the late nineteenth century to the twentieth century significant is that these movements come into view alongside the rise of the nation-state: continuity of the faith by the laity must negotiate not only the distentions of time but the dissensions within global politics as well. To carry on the faith in the twentieth century now involved questions of how both the aims of the faith and the authority of the church were negotiated.

Long before the Second Vatican Council, in which *Lumen Gentium* affirmed the need for the laity to be engaged as "the people of God," having a distinct role to play in the receiving of church teaching, lay Catholics had been organizing for social advocacy and transformation. Some, such as the nineteenth-century Catholic Youth Organization in Italy, were movements intended as social outreach under ecclesiastical supervision.[61] But others, like the Italian Catholic Federation of Students, were organized by lay persons and only later were brought into collaboration with church hierarchy.[62]

The different groups approached the apostolicity of the laity differently, with their approaches paralleling another shift taking place in the Catholic Church—a shift in thinking about the ways in which the church itself is a juridical body, a *societas perfectas*, and the ways in which the church should be conceived of as a movement that makes use of political forms.[63] How these

---

60. Mossimo Faggioli, *Sorting Out Catholicism: A Brief History of the New Ecclesial Movements* (Collegeville, MN: Liturgical Press, 2011), 67. See also John Paul II, *Christifideles Laici* (Vatican City: Holy See, 1988), https://www.vatican.va/content/john-paul-ii/en/apost_exhortations/documents/hf_jp-ii_exh_30121988_christifideles-laici.html.

61. Faggioli, *Sorting Out Catholicism*, 39.

62. Leo XIII's *Fin Dal Principio* (On the Education of the Clergy), in addition to laying out an agenda for the education of priests, connects the decline in clerical education to the popular emergence of lay movements and the need for priests to be able to offer better instruction to these movements: "They will promote among the Catholic laity those institutions which they all recognize as really efficacious in the moral and material improvement of the multitude. Above all they will propose to them the principles of justice and evangelical charity, to which are equally united all the rights and duties of civil and social life, such should be the way in which they fulfil their noble part in the social action." Leo XIII, *Fin Dal Principio* (Vatican City: Holy See, 1902), 15, https://www.vatican.va/content/leo-xiii/en/encyclicals/documents/hf_l-xiii_enc_08121902_fin-dal-principio.html.

63. As Dennis Doyle has characterized it, this is best described as "communion ecclesiology." Doyle, *Communion Ecclesiology*, 11.

questions of the Catholic Church's political nature and cooperation with the hierarchy were answered would, in turn, influence how the laity conceived of their apostolic mission.

We will briefly consider two of these movements to see the contrast. Catholic Action, a strategic form of lay involvement, was authorized by Pope Pius XI in 1922 as "a form of apostolate," a "collaboration of the laity in the hierarchical apostolate." Catholic Action's various suborganizations predated the encyclical *Ubi Arcano Dei Consilio*, in which Pius XI established the movement, but in this encyclical, we find the underlying arrangement in which the apostolic mandate of Catholic Action could be realized.[64] World War I had devastated family, society, and governments, leaving the need for social renewal and reorganization; peace had been "written into treaties. It was not received into the hearts of men, who still cherish the desire to fight one another and to continue to menace in a most serious manner the quiet and stability of civil society."[65]

Catholic Action, in deriving its apostolicity from that of the hierarchy, functioned as an extension of papal influence, involving the laity but led by priests and clerics.[66] Catholic Action's model expanded globally, with the undertones of the church combating the forces that had created societal chaos, including global Communism. By being orchestrated by the priests, Catholic Action was able to expand globally, through various aspects of social life, and in a way that could offer a unified front against Communism and nationalism.[67]

Catholic Action was only the largest initiative of this period, accompanied by new organizations for catechesis, political influence, and education, to name a few.[68] But during this same period, a variety of new associations came into view not bearing the same relationship to the church hierarchy, for various reasons. Particularly after the Second Vatican Council, an increasing number

---

64. Catholic Action was composed of various sub-bodies, including youth, university students, women, and men. Because Catholic Action was composed of numerous sub-concerns, the relationships between the Church and various localities would lead to negotiated truces with fascist governments. See John Pollard, "Pius XI's Promotion of the Italian Model of Catholic Action in the World-Wide Church," *Journal of Ecclesiastical History* 63 (2012): 758–84.

65. Pius XI, *Urbi Arcano Dei Consilio* (Vatican City: Holy See, 1922), 20, https://www.vatican.va/content/pius-xi/en/encyclicals/documents/hf_p-xi_enc_19221223_ubi-arcano-dei-consilio.html.

66. Faggioli, *Sorting Out Catholicism*, 51.

67. As Pollard notes, both Catholicism and Communism were committed in this way to total regeneration of society, but toward different palingenetic projects. Pollard, "Pius XI's Promotion of the Italian Model," 762.

68. Faggioli, *Sorting Out Catholicism*, 61–81.

of lay-directed movements emerged, frequently as contextual responses to political conditions in which the church found itself, but not always with the same relation to church hierarchy, and thus embodying apostolic witness in a decisively different fashion.[69]

The American example of the Catholic Worker movement offers a different account of apostolicity: one of hierarchical blessing, but not direction. Founded in 1933 by Peter Maurin and Dorothy Day, the Catholic Worker movement sought to bring Catholic Social Teaching into the poverty of New York City. Day, from the beginning, conceived of their work as part of the lay apostolate, though the Catholic Worker movement would never be subject to episcopal direction or governance.[70] She emphasizes the works of mercy that the members of the Worker houses do, casting the work of the Worker houses as apostolic in nature. But Day's form yields an expansion of what counts as apostolic, even if it diverged from the intentions of the hierarchy: "Peter Maurin's vision of the city of God included pacifism and distributism. And that is what distinguishes us from much of the lay apostolate today. It is the talent Christ has given us and we cannot bury it."[71]

In her first edition of the newspaper *Catholic Worker*, Day made a friendly analogy between her own work and that of Catholic Action, describing her paper as "quite frankly propagandists for Catholic Action."[72] But though the Catholic Worker movement would affiliate with members of Catholic Action, it made quite clear that it was something different, "having no Mandate from the Hierarchy for this work," though in spirit similar to the culturally regenerative work and apostolic orientation of Catholic Action.[73] Day would elsewhere describe her pacifism and embrace of distributism as consistent with works of mercy and, as such, apostolic. But in exercising the faith in a solely lay-directed way—including a pacifism that has yet to be recognized as a normative Catholic position—Day offers an apostolic alternative to that of Catholic Action. She famously noted that, if asked by the archbishop, she would in fact close the Worker houses. But the Worker houses as such remained

---

69. It is this postconciliar period that gave rise to both Communion and Liberation (a conservative Italian Catholic organization seeking to restore Catholic influence) and Christians for Socialism (a politically progressive group linked to the emerging base communities of Latin America). See Faggioli, *Sorting Out Catholicism*, 96–98.
70. Dorothy Day, "On Pilgrimage, May 1948," *Catholic Worker*, April 1, 1948, https://catholicworker.org/467-html/.
71. Day, "On Pilgrimage, May 1948."
72. Day, *Catholic Worker*, December 1933, 2.
73. Day, "The Church and Work," *Catholic Worker*, December 1946.

dialogical spaces comprising Catholics, non-Catholics, and non-Christians, all of whom were named as contributing to the work of the apostolate.

The apostolicity of the Catholic Worker movement was less totalizing than that of Catholic Action in two ways. First, while the two movements agreed on the need to rebuild a distinctly Catholic culture, and viewed themselves as apostolic movements, the need for explicit direction and connection to the hierarchy remained open.[74] Day's apostolicity broaches the question as to whether apostolicity need be conceived as a map or an itinerary, to borrow the image of philosopher Michel de Certeau—is apostolicity something to be schematized from the top, or learned from the bottom?[75] The map of cultural reformation of Catholic Action requires the coordination of the laity with the hierarchy, while the more tactical engagements of the Catholic Worker movement enter into the ambiguities of a pluralist society, assuming that the works of mercy are normative but that the articulations of the hierarchy are the received framing of what apostolicity looks like, not the final word of their enactment.[76]

Like those of numerous other organizations that maintained connection with but not direction by the hierarchy, the Catholic Worker example indicates the difficulty with apostolicity as articulated in official teaching such as *Apostolicam Actuositatem*: once apostolicity takes root in the soil of the laity, there is no accounting for the direction that it will go. In Italy, for example, two contrasting lay-driven groups, Communion and Liberation and Christians for Socialism, each claimed apostolic continuity with the Catholic Church, and neither contested the need for social teaching, challenged received dogma, or sought to break with the hierarchy. And yet, the two groups maintained distinctly divergent visions of apostolic influence in society because of their detachment from hierarchical jurisdiction. The risk of a fully freed laity, in a politically diffuse world, is the creation of a diffuse and frequently pluralized vision of the apostolate.

In the face of divergent accounts of how apostolic authority functions, particularly when these movements are at a remove from church hierarchy, all might seem lost. But it is here that evangelical examples might offer guidance.

---

74. This would be Day's position, as we see in this article, long before the Second Vatican Council's affirmation of the laity.

75. Michel de Certeau, "Practices of Space," in *On Signs*, ed. Marshall Blonsky (Baltimore: Johns Hopkins University Press, 1985), 122–45.

76. See Myles Werntz, *Bodies of Peace: Ecclesiology, Nonviolence, Witness* (Minneapolis: Fortress, 2014), 144–52.

At first glance, free churches operate without some of the most visible signs of apostolicity—namely, institutional representatives who are signs of congregational unity with other churches and formalized processes of ordination.[77] This has not, however, prevented recognition of some of these groups as apostolic by churches more attuned to the expansive nature of apostolicity.[78] The mark of apostolicity, as an integrated reality, certainly always calls for a deeper habitation, and for churches to repent of error, but does not negate the work of the Spirit within these churches. Let us consider what it is about evangelical networks that warrants this positive assessment.

Evangelical and free churches have predominantly relied on various informal networks and associations, as opposed to binding denominations, making their processes of transmission and apostolicity more fluid than the Catholic examples above. Melani McAlister describes evangelicalism as having an "enchanted internationalism" in which churches join together as international cocombatants against external enemies; global coconspirators for evangelistic strategies; or, at times, covictims of persecutions.[79] Her characterization, though perhaps overwrought, helps us to identify the ways in which free church apostolicity requires active participation in a common mission. To be an inheritor of the faith is to participate in the fate of the whole: whether by supporting the persecuted, voicing active opposition to moral wrongs, or supporting others in evangelism, handing down the faith well goes hand in hand with being a part of networks by which one not only learns how to live

---

77. As Steve Harmon has argued, in writing about Baptists in particular, Baptists have used core creeds of the apostolic faith in their union statements, confessions, and local church covenants, while lacking other, more visible signs of unity and continuity. Steven R. Harmon, *Baptist Identity and the Ecumenical Future: Story, Tradition, and the Recovery of Community* (Waco: Baylor University Press, 2016), 222.

78. See in particular Paul VI, *Unitatis Redintegratio* (Vatican City: Holy See, 1964), 23, https://www.vatican.va/archive/hist_councils/ii_vatican_council/documents/vat-ii_decree_19641121_unitatis-redintegratio_en.html:
> The daily Christian life of these brethren is nourished by their faith in Christ and strengthened by the grace of Baptism and by hearing the word of God. This shows itself in their private prayer, their meditation on the Bible, in their Christian family life, and in the worship of a community gathered together to praise God. Moreover, their form of worship sometimes displays notable features of the liturgy which they shared with us of old. Their faith in Christ bears fruit in praise and thanksgiving for the blessings received from the hands of God. Among them, too, is a strong sense of justice and a true charity toward their neighbor. This active faith has been responsible for many organizations for the relief of spiritual and material distress, the furtherance of the education of youth, the improvement of the social conditions of life, and the promotion of peace throughout the world.

79. Melani McAlister, *The Kingdom of God Has No Borders: A Global History of American Evangelicals* (Oxford: Oxford University Press, 2018), 10–11.

the faith by participation but does so in expansive, informal networks that are shifting.

The example of the Lausanne Conference is a good example here. The Lausanne Conference, which began in 1974, gathered twenty-four hundred broadly evangelical and nondenominational representatives to Lausanne, Switzerland, to discuss missions and to forge a covenant binding the members together. In the resulting Lausanne Covenant, the majority of the text addresses the nature of evangelism and mission, prefaced by soteriological statements. Ecclesiology exists in the document as a way to speak of evangelistic practices: "We affirm that Christ sends his redeemed people into the world as the Father sent him, and that this calls for a similar deep and costly penetration of the world. We need to break out of our ecclesiastical ghettos and permeate non-Christian society. In the church's mission of sacrificial service, evangelism is primary."[80]

Apostolicity, in this example, is a matter of bearing out the apostolic message of salvation, but in a way that subordinates questions of the church's authority to those of *evangelism's* authority. It is important that this last part is clear: church authority serves to perpetuate the task of evangelism, for in the task of evangelism, the church finds its authority. This means, then, that those engaged in evangelism are the ones bearing the authority of the church, and they are doing so in a way that "breaks out of ecclesiastical ghettos" and into new networks of coparticipants.[81] This emphasis on networks, which raised up representative figures through their common participation, was not always ordered around the particular task of evangelism, but still seems to emphasize informal patterns of recognized representative authority as opposed to stable ones.[82]

---

80. John Stott, *The Lausanne Covenant* (orig. 1974; Lausanne Movement, 2009), 51 (para. 6), https://lausanne.org/wp-content/uploads/2021/10/Lausanne-Covenant-%E2%80%93-Pages.pdf.

81. See McAlister, *Kingdom of God Has No Borders*, 85–102, for a full discussion of Lausanne, particularly the tension there over whether evangelism intrinsically had social, ethical, and political dimensions.

82. For a very different example, see Brad Christerson and Richard Flory's study *The Rise of Network Christianity: How Independent Leaders Are Changing the Religious Landscape* (Oxford: Oxford University Press, 2017), which details the interconnections of several prominent charismatic groups, such as the International House of Prayer, Bethel, and Harvest International Ministries. Their work demonstrates the way in which these charismatic leaders exercise apostolicity by way of passing down their influence, whether by formal donor relationships or informal laying on of hands or platforming like-minded leaders. Readers should see this not as a judgment but as a statement about the informal nature of these processes of validation.

In juxtaposing the Catholic Worker example alongside the more diffuse evangelical "network Christianity," I am suggesting that these dynamics of apostolicity as diffuse and involving ongoing negotiation do not break down along Protestant/Catholic lines, or even sacramental/nonsacramental lines.[83] In Catholicism, long before the Second Vatican Council, the question of adaptation and continuity was in the water. But this expansion came not as a smooth process but through conflict, which in turn expanded what Catholicism had to be in order to bear apostolic witness in a new world.[84]

The transmission of the faith—if challenging in a political register—raised significant questions along the axis of race as well within Catholicism. We find Black Catholics asking what it meant for them to be full bearers of the gospel they had received, and what it meant in turn to bear apostolic witness to the next generation, adopting liturgical innovations that drew in new converts and engaging in social activism in ways that were coherent with their own experience of being racial minorities in the Catholic Church. Struggling to be taken seriously as apostolic bearers of the faith, in 1968, the Black Catholic Clergy Caucus, organized in Detroit, would put a fine point on it, declaring that "the Catholic Church in the United States is primarily a racist institution."[85]

---

83. The degree to which charismatic and free-church traditions are sacramental is a question I leave open here, in view of the recent work making the case for sacramentalism in Pentecostalism and nondenominational circles. See, for example, Chris E. W. Green, ed., *Pentecostal Ecclesiology: A Reader* (Leiden: Brill, 2016); Daniel Tomberlin, *Pentecostal Sacraments: Encountering God at the Altar* (Cleveland, TN: Center for Pentecostal Leadership and Care, 2010); Philip E. Thompson, "Gathered Church Sacramentality: Loss and Recovery," in *T&T Clark Handbook of Sacraments and Sacramentality*, ed. Martha Moore-Keish and James W Farwell (Edinburgh: Bloomsbury T&T Clark, 2023), 140–52; Anthony R. Cross and Phillip E. Thompson, eds., *Baptist Sacramentalism* (Carlisle, UK: Paternoster, 2003).

84. Consider, for example, the ways in which Catholicism had been reworked and made cohesive in the contexts of missions colonies. Consider the stories of Black Elk (one of the most famous Lakota converts to Catholicism) and the relationship between Rastafari religion and Catholicism. In both cases, Daniel Castello argues, we find examples of Catholicism entering into a non-Chrisitan space in such a way that the faith handed down is judged and found wanting, and notions of what Catholicism can become are expanded in the process. See Daniel Castello, *Black Elk: Colonialism and Lakota Catholicism* (Maryknoll, NY: Orbis Books, 2005), 158–78. As Castello puts it, in comparing the Ghost Dance and the Rastafari experience with Catholicism in Jamaica, "the Ghost Dance incorporated the Christian narrative in a way similar to that of the Rastafari; the standard of God's justice became the moral framework within which Western colonialism was measured, and the figure of the Messiah would judge the West in an apocalyptic intervention of history" (172).

85. Cited in James H. Cone and Gayraud S. Wilmore, *Black Theology: A Documentary History* (Maryknoll, NY: Orbis Books, 1979), 322. Though the United States Conference of Catholic Bishops had issued official statements on racism, the issue was, as James Cone put it, whether Black Catholics could be "black first and then Catholic." James H. Cone, *For My People: Black Theology and the Black Church* (Maryknoll, NY: Orbis Books, 1984), 50.

Similar concerns emerged in majority Black parishes across the country: Could culturally and politically Black concerns be foregrounded in the church, and what would that mean as far as the transmission of the faith?[86] One version of this answer could be seen in the practice emerging in majority-Black parishes. In Chicago, in the 1930s and 1940s, a live Corpus Christi pageant, featuring an all-Black cast, depicted the life of Christ's suffering and death, drawing thousands.[87] Incorporation of Black spirituals followed suit in various parishes, and by 1968, Black Unity masses—incorporating the aesthetics of the Black Power movement—began to be celebrated, alongside advocacy for better educational conditions in the parish neighborhoods.[88]

Conclusion

Can the Christian faith truly be communicated into the qualitative contours of all of human life, or must human life—as it pertains to questions of race and gender—comport itself to a vision of catholicity that requires certain cultural contours? Protestants and Catholics alike were asking these questions both before and during the Second Vatican Council.

The variegations of apostolicity—institutional and informal, corporate and personal, handed on in continuity or in discontinuity—follow many of the dimensions seen in other marks and have corresponding effects on how other discussions can happen. A church pursuing unity, for example, has to contend with the fact that its material unity cannot proceed in the ways that it did in the past. The apostolic expansion of the church has been made possible by the past, but there are parts of that past that the church cannot use. Catholicity likewise finds its work increasingly complicated by apostolicity, as laity are encouraged to be fully formed as Christians, or to fully engage the work of evangelism, but find that as they do so, their form of faithfulness stretches the edges of how the Christian faith is confessed and transmitted. Holiness, too, finds itself drawn in: apostolicity means, in part, attending to the limits of who can be a representative figure and what behaviors best cohere with that vision. But apostolicity provokes holiness to consider whether

---

86. See Matthew J. Cressler, *Authentically Black and Truly Catholic: The Rise of Black Catholicism in the Great Migration* (New York: NYU Press, 2017).
87. Cressler, *Authentically Black and Truly Catholic*, 102.
88. Cressler, *Authentically Black and Truly Catholic*, 137–42.

God's Spirit may be calling into view persons who embody the holiness of God in different forms.

As we move toward assessing these marks—what they mean for the church of the future and how they might be embodied in the wake of the twentieth century—we must shift gears, moving from description to meditation, to ask, If the Spirit has brought the churches to this place through this history, what might the future require of churches? What is required of Christians to receive this history, to hear it, and to move forward in its light? What might it mean to bear the marks of the church not only as past realities but as living wounds, as questions that remain unsettled?

Conclusion

On Earth as It Is in Heaven
A Modest Proposal for the Twenty-First-Century Church

In the last four chapters, we have seen the landscape of the church in the twentieth century expand, contract, and rearrange. New movements of Pentecostalism, ecumenism, renewal, and realignment left the twenty-first century with a church more variegated in texture and broader in scope than ever before. Answering the question "What is the church?" feels further out of reach than it did before we began. But before we can begin to draw out some provisional insights from our exploration of twentieth-century ecclesiology, I want to ask what it means for the church to be a people in the world, particularly with respect to time, and what this means for the previous chapters.

On Earth as It Is in Heaven: An Ecclesiological Summary

Over the last four chapters, we have explored the claim that the twentieth-century church can be understood as contesting—and not negating—the identity given to us in the form of the four marks. To say that the church is one, holy, catholic, and apostolic is to say that the church is a body given by the Spirit to be complex, transcultural, transhistorical. It is a body of Christ that has, over time, developed striations and dimples, pockmarks and changing hairlines; it is a body that has aged, been renewed, been strengthened and weakened.

I have opted to refrain throughout the book, insofar as possible, from offering evaluative statements about whether or not a church counts as exercising unity, holiness, catholicity, or apostolicity[1] but have presumed that if they confess Christ in the flesh (a work made possible only by the work of the Holy Spirit), they are frail members of Christ's body and, by the Spirit's work, *do* exhibit these things in some fashion. This already takes us beyond a purely dogmatic description of the church and into trying to account for something of the church's lived histories of these claims, as partial and selective as my history of this has been. If we are to name what the church is—if the church is Christ's body in time—then we cannot do without naming the contours and histories. One does not name one's spouse by naming characteristics alone but by telling stories and speaking in particulars; accordingly, ecclesiology, doctrinally speaking, must venture to talk about an act of God that is inflected by time.

The prayer of Jesus given *to* the disciples, the Lord's Prayer, can thus be read as a prayer *for* the disciples, an explication of the complex nature of belonging to this body that is Christ's.[2] The church is the foretaste of God's kingdom in that the church bears witness to eschatological truths in time, worshiping a risen Christ who will yet come again in fullness. The description in the Lord's Prayer gives us an image of a people who bear out this longing in their corporate lives: longing for the earth to be like the heavens is the basis upon which the church engages in worship, self-critical examination, and indeed, testing the gifts that come forth as the church bears fruit in new grounds.

The longing for this joining of God and creation is not easy; it comes with sighs and groans. In each chapter, we have seen how the identity of the church is contested through not only its teaching regarding the marks but how these marks have played out in practice, through its performances and its statements.

---

1. I have done so not in the spirit of inclusive consumerism but in the spirit of taking a testimony at face value, asking not whether a claim is true but in what way it might be true. If the marks of the church are in fact marks that the Spirit gives, and if churches exist as bodies proclaiming the incarnate Jesus only by the Spirit, then it follows that churches confess to be churches of the risen Jesus Christ only by the work of the Spirit. Accordingly, open-minded critical inquiry has been the way forward here. To be part of the one body of Jesus means regarding the mutually exclusive claims of the different parts of the body as *invitations* to discourse and constructive critique, inquiring how the one Spirit works in cohesion and not in chaos.

2. In making this analogy, I am aware that I am eliding the difference between *ekklēsia* and *basileia*, between church and kingdom. I do not, in making this move, intend to diminish the literature of the missional church movement, for example, which sought to stage a reversal of ecclesiocentric thinking. For the history of this theological movement, beginning with the Edinburgh Missionary Conference of 1925, see Darrell Guder, *Called to Witness: Doing Missional Theology* (Grand Rapids: Eerdmans, 2015).

The joining of the heavens to the earth means, among other things, a reception of the gifts of God amid the vicissitudes of time. The entrance of God's kingdom into creation occurs under the sign of struggle—as the clash of God with the gods of Egypt, as Jesus being threatened with infanticide, as the arrest and trial of the witnesses in Acts. The same is true of the church: it is a body created by the work of the Spirit, but as the struggle of the Spirit against the gods of despair, of sexual immorality, of greed, of vice and idolatries.

And so, the stories of the church in the twentieth century bear this mark of contestation. Unity takes place in negotiated ecumenical discussions, but also in asking how wars effect ecclesial disunity. Reflection on holiness, as a reception of God's fullness, leads to questions about what it means to bear witness to that in moral practice. Catholicity, the claim of bearing the whole faith in all of creation, raises the question of how cultural texture and anthropological depth are accounted for. And the topic of apostolicity prompts us to ask what it means to bear witness to the living Word of the Father in the peculiarities of time and the variations of creaturely life.

The presence of God in the world in Christ's own body, thus, does not take an *easy* form, but one in which the people of God bear the mark of this encounter in their collective life: sacrifice. From the sacrifices of Abel and Noah and Abraham to the final sacrifice of Christ, the people of God's corresponding form is to join themselves to their offering. We do not simply offer some *thing* of great value; rather, we offer our *selves* in worship, that we—God's people—might be changed. It is fitting that the people of God fit the form of God's own disclosure: a fire that burns but does not consume gives rise to a people who are changed but not destroyed.

Living Sacrifices in Time

The description I have offered here is one in which contestation is intrinsic to the church being an offering to God, part of how the church is changed not only in its pursuit of faithfulness but in its learning to live with the fullness of its members. These sacrifices are costly, but also intrinsic to being Christ's body: there is no other way.

It is fitting that the church that offers sacrifices to God,[3] celebrating the sacrifice of the Son and thus striving to give to its members in ways that risk

---

3. In the churches of my youth, and of my adulthood, this is persistently equated with the offerings of finances and time. Catholic churches will more readily see this in terms of

partial understandings and valued formulations, should itself be described as a living sacrifice.[4] This description, calling forth the Levitical rites, both affirms and undermines a reading of the church as a material body. For sacrifice is proper only to something material, something that can undergo loss, even if such losses paradoxically make the material more of what it is meant to be. But the "true and proper worship" (Rom. 12:1 NIV) that Paul enjoins us toward is one that feels resolutely *im*proper, for to do it is to surrender ourselves to being led in a direction we cannot map out and, at times, to being led by the hand to places we do not wish to go.

But such is the vocation of the people of God, who, from their expulsion from the garden to their journey through the desert to their times in and out of exile, have been led by God into places they would not otherwise have chosen to go.[5] These journeys—through the world and, as Augustine puts it, "during" the world—are tied together with the vocation of the people of God to come into their fullness as a people. Through their journeys, they lose their Egyptian gods, even while welcoming new outposts of God's people in Alexandria; they lose their taste for the leeks of Egypt and the meats of Babylon, even if the people of God will be asked to take them up again from the gentiles. Such losses—of favored status, of tastes, of homes—are all but promised to the people of God by Jesus. But the loss of such things is not their permanent loss, even if to Israel the taste of leeks and melons never left their memory. That which is true about the people of God—that they are God's own covenant community—is not lost, insofar as being the people of God is first a matter of God's own faithfulness toward Israel and all those included in God's covenant.

As I have described it in these chapters, such losses are not only the sins and maladies that are killing us but the things that have supported us as well—cultural alliances, denominational configurations, and unified doctrinal alignments. The World Council of Churches, in expanding its scope, lost one center of gravity and gained another, more difficult gift: that of new partners among Pentecostals, Catholics, and Orthodox. Churches engaging in debate over women's ordination

---

the Eucharist, that in taking the bread and wine, we are being joined to Christ's own atoning work. Other Protestant churches will take this notion in terms of acts of obedience, sacrifices of service. But in any event, these are co-inhering accounts: to be a sacrifice entails not only our bodily substance but all that our bodies do, consume, and produce.

4. In what follows, I am indebted to Kirsten Sanders, who first helped me to see this motif as connected to the life of the church.

5. Much ink has been spilled on the theme of exile in the church's identity. But the motif of exile as a permanent status of the church makes sense only if there is a point of return; otherwise, exile is simply an endless journeying without a home.

or about the charismatic gifts not only found their liturgies and denominational arrangements complicated but found new depths to their reflections on the apostolicity of the church. But such is the character of the church as a living sacrifice: in the sacrifice, not only is that which is inessential to the thing consumed, but that which gives the sacrifice integrity is as well. Gristle and bone are burned alongside meat—all of it entailed in what it means for a sacrifice to be given.

With this motif of the church in view, we are able to view the contestations of the twentieth century—and indeed, of all the time before it—as less a history of ideas than a history of the Spirit immolating those elements that we wish to salvage from the fire but that were always meant to be transfigured in sacrifice. For entering into the name "church" is not to enter into a set of abstracted attributes, but to enter into a history in which the Spirit continues to make of us offerings through Christ to the Father. This does not mean setting aside the nature of doctrinal arguments, but seeing it in a theological frame: the process by which Christ's body, the church, is remade is not a history of decline but one caught up in the Spirit's work of renewal.

In using this analogy, I want to note one difference: it is not yet clear, at least to the church, what is to be *ultimately* lost. It will do no good to overstate the case with respect to ecclesiology, declaring that the church is Christ's own body and will not vanish or be overcome by the gates of hell. But this is not to say that all things remain so clear. There was a time when the papacy was not, when Rome was not yet the center of Catholic faith. Presumptions that seemed ironclad fell out of use or were walked back significantly. Elements that seemed to be over and done with came back into view, such as an overt emphasis on the Holy Spirit's gifts. This is what makes ecclesiology such an interesting and, many times, infuriating doctrine to study: to confess the church is to confess a work of God that passes through culture and time continuously, catching up cultures, histories, and times disparate from one another but united in the one work of Christ.

The trick is *what to make of these changes*. As opposed to reading this as a narrative of decline—Protestant, Catholic, or otherwise—it is both more interesting and more true to read the church as a body that perseveres, with the hope that God is at work in institutions, arguments, movements, and hearts. As Charles Williams puts it, in reference to Christendom,

> It is an operation of the Holy Ghost toward Christ, under the conditions of our humanity; and it was our humanity which gave the signal, as it were, for

that operation. The visible beginning of the Church is at Pentecost, but that is only a result of its actual beginning—and ending—in heaven. In fact, all the external world as we know it, is always a result. Our causes are concealed, and mankind becomes to us a mass of contending unrelated effects. It is the effort to relate the effects conveniently and without touching, without (often) understanding, the causes that makes life difficult.[6]

As Robert Jenson has argued, it does us no good—nor would it be possible—to wish away whatever events have occurred to shape the church over time, for whatever perceived errors were committed then have created the church now. While arguing that past church pastoral leaders were led unerringly in their theological judgments,[7] he acknowledges that whatever shape this will take in its fullness is yet unknown: "The judgment 'The church has acquired institution x by the leading of the Spirit' must in any case be after the fact; dramatic necessity can be perceived only when the event is there. The church's beginning, it appears, provides no paradigm by which to make such judgments. . . . The church is what she is as an anticipation of her transformation into God. Thus even if the church's beginning were uniform, we should still look forward to see her true shape."[8]

In this book, we have explored contours of twentieth-century ecclesiology, but not as if there were no parameters of what the church has been. Indeed, to explore twentieth-century ecclesiology under the headings of the four marks is to assume not only that these marks are guiding marks for the church but also that they are *true*. In assuming that they are true, one must—as Jenson suggests—presume the truthfulness of the church's past judgments on the church's shape, even if—as he also suggests—the full shape of that body is not yet in view.

Put differently, one can both presume the validity of past judgments and at the same time say that how these marks will appear is in part unknown to us. As we have seen, saying that catholicity is a key dimension of

---

6. Charles Williams, *The Descent of the Dove: A History of the Holy Spirit in the Church* (New York: Living Age Books, 1956), 1.

7. "But if the church made *that* decision wrongly, she is not only materially but methodologically separated from her truth. A church guided by the Spirit cannot 'have been mistaken when it determined what was going to be the norm of faith'" (Robert Jenson, *Systematic Theology*, vol. 2, *The Works of God* [Oxford: Oxford University Press, 1999], 239). Here, Jenson is referring to "an irreversible creedal or liturgical or canonical choice" and stating that choices of this sort are entailed in what constitutes the "future self-identity" (238–39).

8. Jenson, *Systematic Theology*, 2:238–39.

ecclesiology is not the same as saying that catholicity's contours have been fully manifested solely by adherence to the apostles' minimal teaching, in substance and form. If catholicity means attending not only to the qualitative dimensions but to the geographic and cultural ones as well, then—as Jenson suggests—the full shape of the church's catholicity evades us for no other reason than that the church continues to grow and flourish in time. It is not a matter of "making the church" from scratch, as if there had never been a church before, but neither is it a matter of refusing the gifts that God brings through time.

The temptation of living sacrifices with respect to tradition, then, is twofold: either to wholly eradicate tradition or to presume that tradition is an object to be preserved. Some churches, in an effort to participate wholly in the work of God, engage wholesale in the eradication of the past, through either neglect, conscious distancing, or outright purgation of unpleasant figures. This error presumes to know, for example, that the piety of misguided souls of another era was simply bad-faith posturing that had nothing to do with God or that sins of the past did not in fact bear good fruit despite themselves. But being a living sacrifice over time means that the purgation we desire cannot be that which we take up by our own planning; Jephthah's daughter remains dead, though Jephthah's zeal was righteous. Jephthah retains his place in the story of Judges not only as a sign of what not to do but, paradoxically, as a sign of zeal's goodness, however overgrown.

The opposite temptation is like unto it: to try to preserve traditions in a way that would make them invulnerable to the transforming effects of time. This is to treat traditions not as living on in and through the bodies of the faithful and through the practices that shape them but as fixed monuments that must be cared for, incapable of living (unless we make them live). Anne Carpenter, in her *Nothing Gained Is Eternal*, focuses our attention on the nature of tradition as both vulnerable to God's ongoing activity and sustained by God in and through its human agents.[9] To view tradition as that which exists over against humans, as opposed to irrevocably depending upon us,

---

9. Anne M. Carpenter, *Nothing Gained Is Eternal: A Theology of Tradition* (Minneapolis: Fortress, 2022), 164: "Human power, restored to itself, does not act apart from its vulnerability to the present moment. Such power in vulnerability is where God acts and where Christianity most resides. The effectiveness of power here is not in its 'over against,' in the iron of a guarantee whose means is the force of its must. No, this power is discovered in freedom's willing of the other—I might also say, in the free willing of *another present and its future*, one where every 'I' can be" (emphasis added).

means that to be traditioned is to engage with the living God, whose Holy Spirit moves in time, bringing back things we have forgotten and at times letting go of things encumbering us.

Receiving these gifts, however, is itself part of the living sacrifice that the church is. In the ecumenical movement, to receive the gifts of a different Christian tradition fully and truly is not only to risk that one may have been in error on doctrine but also to risk acknowledging that a particular church's present cultural shape has been built on fragments. There are ways of playing this out *ad absurdum*—it would be silly to say that a church is lacking unless it contains every iteration of human identity, for this would mean that a church has never existed at any time or any place. What I mean is more prosaic: a church's receiving of new gifts—either from other churches or because of time's passage—is intrinsic to what Jenson suggests. And therefore, these marks of the church—brought forth in one era—will *by their nature* be contested, expanded, and reconfigured in different eras.

Contestation as Ecclesiological Mark

If the gifts we are talking about here are not only linguistic maneuvers but also that which God makes possible, then the gifts change us. In this image of the living sacrifice, to be a gift *for* God is to be made *by* God into that gift. The sacrifice here is not a self-offering like Cain's, defined by that which we see as reasonable and right, but the gift that is called forth, like Peter's leadership (Matt. 16:18; John 21:15–18), laid on us as the kind of gift we will be, like it or not. Contestation, then, is not just resistance to that which is true, but the process by which the church must discern what it means to receive the gifts of God to the church well and not to resist the changes that these gifts will make. Such a process involves not only receiving new life but letting old life go.[10] This process, again, is not simply sociological but theological—the sacrifice that the church *is* depends on it being the body of Christ the head, the one who was crucified and raised again.

This contestation is, then, one that contributes to the identity of churches as Christ's own time-inhabiting body. Contestation is different than *opposition*, in that it is through the encounter with others that communities are

---

10. For what this process might look like, see Mark Lau Branson, *Memories, Hopes, and Conversations: Appreciative Inquiry and Congregational Change* (Herndon, VA: Alban Institute, 2004).

formed,[11] but also, it is in this way that Christ makes known his identity as the living Son of God. As Hans Frei argues, "Intention . . . is nothing in itself without enactment. Enactment does not merely illustrate, but constitutes, intention . . . [Jesus's] love—enacting the good of men on their behalf—is not to be discerned simply and directly as predominant personal deportment, but as the specific vocation entailed by his mission of obedience to God."[12] In this, Frei points us to this key point: Christ's identity as the Son is enacted precisely as the obedience of the Son intersects with the particularities of his interlocutors: the request of Mary when Jesus indicated that it was not yet his time, the woman who pulled at the hem of Jesus's garment, the punishing blows of the Romans. Insofar as Jesus's identity appears to us in and through his trust in the Father, his identity—his reception, his mission, and his enduring presence—comes in tandem with the Spirit's work to lead, direct, and make this presence full in the world.

This contestation, the mode by which Jesus appears in creation, and the manner by which the church receives and tests the gifts of the Spirit are thus part of how the church comes to life in the world. As Stephen Meawad has rightly written, the hope of the moral life is that we will arrive at a state in which virtue is simple—done for the right reasons, in the right way, in complete cooperation with the will.[13] But during time, he writes, the moral life involves struggle. The same aspiration applies, I believe, to much modern ecclesiology. Sometimes we can treat struggle as an ill-advised phase or as a deficiency of virtue. But in what I have sketched here, contestation—either against sin or, in the church, over receiving the gifts of the Spirit or as a function of polity—is indicative not only of what it means to be a creature in the world but also of what it means to be a member of Christ's body.

Contestation, therefore, is an act by which the church and its members bear out the work of the Spirit, making known the saving presence of Christ, in praise of the Father. This is not because contestation is the thing itself,

---

11. This is the significance of Bonhoeffer's comment about the nature of Christian community when he argues that in community, conflict is not eliminated, but that communities put the wills of various persons into contact with one another as mediated through Christ. A community is not wills operating alongside one another, nor is it the unfettered will of a person left untouched by others, but the bringing of wills into contact with one another in a way that invites mediated conflict. See Bonhoeffer, *Sanctorum Communio: A Theological Study of the Sociology of the Church* (Minneapolis: Fortress, 1996), 73–74, 117–36; and my explication of this in Werntz, *From Isolation to Community* (Grand Rapids: Baker Academic, 2022), 35–37.

12. Hans Frei, *The Identity of Jesus Christ* (Eugene, OR: Wipf & Stock, 1997), 151.

13. Stephen Meawad, *Beyond Virtue Ethics: A Contemporary Ethic of Ancient Spiritual Struggle* (Washington, DC: Georgetown University Press, 2023).

but a mark by which the body of Christ comes into the world, like Jacob, wrestling the angel until it is named and limping. The nature of this contestation is, as Jesus tells the apostle Peter, not one of our own choosing, and thus, there is no way to say in advance what it will require for the church to remain faithful. For there may be some questions to which there is no need to respond, and some questions that we are summoned to answer for which we are ill-prepared. To return to the previous chapters, it is unquestionable that the Western world, by and large, remained flat-footed on questions of race for the better part of the twentieth century, while somewhat better prepared to talk about economics, well-prepared to have discussions about episcopal succession, and unsure how to proceed in the face of populism. This is not to damn the Western church, but to indicate that the contestation over the nature of apostolicity (as I have framed it) required skills and habits that some churches lacked and that could be gained only through contestation. But it is in this same way that we can see the growing pains among the churches not as a long series of failures to act according to their own principles or to somehow grasp their own revolutionary insights, but as God's gracious work by the Spirit to reform a body in need of reformation.

A Church Desired: The Theological Virtues

An account of the church, even one attentive to ethnography and history, is not a sociological account. There is no church as a purely "alternative polity" that is not already a site of God's burning love, lighting the sacrifice anew. These four marks, characterized as they are by turning in history, must thus nest in a larger account of this creaturely body as a sign of God's work. And as such, the four marks find their orientation in the virtues, theological and cardinal, for the church exists as neither a purely spiritual body nor a historical one, but as a theological body, of dust given life by God's Spirit.[14]

Insofar as churches operate within the strictures of time, they are vexed by not only questions of scarcity but also questions of continuance and stability.[15] There is no guarantee that a particular church will survive into the

---

14. The account that follows of the cardinal virtues fully acknowledges, in particular, that the list of the virtues is not uncontested.

15. There is a fascinating body of psychological literature surrounding the questions of scarcity and survival. As Sendhil Mullainathan and Eldar Shafir have argued, summarizing a number of these studies, scarcity (of time, resources, etc.) leads to an inordinate concrete attention and diminished focus on longer-term and more abstract values. When a person is hungry,

next decade, even if plausibly some iterations of the church will survive far beyond demographers' estimates. The temptation of a church to focus on its survival comes with, as we have seen, the complexity of naming a work of God that occurs in time and through material forms. The Holy Spirit works to animate, enliven, and gift the gathered body. But our bodies age, as do the confessional forms our bodies belong to. Even a living sacrifice, renewed in flame by the Spirit, wonders whether it might one day simply be consumed.

It is for this reason that *hope* comes first, for it pulls our lives of ecclesial sacrifice and struggle into a frame we cannot fully know, except to say that it looks somehow like the communion of the Father, Son, and Spirit. Our life together, made possible by the triune God, will not be characterized by sacrifice forever, but will, like Christ, rest from its labor. The church triumphant will be a continuance of the church militant, assumedly (like Christ) bearing its scars and the marks of its struggles both in the world and with itself, but in a resurrected form that it cannot fully anticipate. We can say that the gifting of the Spirit anticipates in our present the life of the world to come, but our contestations of the marks find their animus to continue not in the perfections of time, but in the hope that the wounds of time will be bound up, even if not forgotten.

This propulsion through time, though animated by the Spirit, bears the marks of deliberation and judgments both true and erring, and such is the life of faith. Faith, as a gift of God, names the way in which the body of Christ's existence is not that which is generated by a church's calibration of its ways to what it projects the future to consist of, but a willingness to trust that the future God has for it, whatever that may entail, is inseparable from the love and refining work of God. In the lives of the saints, in the history of churches, in the accounting of the church in Scripture, there are abundant recurrences. History may not repeat itself, but it frequently rhymes.[16] As we

---

for example, they seek food (concrete) and defer questions of "health" (abstract), and when a person has limited financial resources, they focus on "paying bills" (concrete) and not on "being financially stable" (abstract). Representative leaders of churches and denominations, I suggest, think of their own collective existence similarly. This is not necessarily a failure of the virtue of hope, but it is a constriction of the ways in which hope might be understood to take root in a church's practices. Sendhil Mullainathan and Eldar Shafir, *Scarcity: The New Science of Having Less and How It Defines Our Lives* (New York: Picador, 2013).

16. This sentiment is most clear in the essay "The Unreachables," by a peer of Sigmund Freud, psychoanalyst Theodor Reik, who wrote, "It has been said that history repeats itself. This is not quite correct; it merely rhymes." Theodor Reik, "The Unreachables," in *Curiosities of the Self* (New York: Farrar, Straus and Giroux, 1965), 133.

have seen, ecclesiological discussions of the twentieth century over the ordination of women, the role of culture in liturgy, colonization, the entanglements of media in teaching authority—these all are with us now well into the twenty-first century in exaggerated ways.

Such is the mode in which a "living sacrifice" lives by *faith*: it will not emerge unscathed, but it will continue nonetheless. The way to move through time, sustained by faith, is not to say that we have "learned from mistakes." This would mean that time was just, theologically, a process in which we progressively tinker with processes to get things just so, ecclesiastically speaking. *New* mistakes will bear the lingering effects of *old* ones, for the mistakes of the future are frequently conscious attempts to avoid a past we cannot disavow: the past has made us what we are, even if we do not repeat it. The future is linked to the present and will be formed by errors and successes we cannot yet anticipate. Faith is the anticipation of the church that its future will be, like the past and the present, one sustained by the Spirit, even if not perfected.

This deflation of expectation about perfectibility opens up, in turn, our capacity to understand that the love the church inhabits is not one in which the church will exist beyond difficulty or loss, but one that will remain entangled in politics, in surprises, and in time's reversals. If the church, as a living sacrifice, participates in the work of the Spirit, and the church—as the second-century Epistle to Diognetus affirms[17]—remains scattered throughout the world, then the love the church knows is inseparable from the biome of creation: as long as creation endures, so will the church, tethered to the creation that makes it possible, though scattered.[18]

In being a living sacrifice, the church exists only as it is sustained by Christ's promised presence. This presence of Christ is the fire that does not go out upon this altar (Lev. 6:12–13), the faithful and ever-sustaining love of God, which burns even the ashes. To view the church in this way is to say that *particular* churches are not guaranteed perpetual existence but are, like elements caught

---

17. See Epistle to Diognetus 6.1–2: "In a word, what the soul is to the body, Christians are to the world. The soul is dispersed through all the members of the body, and Christians throughout the cities of the world." In Michael W. Holmes, ed. and trans., *The Apostolic Fathers: Greek Texts and English Translations*, 3rd ed. (Grand Rapids: Baker Academic, 2007).

18. For this adjustment in thinking about the connection between the church and world, see Luke Bretherton, *A Primer in Christian Ethics: Christ and the Struggle to Live Well* (Cambridge: Cambridge University Press, 2023), 32–34. In this analogy, Bretherton situates the task of living morally in a matrix in which human life is dependent on and constituted by the humus of creation. I am adopting his notion here as a way of describing the inextricability of the church from creation.

up in the fire, subject to alteration to the point of unrecognizability. And yet, insofar as the ashes remain in the flame, *even the ashes are not lost* but become part of what makes new sacrifices possible. Such is the story of the church in the twentieth century: one in which the marks of the church endure, one in which the gospel multiplied out into new spaces and among new peoples, but in the process risked becoming unrecognizable to itself. In keeping step with the Spirit, the church being recognizable to itself was never the aim, for in remaining a living sacrifice, it was recognizable to God.

After "the Church"

One of the underlying suppositions of this book is that, while there is ultimately one church insofar as there is one Spirit and one Lord (Eph. 4:4–6), contestation—appropriate to a church living in time—is not a stranger but a friend. And in time, we pursue the same Lord, bound together in a manner that requires our mutual correction: it is not possible for a church to remain autonomous, theologically speaking, insofar as what makes a church possible is not its self-constitution but its constitution by the Spirit, who proliferates without dividing. In what I have presented, I have tried to do justice to Baptists, Methodists, Catholics, Pentecostals, Orthodox, evangelicals, and many more, not as self-contained entities subject only to internal critique, but as members of one body now bound to give and receive correction, to give and receive gifts. If the marks of the church are not constructive aims of churches but, rather, that which the Spirit's constitution makes possible, then what emerges in and through a church that professes the triune God is an invitation to a porous existence, open to contestation from new and old.

In this sense—in the sense of differentiated pneumatology, in which the Spirit works in and through the histories, culture, and ethos of particular bodies[19]—there is one church. But attending to the church with the virtues of faith, hope, and love as described above requires us to defer the language of "the church" for the language of "the churches," both to acknowledge the

---

19. As Bonhoeffer describes the life of churches, churches are made alive by the Spirit, who confronts, mends, and operates in the spirit (ethos and culture) of churches. See *Sanctorum Communio*, 157–92. Here, Bonhoeffer is not only working to acknowledge the sociological and anthropological elements at work in churches; he is also doing so in a different way than those who would contend that the relation between God and church is one of projection or language: churches are what they are, as creaturely bodies made possible by the Spirit, with neither aspect of this negated.

divided state of Christ's body and also to affirm the way in which contestation remains an ongoing feature of Christ's body until time's end. This may seem like giving up, capitulation to division, but as I have been arguing, it follows from a commitment to understanding the Spirit's singular work as one that is variegated, in which all churches—new and old—have become inheritors of the same work of the Spirit.

If the theological virtues name how the churches are contesting bodies, then this raises a practical question: *How can this be sustained?* To the theological virtues—faith, hope, and love—we must add the practical virtues to help us navigate time well.[20] In what follows, I do not offer the one-and-only account of how practical virtues might aid us, insofar as the virtues are interrelated, for better or worse: to be lacking in courage affects how one might be just, in the same way that a failure to be just (giving to people what they need) affects how one can be temperate. For a church that desires to be entirely consumed does not need to ask questions of endurance, much less of justice or prudence. There is no need for such a church to concern itself with how to do things sustainably or whether everyone has what they need. But a church that will persist as a living sacrifice, an ongoing offering, must ask these questions.

The Temperance of Oneness

To call for temperance is to call for modesty, for doing a thing neither in excess of what is needed nor in deficiency, and the question of church oneness is most in need of this virtue. Temperance names here a caution against an overzealous desire *toward* loss, as well as a summons to sober investigation about what might no longer be needed. In our study of twentieth-century ecclesiology, the most obvious examples of overzealousness were in the numerous calls for churches to dispossess themselves of their historic commitments regarding sacraments, politics, or tradition. Dispossession for its own sake is not only—as I have argued above—pretending that one's history is not still operative but also treating the past as if it, too, was not the vehicle of the Spirit's work.

---

20. There are multiple accounts of the natural virtues. Aristotle provides, in the *Nicomachean Ethics*, the most well-known and frequently relied-upon account of the cardinal virtues, but elsewhere, such as in *Rhetoric*, he expands this list to include magnificence, magnanimity, and more. Later authors would annex additional virtues to the four cardinal ones, a tradition that we find particularly in Thomas Aquinas.

But the opposite error, in my judgment, takes place perhaps not in intransigence toward change, but in supposing that the temperance called for in *some* areas of church life should be manifest in *all* areas. Consider here the highly contested *Sacrosanctum Concilium*, the Vatican II document concerning changes of the Holy Mass liturgy into languages other than Latin.[21] The modest aims of the document were not only to accommodate to a people unaccustomed to Latin but to convey the historic liturgy in ways that maintained the Mass as a matter of church unity: "Liturgical services are not private functions, but are celebrations of the Church, which is the 'sacrament of unity,' namely, the holy people united and ordered under their bishops."[22] Telling in this description, and its concerns for unity, is that liturgical reforms are a matter of *internal* unity and distinct from questions of ecumenism, which means that, for Vatican II, temperance in one area (liturgy) does not necessarily translate to other questions. Provisions are made for the sake of mission,[23] local parish life,[24] and among the body of priests,[25] but no mention is made of the liturgy's capacity to draw in other Christians, despite the overt ecumenical concerns of the council at large.

Let us see temperance at work elsewhere in these discussions. At times it has been the most direct path of approach to the question of church plurality through a model of subsistence, wherein—as in Vatican II's *Unitatis Redintegratio*—all churches other than the true church persist as "divided brethren," as perhaps "ecclesial communities." In this model, a true church is envisioned to which all others should return, or at the minimum, what other churches have is a residual inheritance made possible by the true church. Temperance invites us not to negate the historical claim of church origins, but to ask a theological question of whether historical priority is the conditioning factor. It is true, for example, that Pentecostal churches of any variety are made possible by both their inheritance from Catholics and, at times, their

---

21. Paul VI, *Sacrosanctum Concilium* (Vatican City: Holy See, 1963), https://www.vatican.va/archive/hist_councils/ii_vatican_council/documents/vat-ii_const_19631204_sacrosanctum-concilium_en.html. Notably, the document preserves the priority of Latin (36), while offering broad concessions to its translatability to accommodate those for whom "the use of Latin constitutes a grave obstacle to their praying the office properly" (101). Temperance, as I have been describing it here, best describes the approach of the document, which is attuned to the connection between the laity and the liturgy but takes an incrementalist, case-by-case approach.

22. Paul VI, *Sacrosanctum Concilium*, 26.
23. Paul VI, *Sacrosanctum Concilium*, 38.
24. Paul VI, *Sacrosanctum Concilium*, 38.
25. Paul VI, *Sacrosanctum Concilium*, 57.

negation *by* Catholics.[26] But this is different than saying that Catholics have not been enhanced by something that (in its earliest forms) was looked upon with great suspicion.

It is the mark of contestation continuing and coming into convergence that allows this kind of unity—this kind of "exchange of gifts"[27]—to occur. Imagine the way, for example, that two people embrace: their connection most easily happens when one body is moving and the other motionless. Making this connection when *both* bodies are in motion is an act that is more prone to failure, misunderstood intentions, or awkwardness.

But the relation between churches is like this last kind: finding union when *both* parties are in motion. If both churches are in fact living entities, then the pursuit of the fullness of unity cannot be done by one inert and one moving partner connecting; we cannot pretend, as early World Council of Church discussions did, that a "younger" church falls under the jurisdiction and energy of an "older" church. Their union must happen by two moving partners converging. Such an act requires temperance, with each partner attuning their movement to the movement of the other, with respect to institutionality, appropriate entrance points into conversation, and virtue. In practical terms, it means false starts, and perhaps—to continue this metaphor—awkward embraces. But what it *cannot* mean is the cessation of activity by one of the partners. For convergence to happen, temperance (the virtue of moderation) requires us to distinguish between excess and deficiency of movement in a communion, and to not assume that the present speed of motion in a communion is in fact moderation.

Let us speak in particulars: temperance will mean asking whether difficult conversations in a communion are being deferred out of fear, and whether long-lost elements of a tradition should be surrendered in favor of formulations that are compelling because of exposure to new partners. It may mean, as we see with the formations of the Church of South India or the Anglican Church of North America, the willingness to converge into a new entity

---

26. For one summary of this particular ecumenical exchange, see the Dicastery for Promoting Christian Unity's summary of the 1990–1997 dialogues: *Evangelization, Proselytism and Common Witness* (Rome: Dicastery for Promoting Christian Unity, 1997), http://www.christianunity.va/content/unitacristiani/en/dialoghi/sezione-occidentale/pentecostali/dialogo/documenti-di-dialogo/testo-in-inglese.html.

27. See here the approach outlined by Walter Kasper, former president of the Pontifical Council for Promoting Christian Unity, in his book *Harvesting the Fruits: Basic Aspects of Christian Faith in Ecumenical Dialogue* (London: Continuum, 2009).

entirely. Or it may mean the coordination of mission, as with the International Mission Conference, or the revisiting of commitments with respect to war, as in late twentieth-century Catholicism. All of these involved some measure of loss, but loss best understood not as abandonment but as integration in light of ecumenical encounter.

The Prudence of Holiness

Temperance alone can lead to unqualified moderation, and indeed milquetoast pluralism in which there is no possibility of the church's being one. The desire for the church to be visibly one, likewise, absent temperance, can devolve into hegemony or idealism, enacting unity either in a way that overcomes not just divisions but also distinctions or in a way that retreats into the ether. And few discussions test both temperance and oneness more than discussions about holiness.

Prudence enters into view here as a question about time: What does it mean that virtue involves not just what our *end* is but also what *our approach* to that end looks like? To be excessively prudent is to demand more than is possible (e.g., to ask a toddler to be wise), but it is also, in this case, to expect more of the people of God than they are capable of. To be deficient in prudence, by contrast, would be not to be aware of the dangers, to attribute whatever people are doing as good, and to refrain from making judgments for a time. In this way, holiness requires prudence as its counterpart, for prudence calls for patience and judgment. If the churches are always in motion, as we saw with our discussion of temperance, then prudence allows us not to name *whether* something is seeking to live in light of God's perfection but to ask *in what ways* it is, and what it means for us to spur on that pursuit.

Holiness, as we saw, is not, first of all, moral rectitude, but an enactment of our nature as creatures made in God's own image. Thus, to pursue holiness is to open ourselves to God's activity of making us more and more into that image. To consider holiness is to ask how it is, first, that creation can bear the image and calling of God, and then, what that entails for the life of the church and all its members. The elevation of the laity, in its ecclesial form, and populism, as its political analogue, both raise the question of what it means that God has called *a people* to be holy, and further, how to reckon with the failures of that people to bear that vocation of holiness well.

To introduce the laity as coequal bearers of God's holiness—in discussions of laity/clergy divides, in charismatic renewal movements, in considering the laity as actors in political life—opens up a disruption in ecclesial life in the same moment that it occasions an expansion of holiness. This is, in part, because questions emerge as to whether the structures that make possible holiness of the laity—as distinct from clergy—or make the ordering of the Spirit possible (prior to charismatic renewals) are no longer seen as quite capable of operating in a new environment with many more agents: the old wineskin may not be up to bearing the new wine.

The question of the charismatic gifts helps us to get at this question in particular: If the gifts of the Spirit are gifts that—as in the case of the earliest Pentecostals—open up leadership to women and men, create interracial leadership structures, and make possible expansive involvement of lay people, what kind of structure can sustain these gifts? Michael Kinnamon provocatively asks this as the question, "Can a renewal movement be renewed?"[28] A fork in the road appears in the form of the church's oneness: Can this variegated form of holiness lead only to further division?

It is here that prudence becomes a contentious ally, both to holiness and also to visions of unity. For just as unity can be produced in ways that obscure underlying dynamics that will pull churches apart, so a holiness that forgets that it is worked out in time can forget that the aim is not *purity* but *holiness*: growing into the fullness of the Spirit's work among us. At the risk of invoking the specter of the White moderate,[29] such a prudence is best characterized as incrementalism—deliberate movement over time in the direction of holiness. Such a holiness does not abandon the vision of God's work among all the people but does recognize that such growth means finding new wineskins capable of bearing such growth. Such new wineskins—to be recognizably wineskins—will have continuity with the old forms, but they are appropriate to the increased volume of the wine.

"Deliberation" is an overused term for how this happens, and it often assumes that the conversation partners in the model are remaining still until such time as an agreement is reached, keeping all other things equal as this one point is decided. Whether or not stasis is an explicit expectation of conversation partners, the presence of movement by conversation partners is part of

---

28. Michael Kinnamon, *Can a Renewal Movement Be Renewed?* (Grand Rapids: Eerdmans, 2014).

29. See Martin Luther King Jr.'s famous "Letter from Birmingham Jail."

why deliberation fails: it does not account for the movement of a people as an internal feature of their life and is frustrated when, as soon as the conversation is concluded, a new conversation is needed—for things have already changed. It is difficult, if not impossible, to prescribe a rule for an object in motion, for the rule will be out of date before it is issued.[30]

What prudence opens up to us in the process here is the possibility of *patient convergence*, not *deliberated unanimity*. If the Holy Spirit is not one to be marshaled for our own outcomes, but the One to whom our lives are called to conform, the unity among the church cannot be manufactured so much as lived into. To borrow Hartmut Rosa's image, the church must look for resonance among its members rather than singularity, must encourage them to move in tandem with others instead of to consolidate.[31] Such resonance involves listening, expectation, and above all waiting—it requires prudence to know when the partners, in their mutual pursuits of the Spirit's work, are approaching convergence and to say, in that time, that a new form of unity has come. The Spirit is the one who brings union, working in and through creation, and the union of created beings can go only as fast as they are able.

Such prudence presumes that each member is pursuing the holiness of God, given already through the Spirit by Christ's work. And such prudence requires patience with what feels like distension, stretching, painful bearing with disagreements that seem interminable. But if it is the Spirit at work, then what seems lost is only in the process of a long journey toward reunion. Prudence helps us to name, then, when we are moving too slowly or too quickly, too eager to grasp what is only the Spirit's to give.

But this waiting is not pining or anxiety. Because our mutual waiting presumes that the Spirit is at work elsewhere in a presently divided body, such waiting involves speaking into those parts of the body that are not yet in communion with us. It is not out of order, then, for Catholics to offer intelligent, informed, and charitable comment on Anglican questions, or vice versa. It is not without merit for Rwandan Baptists to critique the formulations of their compatriots in Singapore or Canada. For such critique is a kind of testing of whether the time for reunion is now, and if not, what hope might be present.

---

30. See Lorraine Daston, *Rules: A Short History of What We Live By* (Princeton: Princeton University Press, 2023), 207–11.

31. Hartmut Rosa, *The Uncontrollability of the World*, trans. James C. Wagner (Cambridge: Polity, 2020), 32–34.

The Fortitude of Catholicity

Such hope pulls us into the difficult business of speaking forthrightly, with future resonance in mind and the Spirit's work as a presumption. For catholicity speaks of the need for the church to hold gifts in common and for its confessions to be that which encompasses the totality of what it means to be God's creatures. Catholicity, as we saw, is not just about ubiquity or comprehensiveness of doctrine but about intensity and depth, connecting the intimacies of what we are as creatures to the fullness of the Spirit's work through Christ. Speaking in this way means venturing limits to the outward journeys of holiness and the well-founded desires for unity—there *are* specific contours to what Christians have confessed, and to confess the faith is to confess it robustly.[32]

Churches that opt for a more biblicist approach, on this reading, are not attempting to be minimalist in their confession or opting for a confession that negates the fullness of the faith. Rather, they can be seen as proceeding with a prudent fortitude, moving forward at a moderate pace in pursuit of catholicity, instead of dissolving entirely what they are for what they might be. In Baptist life, for example, it has become more common to embrace parts of the Christian calendar, such as the seasons of Lent, Advent, and Pentecost, not out of a desire to adopt all parts of the calendar, such as the celebration of the dormition of Mary or the intercession of the saints, but out of a desire to more fully embrace how time itself is infused with the ongoing work of God and repeating narration of God's work in and through time.

But fortitude—the virtue associated with courageous character—speaks not only of the willingness to venture forward (embracing what one's forebears would have thought anathema), but the willingness to do so when it means that we might be unrecognizable in certain ways to our forebears. To embrace a more catholic faith—one that moves beyond the specificities of one's home

---

32. To say "specific" is not to negate the doctrinal plurality surrounding *how* the incarnation means that Jesus is fully God and fully human, or to negate *how* the Trinity is coequally and simply Father, Son, and Holy Spirit. The Victorines are not Bulgakov, and the Dominicans are not identical with the peasants of Solentiname. But in the common confession of faith that frames these different examples is not plurality speaking of different gods, but speaking of the one God of the gospel across time. This unanimity presumes that what is spoken is subject to other speakers—namely, those who have made their speech possible: the apostles and the long line since then of hearers and speakers of the gospel. Accordingly, the speech in one place is connected to the speech in another, contested not out of a desire for ownership but because the participants have mutually received the one gift of Scripture's God.

denomination—is not to opt for an antidenominational, minimalist ethos, but to acknowledge that movement in the direction of catholicity, like movement toward holiness, will mean convergence of God's work in ways that breach the bounds of presently defined denominations.[33]

Such fortitude has, on the one hand, the possibility of being courageous, causing a church congregation to embrace the possibility of it being weird to its own denomination or current networks. But fortitude can also be deficient. For a church can also, in the name of denominational cogency (and not for reasons of theological fidelity), restrict and prohibit because it sees a development as inconsistent with the history of a particular people. Arguably, drawing lines of this kind can be a matter of prudence—one cannot be everything all the time. But this is a common posture, one that appears in both Protestant and non-Protestant forms, with Anglicans suspicious of Catholic remnants within their communion, with Catholics suspicious of the compatibility of Aquinas with Latin American Marxism.

Catholicity must be paired with fortitude, for without it, catholicity may shrink back when it needs to venture a hard word, to argue vigorously for preserving something we might otherwise be tempted to abandon. Absent fortitude, catholicity may likewise hesitate when it needs to embrace heretofore unthought depths of what the gospel of God might want to redeem. That Christ is fully human and came into the world does not mean that God changed, but that every aspect of what humans are is open to God's transformation. And for institutions to embrace this truth requires the courage to inquire, pray, and sometimes, to say no.

With respect to a church's history, fortitude requires—as we saw with holiness—being willing to revisit hard and sinful periods of the church's existence and to reckon with how that history shapes our present. Fortitude

---

33. Whether denominations belong to what churches are in time is an important question. Consider the discussion of this question by Peter Leithart in his book *The End of Protestantism* (Grand Rapids: Brazos, 2016), in which he asserts that denominations will remain until the end of time. By this, I take Leithart to mean that self-selected networks of churches that have family resemblances will remain until the end of the age. But Leithart's vision is more structured and capable of disciplinary procedures than the one that I have in mind, or that I think is theologically defensible.

On the basis of what I have sketched in this book, I agree with his assessment, provided that what we have in mind is closer to networks, which provide connection, opportunity for common worship and mission, and a framework of fraternal accountability across time and geography, but which acknowledge their time-boundedness. Their authority, for this reason, is a proximate one, with the catholic expansiveness of doctrinal commitments that invites curiosity and testing across the network.

means being willing to tell the stories of our procession into the world faithfully and penitently and trusting that the loss of some stories may mean the rebirth of others. For Presbyterians to come to terms with their role in the apartheid in South Africa[34] or in their opposition to Martin Luther King Jr.[35] means that alternate heroes come to the fore, bearers of the gospel whose witness was muted previously. But this fortitude likewise means that the new heroes have feet of clay: they are not pristine, to be defended at all costs, but *new* occasions for our penitence.

For ultimately, catholicity's fortitude means that a church must be penitent in its deepening of faith—that every embrace of the Spirit's purifying work means coming to terms with past, present, and future aspirations of perfection and embracing penitence as a lifelong posture. Here, holiness and catholicity begin to shake hands, with unity waiting in the wings; repentance becomes the occasion for forgiveness among the churches, the opportunity for catholicity to deepen, and eventually, for the unity of the people of God to be like oil in the beard of Aaron (Ps. 133).

The Justice of Apostolicity

Classically, the cardinal virtues are those that make justice possible. It is not possible to be just without being able to courageously do what is needed, in the right manner, and without partiality. Justice, as a virtue, concerns "the habit by which one renders to each his due by a constant and perpetual will," Aquinas argues, encompassing not only the disposition by which we treat others but also the actions we take to ensure that each has what is due to them.[36] And for the Christian, this justice must be fitted with the clothes of faith, hope, and love, so that justice might engage the world charitably, perseveringly, and without despair. This is a tall order for Christian justice, but it is also a fitting description of what is needed for apostolicity to be done well. For churches not only to name their relation to the apostles well but also to live as bearers of the apostolic message and witness, churches must—building on fortitude, temperance, and prudence—give to the past and present what is due.

---

34. Peter Randall, ed., *Study Project on Christianity in Apartheid Society* (Capetown: Christian Institute of Southern Africa, 1972).

35. Joel L. Alvis, *Religion and Race: Southern Presbyterians, 1946–1983* (Tuscaloosa: University of Alabama Press, 1994), 104–32.

36. Thomas Aquinas, *Summa Theologica* II-II.58.1 (Westminster, MD: Christian Classics, 1981).

Conclusion

As with other virtues, there is a deficiency and an excess, a way of missing the mark of virtue. It is possible, on this count, to fail by dismissing the singularity of the apostolic witness, subsuming all of what it means to be apostolic into present appropriations. The Scriptures, which form every church, bear this truth out: all other Christians are naught without the singularity of *those* apostles, the first saints and doctors of the church, who handled Jesus in the flesh. For it is they who teach us to see how gentiles are included in the mission of Israel, what it meant to know Jesus face-to-face, and who can speak to us of the Father's only glory, the incarnate Son.

It is possible, on this count, to also fail by dismissing the witness of the gentiles to the ends of the earth. The inclusion of the gentiles is a work of negotiation, of inviting them into the ongoing work of God, but not expecting that the gentiles will be Israelite, in idiom, mind, or background. The expansion of Christ's body into the world draws in new people, new imagery and ideas, new occasions for the churches to be catholic, one, and holy, but only if they can honor the need to be presently apostolic as well. As we saw, the struggle with apostolicity is a struggle to name how the past and present relate and to call out the full range of those who faithfully bear the apostolic witness for the church into the world. The quest for being just to our past and present presumes, in turn, a commitment to a unity we cannot yet see, to a holiness we will continue to navigate as the gentile mission continues, and to a catholicity now called to go to humans in this place and this time. We cannot be just to the future, for the future is God's alone, but we can trust that to be the church is to be just to those who are already among us, those whom the Spirit is upon to bear apostolic witness today.

Whatever future there is for churches, it cannot be one rooted in fear. It must be one rooted in gratitude for what has been and for what is. For the Spirit is always and ever giving what is needed, bread in the wilderness for the living sacrifices that journey through the world. That we are living *sacrifices* means that there will be more losses yet to come, but that we are *living* sacrifices means that what losses may come will never fully consume us. Of the reading of Scripture, of the journey of virtue, and even of contestation—there will be an end. But of the journey of the people of God with God, there will be no end.

Thanks be to God.

Index

Ad Gentes, 122–23
African Independent Church (AIC), 29–31
Anglican Church, the, 94–96
apartheid, 46–47, 120–21
"Apology to First Nations Peoples" (UCC), 85–87
apostles, the, 128n6, 129
apostolicity
  authority and, 126–32, 137–40
  Catholicism and, 129–30, 133–34, 137–38, 141–47, 148–51, 154–55
  catholicity and, 92–98
  culture and, 128, 130–32, 140–47
  defined, 126–29
  differentiation and, 131–37
  doctrine and, 128
  Eastern Orthodoxy and, 129–30, 137–38
  ethics and, 145–47
  justice and, 136–37, 178–79
  the laity and, 133, 143–45, 147–55
  mass media and, 130–32
  ordination and, 128, 133–37
  polity and, 126–27, 129–30
  Protestantism and, 134–35, 138–40, 143–44, 147, 151–53
  race and, 153–54
  succession and, 128, 137–40
Aryan paragraph, the, 51, 98–99
Aulén, Gustav, 93, 98

authority, apostolicity and, 126–32, 137–40
autocephalous, Eastern Orthodoxy as, 22

Balokole, the, 108
baptism, holiness and, 60–61
Baptist churches, 61–63, 83–87, 134–35
Bediako, Kwame, 140–41
Behr-Sigel, Elisabeth, 67
Benac, Dustin, 2n1
Bennett, John C., 42–43
Black Catholics, the, 103–4, 107, 153–54
bodies, physical, 77–81
body, church as, 164–66
Bonhoeffer, Dietrich, 8–9, 99, 165n11, 169n19
borrowed, holiness as, 57
Bretherton, Luke, 168n18
Bulgarian Orthodox Church, 111
Burkhard, John J., 127–28
Byzantine Rite, the, 66–67

Carpenter, Anne, 163–64
Catholic Action, 149–51
Catholic Church, Roman. See Roman Catholic Church (RCC)
Catholic Worker movement, 150–51
catholicity
  apostolicity and, 92–98, 101–3

  Catholicism and, 103–4, 107, 110–11, 113–14, 118, 122–23
  context and, 97–101, 108–23
  doctrine and, 92–98
  the early church and, 92–95, 101–3
  Eastern Orthodoxy and, 109–11, 120
  economics and, 112–16
  expansion of, 103–8, 114–15
  fortitude of, 176–78
  migration and, 119–21
  mission and, 116–19, 121–23
  Protestantism and, 94–98, 101–3, 105–8, 112–16
  race and, 103–8
  renewal and, 101–3, 105–8
  time and, 92–98, 101–3
  ubiquity and, 96, 116–19
  unity and, 92–98
CELAM. See Episcopal Council of Latin America (CELAM)
charismatic movement, the, 26n35, 59–64, 78. See also Pentecostalism
Chinese Catholic Church, 47–48, 141–44
Christ figures, clergy as, 136–37
Christian civilization, 110
Christians for Socialism, 151
Christifideles Laici, 148
church, kingdom and, 158n2
Church of Christ in Japan, 51–52

181

Church of South India, 52
Church of Uganda, 107–8
civil rights movement, American, 48–49
civilization, Christian, 110
colonialism, 32–33, 47, 117–19, 141
communication, apostolicity and, 130–32
Communion and Liberation, 151
communion theology, 24. *See also* Vatican II
Communism, catholicity and, 109–11
community, conflict and, 165n11
Cone, James, 48–49
confessions, church. *See* apostolicity
conflict. *See* war
Congar, Yves, 7
contestation, 18–22, 41–42, 159–70
context, 25, 70–71, 97–101, 108–23
continuity, 129–32. *See also* apostolicity; time
convergence, patient, 175
crisis, uses of, 2n1
crucifixion, apostolicity and, 144
crusades, evangelical, 105–6
culture
  apostolicity and, 128, 130–32, 140–47
  catholicity and, 108–11
  holiness and, 70–77
  unity and, 42–45, 52–54

Daneel, M. L., 30–31
Day, Dorothy, 150–51
deliberation, prudence and, 174–75
denominations, 37–38, 177n33. *See also* polity
diaspora, Orthodox, 66, 120
differentiation, 58–59, 64–71, 131–37
discovery, 18–22. *See also* contestation
dispensationalism, 39n83

disruptive, holiness as, 61–62
doctrine, 15–16, 36–42, 52–54, 63–64, 92–98, 128
Du Plessis, David J., 27
Dulles, Avery Cardinal, 94

early church, the, 64–71, 92–95, 101–3
East African Revival, the, 107–8
Eastern Orthodox Churches
  apostolicity and, 129–30, 137–38
  catholicity and, 109–11, 120
  holiness and, 64–67, 72–74
  unity and, 22–25, 48
economics, 112–16, 144–45
ecumenism, enforced, 51–52
El Salvador, 51, 118–19
ELCA. *See* Evangelical Lutheran Church in America (ELCA)
electronic media, apostolicity and, 130–32
enforced ecumenism, 51–52
Episcopal Council of Latin America (CELAM), 144
ethics, 42–45, 145–47
Evangelical Lutheran Church in America (ELCA), 135
evangelicalism, 38–42, 105–7, 151–53
evangelism. *See* mission
exile, ecclesiology and, 160
expansion, catholicity and, 103–8, 114–15

faith, virtue of, 167–68
FGBF. *See* Full Gospel Baptist Fellowship (FGBF)
Fin Dal Principio, 148n62
First Peoples, holiness and, 85–87
fortitude, catholicity and, 176–78
four marks, the. *See* marks, ecclesiological
fraternal, unity as, 16–17
free church apostolicity, 152–53
Full Gospel Baptist Fellowship (FGBF), 62

fundamentalism, 36–38
Fundamentals, The, 37–38

gay and lesbian ministers, ordination of, 135–37
gender, ordination and, 67, 133–35
gentiles, apostolicity and the, 179
geography, church. *See* ubiquity
German National Church movement, 50–51, 98–101
gift, holiness as, 57
gifts, ecclesiological, 164, 174
globalization. *See* ubiquity
government, church and, 72–77, 148–51
Graham, Billy, 39n83, 105–6
"Great Man" storytelling, 4
Greek Orthodox Church, 74

healing, holiness and, 77–81
hermeneutics, 36–42
heroic, history as, 4
hesychastic prayer, 65–66
hierarchy, holiness and, 58–59, 64–71
Hirsch, Emanuel, 99
history, 39n83, 101–3, 137–40
holiness
  baptism and, 60–61
  Catholicism and, 58–59, 69–71, 83, 87–89
  the charismatic movement and, 59–64, 78
  differentiation and, 58–59, 64–71
  Eastern Orthodoxy and, 64–67, 72–74
  healing and, 77–81
  hierarchy and, 58–59, 64–71
  populism and, 64–77
  Protestantism and, 61–64, 67–69, 75–76, 83–89
  prudence of, 173–75
  race and, 70, 83–87
  repentance and, 81–89
  unity and, 55–64
  worship and, 64–71
Holscher, Kathleen, 145
Holy Spirit, the. *See* Spirit, the

Index

hope, virtue of, 167–68

incarnation, holiness and, 77–81
India, Church of South, 52
individualism, 66
institution, church as. *See* polity
instruments, musical, 102n24

Japan, Church of Christ in, 52
Jephthah, 163
Judaism, 50–51, 99
justice, apostolicity and, 136–37, 178–79

KHC. *See* Korean Holiness Church (KHC)
kingdom, church and, 158n2
Korean Holiness Church (KHC), 60–61

laity, the, 64–71, 133, 144–45, 147–55, 174
Lambeth Conference, Anglican, 94–95
Latter Rain Pentecostal movement, 143–44
Lausanne Movement, the, 41–42, 153
LGBTQ+, ordination of, 135–37
life, apostolicity of, 128
Life Is Worth Living, 130–31
liturgy, 64–71. *See also* polity
living sacrifices, 10–11, 159–64, 167–69
local, church as, 116–23
Lord's Prayer, the, 158
love, virtue of, 168
Lumen Gentium, 58–59

managerial culture, apostolicity and, 131–32
manualist tradition, the, 146–47
marks, ecclesiological, 5–9, 164–66. *See also* apostolicity; catholicity; holiness; unity
mass culture, apostolicity and, 131–32
materiality, 140–47, 160

Maurin, Peter, 150
MCC. *See* Metropolitan Community Church (MCC)
media, mass, 130–32
medical missions, 78–81
medium, apostolic, 129–32
Memory and Reconciliation (RCC), 87–89
Methodists, holiness and, 67–68
Metropolitan Community Church (MCC), 135
migration, catholicity and, 119–21
mission
  catholicity and, 116–19, 121–23
  holiness and, 78–81
  unity and, 19–22, 31–36, 38
morality. *See* ethics
Mortalium Animos (1928), 15
musical instruments, prohibition of, 102n24

Nagasaki, church unity and, 50
Nairobi Assembly, WCC, 112
nationalism, 49–52, 71–77
Native Americans, holiness and, 85–87
neo-evangelicals, 39n83
network Christianity, 152–53
New Delhi Assembly, WCC, 112
Newbigin, Lesslie, 29
Nigerian civil war, the, 28–29

Ockenga, Harold John, 105–6
one, church as. *See* unity
"Oneness" Pentecostal movement, the, 28n44
ordinary-extraordinary, apostolicity as, 127n3
ordination, apostolicity of, 128, 133–37
origin, apostolicity of, 127
Orthodox Churches, Eastern. *See* Eastern Orthodox Churches
outreach. *See* mission

papacy, the, 17, 24–25, 129–30, 138
parachurch organizations, 106–7
patient convergence, prudence and, 175
PCR. *See* Programme to Combat Racism (PCR)
penance. *See* manualist tradition, the
Pentecostalism, 26–29, 63–64, 101–3, 134, 143–44
perfectibility, ecclesiological, 168
Pius XI, 110–11
plurality, unity and, 18–22
politics, 72–77, 148–51
polity, 14–25, 58–62, 126–27, 129–30
populism, holiness and, 64–77
Porvoo Common Statement (1989), 139–40
poverty, 112–16, 144–45
prayer, holiness and, 65–66
primacy, apostolic, 138
Programme to Combat Racism (PCR), 46–47
prosperity gospel, the, 115–16
Protestantism
  apostolicity and, 134–35, 138–40, 143–44, 147, 151–53
  catholicity and, 94–98, 101–3, 105–8, 115–16, 118–21
  holiness and, 61–64, 67–69, 75–76, 83–89
  unity and, 18–22
prudence, holiness and, 173–75
Puebla Assembly, WCC, 114
purity, prudence and, 174

quantitative catholicity. *See* ubiquity

race, 45–49, 70, 83–87, 103–8, 153–54
Rauschenbusch, Walter, 34–36, 75–76
RCC. *See* Roman Catholic Church (RCC)
redress, holiness and, 81–89

Reich church, the. *See* German National Church movement
renewal, church, 101–3, 105–8
repentance, holiness and, 81–89
restoration, church, 101–3
Restorationist Movement, the, 102–3
retrospection, holiness and, 81–89
revivals, church. *See* renewal, church
Roman Catholic Church (RCC)
　apostolicity and, 129–30, 133–34, 137–38, 141–51, 154–55
　catholicity and, 103–4, 107, 110–11, 113–14, 118, 122–23
　holiness and, 58–59, 69–71, 83, 87–89
　unity and, 14–18, 47–48, 171–72
Russian Orthodox Church, 23–24, 73. *See also* Eastern Orthodox Churches

sacrifices, living, 10–11, 159–64, 167–69
SBC. *See* Southern Baptist Church (SBC)
scarcity, churches and, 166–67
Scripture, 36–42
Second Vatican Council. *See* Vatican II
selectivity, historical, 4–5
sex, ordination and, 135–37
Sheen, Biship Fulton, 130–31
sin, holiness and, 81–89
slavery, holiness and, 83–87
sobornost, 109–10
social action, 34–36, 42–45, 75–77. *See also* mission
Social Gospel movement, the, 34–36, 75–76
social sin, 83, 87–88
Southern Baptist Church (SBC), 83–89, 134–35. *See also* Baptist churches

specificity, catholicity and, 176n32
Spirit, the, 5–9, 26–31, 59–62
Spiritan movement, the, 59n10
spiritualism, undefined, 98
state, church and, 72–77, 148–51
subsistence, unity and, 16–17
succession, apostolic, 128, 137–40
supporting, culture as, 108–11
survival, church, 166–69
symphonia, Orthodox, 72–77

taxation, holiness and, 74–75
television, apostolicity and, 130–32
temperance, unity and, 170–73
time, 81–89, 92–98, 101–3, 159–64, 166–69. *See also* apostolicity
tradition, ecclesiology and, 163–64
Trinity, the, 63–64
truth, ecclesiology and, 162–63

ubiquity, 96, 116–19
ubuntu theology, 120–21
UCC. *See* United Church of Canada (UCC)
Uganda, Church of, 107–8
undefined spiritualism, 98
Unitatis Redintegratio, 16–17
United Church of Canada (UCC), 85–89
unity
　Catholicism and, 14–18, 24–25, 43–44, 47–48, 171–72
　catholicity and, 92–98
　civil rights movement and, 48–49
　colonialism and, 32–33, 47
　contestation and, 18–22, 41–42
　culture and, 42–45, 52–54
　doctrine and, 15–16, 36–42, 52–54, 63–64
　Eastern Orthodoxy and, 22–25, 48
　ethics and, 42–45

holiness and, 55–62
mission and, 19–22, 31–36, 38
nationalism and, 49–52
Protestantism and, 18–22, 26–42, 45–47
race and, 45–49
social action and, 34–36, 42–45
temperance of, 170–73
war and, 28–29, 49–52
universality. *See* catholicity
Uppsalla Assembly, WCC, 112

Vancouver Assembly, WCC, 112–13
Vatican II, 16–18, 24, 43–44, 58–59, 144–47, 171–72
Velvet Revolution, the, 111
vernacular, apostolicity and the, 140–41
virtues, practical, 170–79
virtues, theological, 166–69
visible, holiness as, 77–81
vivifying, charismata as, 60–61

war, 28–29, 49–52
WCC. *See* World Council of Churches (WCC)
witness. *See* mission
WMC. *See* World Missionary Conference of 1910 (WMC)
women, ordination of, 67, 133–35
Worker-Priest Movement, the, 70–71
World Council of Churches (WCC), 18–22, 45–47, 63–64, 112–15
World Missionary Conference of 1910 (WMC), 19, 31–36
World War II, 49–52
worship, holiness and, 64–71. *See also* polity

Yeago, David, 96n9
"younger churches," unity and, 32–33

Zion Christian Church (ZCC), 47